*...rden*

A HISTORICAL GUIDE TO
TRADITIONAL CROPS

A garden writer in a well-ordered kitchen garden; the frontispiece from *Every Man his Own Gardener* by John Abercrombie (an edition of 1800)

# The
# Kitchen Garden

## A HISTORICAL GUIDE TO
## TRADITIONAL CROPS

## DAVID C. STUART

ALAN SUTTON
1987

ALAN SUTTON PUBLISHING
BRUNSWICK ROAD · GLOUCESTER

Copyright © David C. Stuart 1984

First published 1984
by Robert Hale Limited

This paperback edition published 1987

British Library Cataloguing in Publication Data
Stuart, David C.
The kitchen garden: an historical guide to
traditional crops.
1. Gardening — Great Britain — History
2. Plants, Edible — Great Britain —
History
I. Title
635      SB451.36.G7

ISBN 0-86299-453-5


Cover picture: detail from Golding Constable's Vegetable
Garden by John Constable; Ipswich Museum, Suffolk.
Photograph: The Bridgeman Art Library

Printed in Great Britain by
The Guernsey Press Company Limited
Guernsey, Channel Islands

# CONTENTS

# ILLUSTRATIONS

*Names in brackets refer to the
Bibliography of Picture Sources overleaf*

# BIBLIOGRAPHY OF
# PICTURE SOURCES

Abercrombie, J., 1800. *Every Man his own Gardener*
Austen, R., 1653. *A Treatise on Fruit Trees* (1753 edition)
Blackwell, Elizabeth, 1734. *A Curious Herbal*
Bonnefons, Nicolas de (trans. Evelyn), 1658. *The French Gardener*
Bradley, R., 1718. *Gentlemen and Gardeners' Calendar*
Duhamel, E., 1825. *Traites des Arbres etc.*
*Florist and Pomologist*, 1863
Gerard, John, 1597. *The Herball*
Hooker, W., 1817. *Drawings of Fruits*
Lawson, William, 1618. *A New orchard and Garden* (1656 edition)
Loudon, J., 1822. *Encyclopaedia of Gardening*
Martyn, Thomas, 1792–4. *Flora Rustica*
Parkinson, John, 1629. *Paradisi in Sole Paradisus Terrestris*
Parkinson, John, 1640. *Theatrum Botanicum*
Rea, John, 1665. *Flora, or a Complete Florilege*
Redouté, P. J., 1827–33. *Choix des plus belles fleurs et fruits*
Vietz, Ferdinand, 1819. *Icones Plantarum etc.*
Vilmorin-Andrieux, Mme, 1885. *The Vegetable Garden*

## ACKNOWLEDGEMENTS

Grateful acknowledgement is made to the Lindley Library, The Royal Horticultural Society, for their assistance and permission to reproduce illustrations from the volumes listed above, and also to Eileen Tweedy who undertook the photography.

# FOREWORD

This book developed from my own interest in growing fruits, vegetables and culinary herbs. As I began to look at the history of each crop, I soon found that almost every species has a fascinating past, and one often deeply enmeshed in our own history. The way in which the plants have been brought into cultivation, and subsequently developed or dropped, has reflected many aspects of political and social change, as well as changes in religious and scientific thought. Even a humble salad plant likes the lettuce, whether in a plastic bag in the supermarket or crisp and fresh in your garden, has a history which is worth telling.

Many modern books on crop evolution tend to concentrate either on the earliest period of domestication or on the modern technical advances made possible by genetic research. The middle ground, the ways in which our ancestors actually used and grew the plants, is often ignored. Consequently, I have tried as far as possible to integrate modern crop research with the garden books, herbals, cook-books and plant histories of the past. Most of the sources used contain a great deal of further information, and I hope that the system of references will enable any reader interested in a particular crop to find out more about it.

In each entry I have tried to include as much as I can about the origin and early migrations of each crop, about the integration of each one into European, and especially British, gardens and cuisine and about the medicinal uses they were once thought to have. Where I have found especially attractive and forgotten ways of preparing the plant for the table, I have included those as well. A number of the less common crops can make very attractive garden plants as well as providing food, and I hope that some of the entries will encourage gardeners to try something new to them.

Worldwide, the number of plant species in domestic use is immense. I have restricted this survey to those crops that can be grown by almost anyone in the temperate zone (especially in the United Kingdom), fortunate enough to have a garden. I have also included a number of plants that were once produced at home for the table but are now either no longer is use or grown only in much warmer climates. Consequently, some fruits like banana and mango, widely eaten today, are not included because they have never been a serious crop in the greenhouse. Pineapples, lemons and oranges are included because substantial crops were once profitably obtained under glass. Likewise, rampions and skirrets, which were once important outdoor crops but are very rarely seen today, are included. Crops which have only been in very marginal cultivation (the dandelion is an example) have been left out.

Of the herbs, the main ones likely to be found in today's kitchen have been included; most rare flavourings (laurel leaves, for instance), as well as all those whose uses seem to have been entirely medicinal, have been left out. A note of caution, though: a large number of culinary plants have been regarded as possessing medicinal properties. These are often of interest, and I have included them. However, the book is in no way intended as a history of herbalism or as a herbal itself. If you feel inclined to try out the medical properties of the plants in the vegetable patch, you should first study some of the modern books that fulfil that function.

The Latin names given for each crop are generally taken from recent sources, the most important being *Flora Europea*. Because that work gives only an abbreviation for the author of each Latin name, this can sometimes look rather daunting for the non-botanist. So I have included each person's name in full. Where there are two names given, the one in brackets refers to the author who first described the plant. The other name refers to the botanist who transferred the plant to another genus and thus made a new combination.

For some of the major crops, especially in the main fruit-tree species and even more particularly in the cabbage and its allies, both the taxonomy and the nomenclature are extremely complex. For these plants, various Latin names are in circulation. While some are more correct than others, there is no absolute test for their 'correctness', a situation which gardeners and botanists may bemoan but must accept. I have followed whichever source seems to me the most reliable, putting synonyms in brackets.

The locations given alongside or immediately below the Latin name refer, in general, to the area of initial domestication if this is known and if it differs from the overall range of distribution of the species. It is intended as a quick guide and is amplified in the text.

Lastly, no history of kitchen garden plants is complete without at least a brief look at the development of techniques for propagating and growing them, and of the gardens in which they were grown. Many techniques from earliest times are still in use (after all, the nature of plants does not change), others have very fortunately been dropped from the gardener's repertoire. Only a few could be usefully revived. Of the gardens themselves, the highly cultivated and exceptionally productive examples of the eighteenth century are described in some detail, but I have also tried to give a brief outline of the sort of kitchen gardens that led up to that remarkable period.

I hope that the book will encourage the gardener to try to enlarge the range of crops that he or she grows, or at least to look at what does grow in the garden with new interest. The kitchen garden can be a place of fascination and delight, as well as abundance.

Belhaven 1983

# INTRODUCTORY

## *Origins*

Any animal that eats plants must, if it is to survive, be to some extent a botanist. Man, even when every individual was still a hunter-gatherer, was certainly one of the best. When permanently settled villages began to form, crystallizing out of the constantly shifting network of the human population, Man had already found many plant species that could be cultivated, cooked or stored, and the gardener–farmer already knew how to harvest and plant seeds. Many of the crops known to the earliest villagers we still eat with delight, and while some crops have developed over the millennia into more productive or more delicious forms, a surprising number are still very similar to those grown in the earliest gardens.

Village life and the arts of agriculture and horticulture took root in different places and at different times. It is impossible to know to what extent the wandering hunter-gatherers may have carried plant seeds about with them, but as village life developed and began to expand, gardeners generally made use of the edible plants in the local flora. Plants themselves have a complex distribution, the result both of their own evolution and of climatic, geographical and other factors. Consequently, the garden crops varied considerably from area to area. As the village 'idea' spread, or as the gardeners themselves moved on, the range of each of their crops spread too.

Because so many species had entered the garden in prehistoric times, we have to rely on oblique and imperfect information when looking for a crop's origin. The place can most easily be determined for those crops that have a wild progenitor with a restricted geographical range, in which case it is reasonably safe to assume that cultivation began within the range of the original species. Another means of identifying the location of origin is contained in the phrase 'centre of diversity'. This suggests that the place of origin of a crop is often marked by the survival of numerous types of that crop either still in cultivation (as with wheats in Turkey) or now as part of the wild population (as in some of the stone fruits). While this can certainly show where a crop has been important to Man at some time in the past, because the interaction between the gardener and his crops is so complex, it does not necessarily show the original location of domestication. Many centres of diversity must have been lost, through either climatic change or the superimposition of later phases of agriculture. Even those that remain are very much under threat. Further, quite a number of crops have several centres of diversity, though these can have widely different levels of complexity. There is no really satisfactory way of determining which is the earliest; it is usually suggested that the area showing most diversity is the oldest.

In general, the archaeological record, while throwing brilliant shafts of light on some crops, sheds light on very few. Most interest has so far centred on major agricultural crops which in any case, being the most common, have left the largest number of remains. Not very many kitchen garden plants leave material for the archaeologist, though recent work on comparatively modern gardens, especially those of Pompeii, has yielded some fascinating information (47).*

As the entries show, present-day knowledge of the origin of many crop plants can only assign them to the most vaguely defined geographical regions and equally vague epochs. Probably for many their early history is forever lost. In some cases, even the original species first taken into cultivation has been lost, and while some crops have been so modified by their domestication that they have lost all contact with any known wild species (the onion is an especially interesting example), others are still hardly to be distinguished from wild plants (lamb's lettuce, sweet cicely, salsify and scorzonera are but four scarcely modified crops). Most of these are of minor horticultural importance and seem to have hovered for thousands of years on the margins of horticulture. They can hardly be said to have an 'origin', though their geographical ranges have often been extended far beyond their original and natural ones. As a group, they grade into species which have scarcely even entered the garden at all, though sometimes playing a useful role in the kitchen. Gathering food

---

*Numbers in brackets refer to sources listed in the Bibliography.

plants, especially salads and pot-herbs, from the wild is much more widespread today in the rest of Europe than it is in Britain, where, it seems restricted to brambles, rosehips, elderberries and a few others. Elsewhere, the range of species commonly used is large, embracing everything from grape hyacinth bulbs (*Muscari comosum*), in countries where it is a tolerated weed of field margins, to wood sorrel. However, whatever the place and date of a crop's origin, a successful crop soon extends its range. It can flow along the routes of communication between communities, where its reputation for excellence (whether of taste, of medical or magical properties or of some advantageous aspect of its husbandry) makes gardeners who do not have it want to grow it.

The kitchen garden flora can thus be dramatically altered by historical events. There are some excellently documented examples from Roman times, where men associated with the expansion of that nation found valuable crops growing in newly conquered territories and sent them back to Italy, from whence they spread throughout Roman dominion (see especially Peach, Melon and Cherry).

The Roman occupation of Britain saw an unprecedented number of new crops introduced. Roman gardens in this country, at least in the more settled areas where people were wealthy enough to enjoy comfortable living, would have grown figs, vines, apricots, peaches, globe artichokes, cucumbers and melons, all almost certainly new to these shores. Little is known of the details of their gardens, but it is likely that they were not appreciably less abundant with delicacies than their contemporary equivalents in Italy.

Of course, many heavily domesticated crops, having once colonized an area, are then generally dependent on the continuation of husbandry if they are to remain there. Remarkably few make successful wildlings. It has often been assumed that after the Roman withdrawal many Roman introductions died out fairly swiftly, only to be reintroduced during the sixteenth century. However, Roman methods of husbandry may not have vanished as completely as was once imagined. Gardening traditions seem to have an astonishingly long life, and in any case Roman books on husbandry continued to be read throughout the Middle Ages. Of course, the ability to read and write was found largely among members of religious institutions, at least in the early part of this period. The institutions themselves also were very prosperous but, more important, after the fall of Rome they

'Skill and pains, bring fruitful gains': a walled orchard from Lawson's *A New orchard and Garden*

preserved intact within their walls many elements of Roman life. The cloister gardens and the orchards, filled with roses, vines, lilies, figs, cherries, box, rosemary and myrtle were tended and planted in a way that most Romans would have recognized.

This was certainly the case elsewhere in Europe. The lovely poem *Hortulus*, written by Strabo in the middle of the ninth century, describes the conversion of a nettle-filled courtyard by his door into a delightful garden filled with herbs, vegetables, flowers and fruit. The garden was modelled on passages in the *Georgics* of Virgil, and its third line makes a reference to the gardens of Paestum.

If many monastic gardens remained fruitful and beautiful, it is difficult to imagine that secular gardens were mere wastelands. By the twelfth and thirteenth centuries, landowners were themselves becoming more prosperous. The Domesday Book mentions vineyards, not all monastic, and William of Malmesbury describes abundant gardens at Gloucester. In the late part of the period, Chaucer mentions many sorts of fruit and vegetables and even describes the form of a poor woman's garden. It is easy to imagine that some of his more pleasure-loving characters could not have been immune to the delights of gardening, or at least to the gastronomic pleasures that having one allows.

In the sixteenth century two things happened that brought in a second flood of new plants. These eventually altered the look of both flower and kitchen garden forever, not only because of the new additions but also because of the plants that they ousted from cultivation. Both happenings are associated with the phenomenon called the Renaissance (there had been other lesser renaissances throughout the Middle Ages, but this one was rendered more powerful because many more people could read, books were becoming cheap, and wealth and the pursuit of pleasure were more widely available). Each one was to do with a different sort of exploration; one was a new passion for the study of nature and its variation as it really is, not as the garbled versions of Classical authority said it was. The other was a passion (often stemming from fairly base motives) for geographical discovery. One result of the first was that the gardeners of Henry VIII and his courtiers eagerly scoured Europe for new varieties of fruit and vegetables. A result of the second was the discovery of the Americas from the early fifteenth century onwards, and their pillage soon afterwards.

For British gardeners, the sixteenth century must have been a period of great excitement. Peaches, apricots and melons became, for the rich, common fare. From the New World, Jerusalem artichokes, potatoes (both sweet and ordinary), tomatoes, sweet corn, French beans, runner beans, marrows and pumpkins became delicacies. Though a few sixteenth-century writers (and their followers) claimed that gardening in Britain only began in that century, it is not fully clear how much the purely technical side of gardening improved during the Renaissance. None of the gardening books and herbals that appeared in the second half of the century implies that the techniques of husbandry they describe are newly learned. It is certain, though, that they became more widely used.

The invasion of Europe by American crop species was really the last wave of a wider invasion of what were to become extremely important crops. The increasing contact with the Orient during the seventeenth century and later, while it added many marvellous plants to the decorative garden, did little for the kitchen and the table. One reason for this is, of course, that there is no major barrier to the distribution of crops, seeds or men, and most of the important food plants had had plenty of time to arrive at wherever they could be used. However, a few new plants did arrive. In the nineteenth century the mandarin orange became known in the West, and it is now widely grown in European countries with a suitable climate. Various radish cultivars were brought in, as well as Chinese cabbage types, only now establishing themselves in the garden.

It is extraordinary that by the time the art of writing had appeared amongst what had become nations based on the domestication of plants and animals, not only had the origin of many crops passed into mythology, or been altogether forgotten, but the exploration of the world's flora for food plants was already virtually complete. Only a very small proportion of plant species have been brought into domestication since written records began. Of course, the actual process of domestication still continues as crop species are adapted to suit new needs or to fulfil old ones more efficiently.

What has happened, however, since the seventeenth century is that the sexual nature of plant reproduction was established. By the eighteenth century the deliberate creation of new varieties of already well-known species was seen to be both possible and easy. Consequently, the potential for improvement inherent in many crop species was gradually revealed. With the twentieth century development of an understanding of genetic mechanisms, the search for improved varieties has become even more efficient. Indeed, new varieties have sometimes been so successful as to endanger the survival of innumerable older varieties and the possibly useful genetic material that they contain.

If the kitchen garden flora has seen such remarkable developments over the last two thousand years, why, it may be asked, do we often eat so dully? While it is reasonably easy to show the events behind the acquisition of new crops, the occasional loss is sometimes not so easy to explain. Some are ousted by new and more useful ones (as the potato pushed many other root crops from the garden) or developments of already extant ones (the lettuce was known from ancient times, but its immense development from the eighteenth century to the present day has meant that many once popular salad crops are now rarely seen). Quite often it seems to be merely fashion that determines what is or is not grown (see, for example, the histories of Jerusalem artichokes and cucumbers). Britain seems particularly distinguished in this respect, now scarcely growing not only a large number of worthwhile crop species but also whole sections of the crop species that can be grown. A look through almost any Continental seed or fruit catalogue will reveal all sorts of interesting things, many of which grew here in the past and were then admired. It is difficult to suggest a reason for this; perhaps the earliness and extent of the urbanization of our population has led to a much greater division between people whose lives are dominated by towns and cities (the majority) and those who are dominated by the seasons. As the range of market produce is determined by what the townsman will buy, and not what the countryman can produce, crops and varieties forgotten in the cities soon get forgotten in the country also. Even good ways of eating what is produced have vanished, and so both our gardens and our tables have become less interesting than they should be.

## *The Walled Garden*

In the earliest settlements, there was probably no distinction between areas under cultivation of staple crops and those used for less important ones. However, the idea of a 'garden', in the sense of a safe and protected area set aside for the pleasure of the owner (providing crops as well as flowers, and a place for recreation), seems to be remarkably ancient. Although most archaeological information seems to be based on the gardens of the powerful, at least in the Middle East, the basic plan of so many gardens contains the same elements that it is likely that humbler and lost gardens were similar.

Curiously, the garden plan has survived almost as well as the crop species which the first gardens contained. The ancient gardens or 'paradises' of Mesopotamia combined pomegranates, figs, roses, lilies and palms within a square walled garden, having a cruciform arrangement of paths and watercourses. The design represented an ancient world-map, one that has been found drawn on pottery as early as 4000 BC, and from various locations in the Middle East and eastern Mediterranean region. The world, either round or square, had the tree of life (often a date palm) growing at its centre. Twined around this were four snakes (occasionally just one), as symbols of the atmosphere or winds. Four streams issued from the tree's base and flowed to the four points of the compass, thus dividing the world into four continents. In gardens, the plan usually allowed a pavilion or living-quarters at the place where the tree of life should have stood, and four gates, of which the southern one was, and continued to be, the most elaborate.

In Persia, in the centuries following the birth of Christ, the four-square garden plan was used for the vast hunting parks of

A seventeenth-century French kitchen garden showing the trellis
supports for fruit

the Sassanian palaces. It was found all over the Middle East (often in elaborate forms) and, of course, throughout the Roman Empire, where it could be either a garden plan or an army camp. One of the gardens excavated at Pompeii, a vineyard garden also used as a place of resort, was planned four-square, with the central path probably shaded by a long pergola of vines, and the cross-paths terminated by dining couches and tables, also shaded beneath vines. Other gardens of the same town may have contained mixtures of vines, fruit trees, vegetables and flowers (47).

In northern Europe, the four-square plan (with an adjustment of crops to suit the cooler climate) probably survived the Roman withdrawal. The area enclosed seems to have been divided up into a large number of beds, raised a hand's breadth above the general soil level and held up by wooden boards. Strabo (96) had his made up in this way in the ninth century. By that date, masonry walls for gardens seem to have been rare, and early illustrations usually show wattle barriers (probably the cheapest means of enclosure), though a number show walls of heavy timber baulks with pointed tops, looking very like the defensive pales used for most prosperous dwellings. By the thirteenth century some small gardens seem to have been enclosed by another defensive feature, the ditch and dyke. Chaucer, in the 'Nonne Preestes Tale', describes the garden in which Chauntecleer was too proud, as:

> A yeard she hadde, enclosed al aboute
> With stikkes, and a drye ditch with-out.

Its owner was of humble status, so perhaps such enclosures were very common and much older than their first description.

By the sixteenth century, though some people were already sufficiently prosperous to build themselves walled enclosures for all their gardens, it was quite common for the garden to be hedged. Estienne and Liebault say that, 'the hedge shall be planted likewise with hazell trees, gooseberry bushes white and red, pepper trees, curran trees, eglantines, brambles, woodbinde, the wilde vines, both the hollies, elder trees, intermingled now and then with whitethorn, wild apple trees, and apples of paradise, service trees, medlars and olives'. The result must have been both productive and beautiful to look at, as well as being impervious to 'cattel' and malevolent men. The dyke and ditched enclosure also seems to have remained a popular alternative, for Lawson suggests such a thing, possibly moated, for orchard-gardens early in the seventeenth century. The outer surface of the bank was to be planted with quickthorn (a planting later used for cheap ha-has), while the bank itself was to be

> level on the top, two yards broad for a fair walk, five or six foot higher than the soil, with a gutter on either side, two yards wide and four foot deep, set without with three or four chefs of thorns, and within with Cherries, Plums, Damsons, Bullis, Filbirds (for I love those trees better for their fruit, and as well for their form, as Privit), for you may make them take any form [he is suggesting that they be pleached or trimmed]. And in every corner (and middle if you will), a mount would be raised, whereabouts the wood may clasp, powdered with woodbine, which will make with dressing, a fair, pleasant, profitable and sure fence.
>
> Moats . . . will afford you fish, fence, and moisture to your Trees, and pleasure also, if they be so great and deep that you may have Swans and other water-Birds, good for devouring vermine, and boats for many good uses.

Later in the same century, with landowners and merchants becoming increasingly wealthy, masonry walls for the gardens became quite commonplace. Celia Fiennes, in her travels through England towards the end of the century, saw many examples. Of Mr Rooth's garden at Epsom she wrote:

> The first garden is square the walls full of trees nailed neat, and apricocke, peach, plumb, necktarine, which spread, but not very high, between each is a cherry stipt up to the top and spreads then composeing an arch over the others, there are borders of flowers round and a handsome gravel round . . . out of this (which is fenced by a breast wall with iron palisadoes painted blew with gilt tops) you ascend severall stepps through an iron-work'd gate to a ground divided into long grass walks several of which ascend the hill, and between the ground improv'd with dwarfe trees of fruits and flowers and greenes in all shapes, intermixt with beds of stawberyes for ornament and use, thus to another bank. . . .

She was writing only a few decades before the changing fashion swept away the iron work, most walls, gravel rounds, avenues, topiary and canals, leaving the kitchen garden as the only surviving fragment of ancient traditions.

Of the gardens' decoration, and contributing much to its human occupants' pleasures, the pavilions have been a constant element. Roman gardens had them, often of trellis work twined with vines. The same materials were often used to make shady walks along the inside of the walls. Early medieval gardens had exactly comparable structures, and hundreds of medieval engravings and miniatures show such delights. They continued into the sixteenth century. To quote from Surflet's translation of Estienne and Liebault:

> Even so shall the kitchen garden be set with turrets of lattice fashion, covered over with Bordeaux vines . . . for verjuice . . . the fashion of the arbour shall be in manner of a shadowie place (for arbours are costly to maintain), to that end you may drawe certaine beds underneath, or some floore of herbs, which crave no great cherishing and refreshing, leaving notwithstanding an alley of three foote bredth, both on the one side and on the other, for the dispatching of such work as is to be bestowed upon the arbour.

It was sometimes suggested that British arbours were to be covered with apple trees rather than vines, though vines would have yielded here the verjuice that Estienne suggests as the reason for growing them.

Grand gardens had masonry pavilions. Bernard Palissy described a very grandiose project for ceramic ones in *A Delectable Garden* of 1563 (the elaborate ceramic decoration was to be of his own devising and manufacture). He said:

> As at each of the four corners of the said garden there shall be a cabinet . . . [of these] there will be another which shall be made like the shelves of a merchant to hold a diversity of fruits, such as plums, cherries, figs, and other similar kinds. Also, there will be one, which shall be most useful, in which to set up a furnace to distill waters and essences of sweet-smelling herbs. There will be other rooms for the storing of fruits and all sorts of vegetables, such as beans, peas, lentils, and others of the same kinds. . . .

In the seventeenth century, not only were pavilions much in use but the gardens were also decorated with mounts, sundials and statuary, and some owners even stationed troupes of musicians in the orchard and kitchen garden to add to the delight.

In the eighteenth century, the pavilions in walled gardens were to become quite grand, with marble surrounds to the fireplaces, and elaborate plasterwork. The leafy arbour remained popular in humble kitchen gardens, and even by the end of the nineteenth century such gardens often had wirework arbours covered with runner beans, in which to while away a quiet hour and watch the crops slowly coming to ripeness.

Of the raised beds described by Strabo and illustrated in so many medieval paintings, most seem to have been plain rectangles, each devoted to a single crop. There is little suggestion, as far as I can discover, that they were ever used (at least in Britain) as decorative elements in their own right. The elegant reconstruc-

A parterre design showing the decorative beds suitable for flowers or fruit

tion of a medieval garden at Villandry, with its decorative parterre of vegetables, should not be thought of as a typical example. Only one or two of the sixteenth- and seventeenth-century garden books that give plans for knots or parterres suggest that the same plans could be used for fruit gardens, so perhaps an occasional gardener used them for the vegetable garden as well. *The Four Books of Husbandrie* states that: 'The beds are to be made narrow and long . . . five [foot] in breadth, that they may be easier weeded: they must lie in wet and watrie ground two foot high, in dry ground a foot is sufficient. If your beds lye so dry, as they will suffer no water to tarry upon them, you must make the spaces betwixt higher, that the water may be forced to lie. . . .' The beds were often called 'floores', with the paths between them about three feet wide (36), and were supported, as were Strabo's, by boards commonly painted a stone colour (28, 83).

The use of beds of various sizes, and with no particular ground plan, survived well into the eighteenth century. However, advanced gardeners were certainly once again using the ancient four-square arrangement by 1659, though it seems to have been regarded as a French way of doing things (85). It may be that, by the time masonry walls for gardens were common, the same prosperity allowed the ground to be drained adequately and so did not need permanent and raised beds. Such a development allowed a more rational, as well as ceremonial, plan for the kitchen garden.

As with clothes, carriages, horses, houses and food, the prosperous owner was much concerned with displaying his wealth in the kitchen garden. Whatever its degree of architectural show, its size alone was always an indication of the size and status of the household it served. There was considerable discussion, particularly in the late eighteenth and early nineteenth centuries, about what sort of garden was suited to each class of household, and even what sort of crops it should contain. For instance, a cottager's garden should be large enough to allow the family to eat healthily, but not so large as to demand time for its maintenance that would better belong to the cottager's employer. The range of crops deemed suitable for such a garden was rather meagre and excluded several plants, such as onions and broccoli, now regarded as essential in any garden.

The farmer's kitchen garden, if he was moderately wealthy, was sometimes as large as an acre and commonly walled, and it would have had a full-time gardener devoted to its care. Such a garden could produce both onions and broccoli, perhaps even asparagus and artichokes, but white currants would be grown in place of grapes, and apples, pears and plums, and probably cherries, would be the only wall fruit. A garden appropriate for the gentry might consist of five acres, with hotbeds, melon frames, heated walls and glasshouses. It would produce peaches, nectarines, grapes, pineapples, figs and the commoner fruit out of season. Such families, of course, commonly comprised large numbers of people, and it was for such households that Jacob published *The Country Gentleman's Vade Mecum* in 1717. Under the heading 'Annual Expence of a large Family . . . containing about 25 or 30 Persons in Number, as aforesaid, to be maintained genteely and plentifully, in a Time when Provisions are of moderate Price . . .', he lists the following amounts:

In Meat and Drink, about £400 at least: Expence for Stables for Six
Coach-Horses and Two Saddle Horses, besides the Plow-Cattle and
Deer, in Corn about £80, in Hay and Straw about £100, Twenty
servants Wages about £170. Eight or Ten Liveries about £50 or £55
. . . Expence of fine gardens kept handsomely in Repair, about £80
. . . Wine for the Family of all sorts, about £100 or £125. Cloathes
and casual expences about £200 per Annum.

So the whole Expence of the Family, taking in everything according
to this Computation, may amount for £1200 to £1500 per Annum,
according as it is managed.

One hundred years later, the cost of running a five-acre kitchen
garden was itself £400 a year, varying slightly according to the
nearness or otherwise of a source of coal for heating walls and
glass. The head gardener's wages accounted for only £85 of the
total.

Minor aristocrats, or their financial equivalents, needed for
their households a kitchen garden of eight acres or so. The
increase in social magnificence was marked by no new crops,
though the additional resources were marked by an increased
interest in the out-of-season, with perhaps pineapples being
available throughout the year. For great magnates, kitchen gardens were sometimes of fourteen acres or even more. One
Scottish example at Dalkeith Palace had four hundred feet of
melon frames, a stove house for forcing cucumbers, cherries and
pineapples (all three available all the year round) and two vine
houses each fifty feet long.

Almost all these gardens, from the fairly modest right up to the
very grandest examples, were, at their peak, quite standard in
plan. They were often square or rectangular, with the inside of
the topmost wall facing south. Rectangular gardens always had
the longest axis running east to west, giving a long south-facing
wall for the production of the most valuable fruit. Of course,
most of the old formal gardens had been rectilinear, and the
plan remained for what had become the only walled garden.
In the eighteenth century there was much debate about the ideal
shape for the kitchen garden; it was often said that the rectangular ones were too draughty. Occasionally circular, elliptical,
D-shaped and even trapezoid ones can be found, though they
are, on the whole, fairly rare. Presumably they did not give
sufficiently improved conditions within their walls to make
them generally accepted. Even rarer are the gardens with concentric walls, one garden within another (the innermost part of the
only one I know which is still extant is exceptionally sheltered

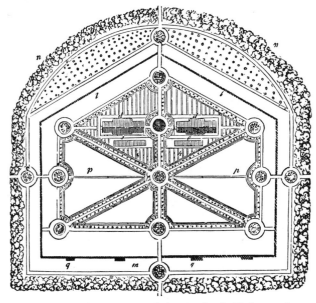

Early nineteenth-century grand planning for the kitchen garden

and warm). They were obviously very expensive to build.

The gardens usually had three entrances which in grand examples were often given some architectural embellishment. The main one, where possible, was in the southern wall. As the productive surface faced north (and so was only suitable for morellos, filberts and currants), it was less valuable, and it also had the advantage that any visitor coming through the entrance was immediately presented with a view of the inside of the north wall, with its ranks of peaches, nectarines, apricots and, when the garden was grand enough to have them, vine houses and pine stoves. Side entrances were often wide enough to allow carts to enter the garden, to bring in litter from the stables and to carry produce to the kitchens. The entrances were often adorned with jasmine, honeysuckle and roses.

The walls themselves were rarely less than twelve feet high, and often seventeen. Where possible, they were faced on the inside with brick, a material retaining heat much better than stone. The coping at the wall head generally projected inwards for several inches to keep drips from the espaliered fruits below, and it is also common to find, just below the coping, the hooks for the attachment of matting or the light frames used to protect fruit buds from late frosts, and maturing fruit from early ones.

The layout, at least by the late eighteenth century, had become fairly standardized. From the entrance in the southern wall the main gravelled walk ran due north. This was frequently flanked by beds of flowers, very rarely of new and exotic introductions, most often of those flowers traditionally associated with the kitchen garden; lilies, pinks, violets, borages, roses, hepaticas, lavender, marigolds and the rest. A number still had kitchen uses in the eighteenth century. The beds also grew most of the herbs required for the house, whether for the table or for the well-being of the inhabitants. Behind these flower beds were light rails built generally to support espalier apple trees or gooseberries. Many apple trees can often be found still growing in this position. Halfway up the main path was one running east to west. This rarely had flower borders, though it was commonly bordered with currants or gooseberry bushes, or in lesser gardens with strawberries, chives or parsley. Where the paths crossed was sometimes decorated with a water tank or fountain. Paths also followed the walls, usually leaving a bed as deep as the wall was high between the path and the wall.

The main paths therefore divided the gardens into quarters. This allowed a four-part rotation of vegetable crops, often with one quarter grassed over each year and used as a drying green, though in some gardens a full four-part rotation was used. The crops themselves were sown in narrow strips, usually three or four feet wide, with narrow paths between. These paths and plots were temporary, being dug over each year, and so did not form permanent structures. The beds between the walls and the peripheral paths either followed the rotation of the quarter nearest them or were, more often, used for those permanent crops (rhubarb, artichokes, asparagus, seakale, strawberries and raspberries) which do not fit into a rotation. Behind the beds of such crops, a space was left to allow for the feeding and maintenance of the wall fruit.

The north wall of the garden, being the sunniest, was always the most elaborately treated. Even quite modest gardens often had a glass house built against the central part of the wall, for vines, pineapples or early peaches, figs and nectarines. In some gardens the entire wall was given over to glass. Where the head gardener did not have quarters in the main house, he was quite often given a small house built against, or forming part of, this wall. His house was frequently central and often given quite decorative architectural treatment for it terminated the view up the main axis of the gardens. This position also enabled the custodian to keep watch over the garden's valuable contents. In prosperous gardens, the gardeners' quarters were combined with a garden pavilion or orangery, often quite grandly furnished and decorated. The pavilions were used as the winter home for lemon or orange trees, myrtles, bays and oleanders and as pleasant places of retreat for the owner and his family in the summer. Lesser gardens sometimes just have an alcove for a seat (with a pleasant view down through the apple trees); much grander ones may have a pair of pavilions, one at each end of the top walk, and a few even had a pavilion in each of the corners of the garden (one I know has four Greek temples, all, alas, in ruins).

On the east- and west-facing walls, the 'lesser' fruits were planted: apples, pears, plums, cherries, damsons and greengages, and very rarely mulberries, medlars and quinces. When the gardens were being newly planted, or when old fruit trees had to be replaced, the new trees were planted in their final spacings, and the intervening spaces were filled with gooseberries and red-currants to give a quick yield. These soft fruits were gradually removed as the more important trees grew to fill the spaces allotted to them. The inside of the south wall, apart from the trees already mentioned, was also used for those currants required later in the season. The bed in its shade was used for rooting cuttings from all parts of the garden and for those salad plants, especially radishes and lettuces, not needing high levels of light.

For growing cucumbers and melons and smaller vegetables out of season, the hotbeds and frames were often outside the walled garden and in the area to the north where stood most of the sheds for storing fruit, seeds and garden equipment (and, in illiberal households, for housing the under-gardeners, apprentices and weeding women). Well-designed walled gardens were entirely surrounded by a broad, open area called the 'slips'. This was often planted up with an informal arrangement of currant and nut bushes, myrobalans and bullaces, cornelian cherries and barberries. The outer surfaces of the garden walls themselves were only rarely used for productive plants of any value, for pilfering was reckoned to make it pointless. They were left bare or given over to decorative climbers. The slips themselves were surrounded by dense plantations, with holly and other ever-greens being preferred as they gave shelter from the wind throughout the year. Where there was not enough space to devote such a large area purely to protecting the walled garden from the gale, the slip's plantation was made of productive trees like service and walnut.

By the end of the 1820s, attempts at codifying the sumptuary aspects of the kitchen garden seem to have petered out. Three decades later the gardens' decline had begun. Associated with this decline seems to have been the stripping away, for however rational reasons, of its flowers. Modern kitchen gardens confine themselves entirely to fruit and vegetables and are rarely attractive places to be in. They are often tucked away in some corner where they need not be seen. Such a clear-cut and destructive distinction between departments of the garden represents an enormous break with an immensely long tradition. In the earliest gardens of all, fruitfulness was one of the most desired characteristics of the 'paradise', and pleasures of smell and sight were thought as important as the pleasures of eating. Even by medieval times, when stately gardens were beginning to separate the kitchen garden from the more formal parts, the kitchen garden was made a place of pleasure by the simple fact that many flowers either had extensive uses in the kitchen or were important cures for the ailments of Man and his animals. Even when these plants had begun to drop out of use, during the sixteenth and seventeenth centuries, they remained as traditional inhabitants of that part of the garden. Such plants included violets (used to decorate and flavour many dishes and to cure fevers, headaches, ulcers and carbuncles), pinks and carnations (crystallized or turned into conserves to 'comfort the heart' and to stave off fevers and plague) and the white lily (*Lilium candidum*), a flower justly popular long before the Romans grew it (it cured everything from tumours of the genitals to scalds). The list can go on through winter cherry, cowslip, primrose, sea holly, hepatica, marigold, various sorts of rose, gentians, blessed thistles and the rest.

This fusion of beauty and commodity seems to have enabled the gardener to see all his crops as beautiful, and though modern gardeners might not want statuary or consorts of viols among their cabbages, the addition of a few patches of the old kitchen garden flowers might revive interest in all the possibilities of that part of his domain.

Perhaps the walled garden, towards the end of its peak, was less delightful than Lawson's ideal. Perhaps it had lost too many of the plant species associated with outmoded habits of eating and curing disease. For all the immense range of culinary species it contained, for all the manifold skills shown by its gardeners, it might also have contained the seeds of its own decay. By the middle of the nineteenth century, with a few exceptions, the kitchen garden seems to have become less a place of resort and, together with the stables, the kitchens and the other insalubrious parts of the house and grounds, to have become part of the realm of the servant classes. After the First World War, political, social and economic changes affected all classes of society. The walled gardens became weedier little by little, the espalier trees less well pruned, and broken panes of glass in the vine house were not replaced. The plasterwork of the pavilion was soon damp and mouldy, and the marble fireplace smashed by vandals. Pineapples became cheaper to buy than to grow, then peaches (but how much less delicious), and then finally even cabbages and potatoes.

Today, I see walled gardens given over to brambles and nettles, put down to sitka spruce, used as nursery gardens or even converted into 'leisure complexes' with bright blue swimming-pools, concrete paving, barbecues and not a plant to be seen. However, most lie forgotten and in ruins. Of the few that are maintained in anything like their original state, most of the produce has to be given away or sold. Modern households no longer need the immense abundance that the walled garden can produce.

# Magic or Medicine

It is easy to imagine nowadays, that the present pace of what we like to think of as advance has been more or less constant century after century. However, this is by no means the case; for over a thousand years following the withdrawal of the Roman army from Britain, the arts of horticulture seem to have remained fairly static or even to have declined. When, in the late sixteenth century, new herbals and books about husbandry and gardening began to appear, their authors wrote not only from their own personal experience of plants but also with a new awareness of surviving Greek and Roman texts that augmented a gardening tradition that was still firmly based on Roman models.

While the herbalists invoked Classical authority to uphold the efficacy of their cures, the same authority enshrined a horticultural system that contained a substantial amount of purely magical belief. Some of these beliefs are so strange that it is difficult to imagine even an observant Roman gardener giving them credence (indeed, Pliny the Elder, in the first century AD, seems to have been sceptical of them). Nevertheless, many of these beliefs remained part of the gardening tradition and were still being advanced as perfectly normal practice in the late sixteenth and early seventeenth centuries. While of course many plants were important for magical rites of various sorts, most of the 'husbandry' magic is concerned with crop formation and transformation, as well as with crop yield.

Of formations, an example is the very ancient belief that asparagus could be obtained by burying a ram's horn in which a number of holes had been drilled. Other examples are given in the entries for a number of crops. The transformations may have arisen (at least in some cases) as a means of explaining genetic differences in crops whose origin was not understood. For instance, curly parsley could be obtained by heavily rolling young seedlings of the flat kind; strongly flavoured tarragon could be obtained by planting flax seed that had been embedded in an onion. Transformations in fruit were commonly thought to be effected by grafting. In some beliefs, the magic is a sort of near-miss to reality. Large leeks could be obtained by wrapping a pinch of seed in fouled linen or a piece of goat's dung and planting one such packet for each leek required. The belief was that the seeds fused and produced a large single plant, but of course the linen and dung would have acted as fertilizers to any seedling that did actually see the light of day. For some reason leeks seem to have had quite a number of odd beliefs attached to them, and many gardeners still remove the tops of the leaves to make them grow larger. This has been happening at least since Roman times and has no effect whatsoever.

More obscure is the horticultural effect of bad temper. Several herbs, basil being the most important, were believed to grow better if sown with curses and hatred. Basil is so heavily wrapped in mystery anyway that perhaps the curses are the last echoes of ancient fears, but this does not seem to be the case for the other crops. Indeed, ancient attitudes to some plants have generally had a remarkably long life, and for some still current in the eighteenth century, even the Romans seem to have forgotten the original purpose of the fear (see particularly the entries for Cabbage and Walnut). Some delicious crops introduced from the Americas in the sixteenth century were still regarded with suspicion in the twentieth. Some of the old beliefs also had a remarkably wide geographical range, perhaps a sign of their very great age. For instance, pumpkins (an American crop) and cucumbers (a Eurasian one) were both supposed to suffer if tended by a woman during her period.

Of magic associated with crop improvement, there are innumerable examples. Before any knowledge of the possibilities of plant breeding, attempts at altering plants must necessarily have been magic. Seeds were soaked in all sorts of fluids to influence taste or colour. Sweet fruit was produced, it was believed, by soaking seed in honey or rosewater, and red cabbages could be obtained from the seed of green ones by soaking them in wine lees. Other such beliefs were current until at least the end of the seventeenth century, even though both Gerard and Parkinson pointed out much of the superstition. Parkinson reports experiments he did before 1629, especially on colour transformations in flowers, as well as on the influence of the moon, and concludes on a lofty and pious note: '. . . if any man can forme plants at his will and pleasure, he can do as much as God himself that created them. For all the things they would adde unto the plants to give them colour, are all corporeal, or of a bodily substance, and whatsoever should give any colour unto a living and growing plant, must be spirituall: for no solid corporeal substance can joyne itself unto the life and essence of a herbe or tree. . . .' In spite of such sound thinking, fifty years later the eminent John Evelyn could report, presumably with no ironic intention, a bizarre experiment on runner bean seeds (q.v.).

Of ancient importance for both religious and magical beliefs, the moon seems to have long played an important role in the garden. Even Evelyn observed its phase when planting onion seed, and other writers suggest its importance in other crops, though particularly for salad plants. It is not entirely clear how much the moon was seen as having an influence on growth (though the cucumber was entirely dependent upon it) or simply as a reminder to plant a new row.

However, though the moon's importance, at least as far as kitchen produce was concerned, seems to have waned during the close of the seventeenth century, it remained important for the medicinal plants of the garden. In 1652 Nicholas Culpepper published his famous book *The English physitian: or an astrologo-physical discourse of the vulgar herbs of this Nation. . . .* This combined two very popular disciplines into a single system and was immediately and immensely popular. Fifty editions appeared over the next two hundred years, and indeed it seems to be returning to popularity. It is extraordinary that its success should be founded not on a simplification of the rather haphazard structure of seventeenth-century herbalism but on greatly increasing its complexity. It did, though, add to the number of reasons why a course of treatment should fail, and if something as grandiose as the planetary system itself could be invoked, so much the better.

It is difficult now to imagine the need for, and importance of, the herbal and herbal plants. There were, of course, no other medicines, and there was no understanding of the way in which infections are spread or even of ordinary dietary needs. While a number of the old herbalist's plants are still important in medicine, before 1700 almost all plants in the garden, and many outside it, were believed to have medicinal uses. Indeed, at a time when Man was seen as the central animal species of the universe, and his planet as the one about which all the stars revolve, it must have been hard to think that any plant could exist for its own hidden purposes and be of no use to him. As the experimental method seems only rarely to have been used (Gerard quotes an early and alarming example, cited here on p. 210, various attempts were made to systematize an unknown plant's properties. The 'doctrine of signatures' was one of the most important of these; it suggested that each plant revealed, by some visual characteristic, its herbal nature and thus indicated what it could be expected to cure. It is therefore not surprising that a walnut, with the brain-like appearance of the kernel, should be used for maladies of the head or that so many plants with yellow sap, or yielding a yellow dye, should have been used in the cure of jaundice.

In general, plants still used medicinally developed their 'correct' usage early. However, for the vast majority of medicinally inactive plants, their ingestion may, particularly for the poorer classes in society, have provided a source of vitamins. So many plants are listed as having unspecified but beneficial effects that it is tempting to see them merely as an addition to a diet deficient in vegetables.

Culpepper's was the last influential herbal to appear, and although popular for so long, amongst moderately educated people, herbalism was already beginning to fall into disrepute by the time the book appeared. In 1665 John Rea wrote in his excellent *Flora, or a Complete Florilege* that,

> ... after considering the whole Series and business of the Book, I concluded with experienced Builders, that it were better to make use of some of the best materials, in the erecting of a New peice, than to

repair and accomodate the Old; fitter to be fashioned into the form of a Florilege . . . than to continue in the old method of an Herbal, and instead of the old names, uncertain places and little or no virtue [here he means medical virtue], to insert some other things much more considerable.

Nevertheless, the old, and often ancient, medicinal uses of our kitchen garden plants are of interest as much from a sociological and historical point of view as from medical ones, reflecting as they do the fears and preoccupations of earlier generations. For instance, a very large number were held to be a protection against the plague, though none can have been effective. Parkinson lists no less than seventeen garden plants, including rosemary, garlic and rue. The various sexually transmitted diseases had almost as many cures, the most famous being rhubarb, though others included heartsease, soapwort, box and larch (this last was mixed with amber). Between seven and fourteen plants were used 'to promote Venery' and included Welsh onions and chickpeas, whereas only one (lettuce) was commonly used to cure 'Colt's evil, or immoderate lust'. Rue had opposite effects on opposite sexes. Quite a number of appetite-affecting plants were to be found in the salad bowl, though I have not come across any suggestion that salads were orchestrated to produce any particularly desired effect. Knowledge of plants' properties were so widespread that a guest would easily have been able to see if anything untoward was intended. Certainly a meal including artichokes would have had an unequivocal message for Roman as well as seventeenth-century guests. Almost all the sixteenth-century American introductions were regarded with excitement or disapproval, depending upon temperament or circumstances, and aubergines and tomatoes were especially dangerous. Indeed, the latter were called 'love apples' well into the twentieth century.

For the sexually modest, culinary dangers were rather widespread, and in 1657 William Coles lists artichokes, sea holly (used in comfits), potatoes, rocket, chocolate, satyrions (orchid roots, often candied) and dragons (a type of arum much grown in seventeenth-century gardens) among the thirteen plants which he says provoke lust. For cooling it off, he suggests the chaste tree, cannabis and hemlock (the dosage of the last must have been careful indeed, or life as well as lust would have been extinguished).

For women, a large number of kitchen garden plants and herbs were required for all the difficulties of menstruation and childbirth. Some methods of use were bizarre. For many centuries women seem to have been excluded from the kitchen garden during their periods.

Generally, a quick glance through any herbal will show a population widely afflicted with ulcers, tumours, suppurating wounds and 'worms in the ears', as well as in the gut, frequently bitten by snakes, scorpions (many recipes are given even in British herbals) and mad dogs, afflicted by the wildest passions of all sorts (knife and sword wounds could have had a garden of cures to themselves), withered members, withered breasts, acute depressions (judging from the number of cures for low spirits and melancholia, the world up to the seventeenth century was an even more daunting place than it later became) and many pictur-esquely described ailments that are difficult to identify. There was also an immense obsession with gaseous and other move-ments of the gut.

# Husbandry

As crops and the gardens that contain them evolve, so do the techniques of husbandry, control, protection and crop develop-ment. While the improvement of crop performance must have been, and often still is, seen by many gardeners as being mainly to do with crop yield, it can also be concerned with the timing of that crop. The timing of ripening does, of course, have a genetic component, but it can also be related to purely technical matters.

I do not doubt that it must always have seemed that the delight of the first of a crop would be increased if it could be had even earlier than the usual resources of nature allow. The Romans seem to have used frames to produce early crops and to have grown melons and cucumbers in earth-filled baskets, moving the plants from sheltered spot to sheltered spot as the sun moved around the garden or house. Roman frames were perhaps glazed with sheets of translucent mica or talc, and though this must have been relatively cheap (compared, that is, to glass), only a few large structures seem to have been built which made use of it. There are suggestions that at Pompeii a few structures existed for overwintering lemons and other tender plants (47). One of them has remains of post holes for the temporary shelters built round the plants at the start of the cold weather (this was tried in England in the seventeenth century). Another is reported as having a series of shelves for holding plant pots. In the eighteenth century Sir Joseph Banks inferred from a verse of Martial's that some mechanism did exist elsewhere in Italy for forcing cherries (just introduced to Europe at that time) and peaches. However, Pliny related that roses were forced by simply watering them with warm water, so perhaps something similar was also done with fruit.

The Emperor Tiberius, who needed cucumbers as a medicine, had potted plants grown in frames placed over pits of rotting dung; otherwise there are rather few references to the Romans using this method of heating for other crops, though the rotted remains of the dung were highly regarded as fertilizer. Perhaps in the warmer climate of Italy its use was not widely necessary. Within our colder shores, it still seems to have been used very little until the middle of the sixteenth century. It was, at least partly, dependent on the use of glass, whether as a bell-jar (a one-piece cloche) or in sheet form for the glazing of boxes or frames. In very grand establishments, glass had been cheap enough to use for garden buildings at least since the middle of the sixteenth century (Lord Burleigh had a purpose-built orangery by 1561, and there are European references to heated garden houses being used for the same purpose dating from the fifteenth century), but it was some time until it became cheap enough to risk in the average garden. The bell-jar seems to have been one of the first forms widely used and in fact survived for a remarkably long time, still being seen in the early part of the twentieth century. Nowadays there are many plastic equivalents.

The first sort of hotbed was extremely simple. A trench three or four feet across was dug about a yard deep. It was two-thirds filled with horse dung that did not contain too much straw, and the trench was filled up with topsoil. The warmth from the fermenting manure warmed the soil, and after the first intense heating was over, the soil was planted with seeds or seedlings. Sometimes the heat was kept in at night with light matting, the plants being exposed to the wintry elements during the day. More effectively, bell-jars were placed over each young plant, the only disadvantage being that the heat rising from the dung brought up water vapour and the atmosphere beneath the glass became extremely humid. In large establishments, an apprentice gardener was employed to prop the glasses up on pieces of twig, to give much-needed ventilation during daylight hours.

The heat in the bed lasted for about two months, so the young plants had to be moved onto new beds when the heat of the old

Wall screens, cloches, bell-jars and potted fruits shown in a charming early eighteenth-century garden

ones began to fail. Sometimes they were grown in baskets (on the Roman model), so making the plants' removal easier. More generally, and especially in the seventeenth century, the beds were used at the beginning of the spring or at the end of the summer. In the early spring they were used to produce early seedlings of melon and cucumber, or peas and lettuces that were later allowed to mature in the open air. In autumn the beds were often prepared in late September and were used to give a December crop of young peas or other delicacies (68).

However, because the manure was in a trench, with a weight of soil and handglasses on top, compaction occurred, access to oxygen was reduced and the fermentation, and so the heat it produced was not used in the most efficient way. A better scheme was soon found to lie in building the manure heaps on the soil surface and not in a trench, and to pile the soil for the plants on top. The pile was kept in place at front and back by boarding or brickwork, and if the back was higher than the front, glazed lights could be placed over them, making perfectly heated frames. This arrangement seems to have been fairly common by the end of the seventeenth century. Condensation was again a problem. In the following century, when gentlemen often had huge ranges of frames for growing melons, apprentice gardeners were often employed to keep the glass wiped clear of droplets that might fall onto the precious plants and cause rot. At night the most elaborate frames had blinds of flannel that could be drawn over the plants to fulfil the same function. In very cold weather, matting was also put over the outside of the glass to conserve heat.

By the early nineteenth century, some exceptionally elaborate frames were in existence. With permanent walls, these had complex systems of grilles and sliding panels enabling the spent manure to be dug out, and replaced by fresh, without disturbing the growing plants in the soil above. Frames of this sort could be used throughout the winter and so produce crops for all of that season. They were especially useful for pineapples, the dampish warmth and ample supply of nitrogen suiting them well. Gardens that could not aspire to proper glasshouses frequently had pine or melon frames to give their owners a reasonable taste of luxury. Even the grandest gardens had melons grown in frames, where they can still be made to do exceptionally well. The moisture from the manure must have vastly reduced one present-day scourge: red spider.

The other important eighteenth-century means of providing

warmth, although initially in this case for fruit trees only, was also thought to derive from Roman precedent (57). That the Romans heated their villas and bath-houses by means of hot air conducted underneath the floors was well known by that date. There was some suggestion that a similar method had been used in the walls, with a flue winding back and forth, as well as up, inside the structure of the wall. By the early eighteenth century, most moderately grand kitchen gardens had solid walls, the most efficient of them built with stone. By the 1720s the north wall of the enclosure was being built with broad flues running up between the inner skin and the structural part of the wall. The flue terminated at its lower end in some sort of fireplace, serviced from outside the garden, and at its upper end by a chimney perched on the wall-head and sometimes given decorative treatment, disguised as a Classical urn or piece of statuary. In the early eighteenth century, the fireplace was a simple one (though closed stoves were in use by that date elsewhere in Europe). When the fire was lit (sometimes with difficulty, as the almost horizontal flues did not draw well when cold), the fire burnt up, bringing the wall quickly to a high temperature, then burned down in a few hours and needed refuelling. When the hot-wall was in use, most often in autumn to ripen off tender or late fruit and wood, some poor gardener had to get up every few hours throughout the night to ensure that the fire kept burning. If possible, peat was the preferred fuel as it burnt more slowly than coal or wood and produced a more even temperature.

One fire could be used to heat about forty feet of wall, but because of the intense fluctuations of temperature, if coal-fired, the trees had to be grown on trellis frameworks fixed five or six inches in front of the wall surface, so that they were not scorched when the wall was at its hottest. Later, in the early nineteenth century, stoves finally replaced open fires, giving an even temperature to the wall and a full night's sleep to the gardener.

There was clearly an enormous heat loss from the wall. However, many fruit walls, even those without flues, had hooks along the coping (the rusted remains can often be seen), from which light fibre matting could be hung on cold nights to keep frost from the young fruits. In some grand gardens the mats formed outsize roller blinds. On heated walls, the mats also kept in some of the heat, but they were fragile and needed constant supervision and repair. Something more permanent was clearly necessary. One early development was the use of light frameworks of wood that hooked onto the top of the wall and sloped down to the ground. The frames were kept light in weight by 'glazing' with oiled paper or linen (the oiling made both more translucent and more waterproof). Kept on during the day, they kept in warmth then, as well as at night when the fires were lit. After the fruit had ripened, the frames were removed, only to be used again to protect early flowering trees, especially apricots and peaches, when bad weather threatened during the early spring. Present-day gardeners with wall fruit could usefully have something similar, using plastic sheeting instead of paper or cloth.

When glass became sufficiently cheap, these moveable frames could be glazed, making them very heavy and cumbersome but also far more efficient. Indeed, early ones were often left in place until hot weather forced their removal. Clearly such structures were very close in form and use to a lean-to greenhouse, and these seem to have developed by the early 1700s. They made possible immense advances in the culture of the more valuable fruits, especially peaches and nectarines, figs (of the more delicious types that will not ripen outdoors) and some of the late maturing grapes, especially the muscats.

Once the new lean-to houses had been in operation for some while, disadvantages came to light. The wall flues, even when well regulated, gave a very dry heat. This encouraged a number of pests, but as such houses were so widely used for peaches and their allies, the worst of these was the terrible red spider. Anyone who had tried to grow these fruits under glass will know that they need almost daily hosing down or spraying to keep them free. In the days before running water was available in the owner's house, let alone the garden, and long before the existence of the hosepipe, the spraying was done with syringes or hand pumps: a terrible job.

Nevertheless a source of humid heat was available: the hot-bed. These were soon to be seen built along the centre of the new glasshouses. Red spider, disliking the moisture, became less of a problem. The heat was fairly constant and could be managed within a narrow temperature range. Pineapples were often planted directly on the top of the beds. Lettuces and peas were sown for early crops. Potted strawberries, cherries, figs, peaches and sometimes even mulberries could be forced by bringing them into the warmth at the appropriate times. All that was needed for such luxury – apart from a regular supply of glass, since about a third of the fragile 'crown' glass needed to be replaced every year (57) – was a stable large enough to provide the fuel.

Manure heat did not, however, remove the need for wall flues, for the heat still needed boosting in the coldest weather. Various ways were tried to improve the flued wall's efficiency, including mounting flues in the form of terracotta pipes on the inner surface of the wall so that there was less heat lost through the main fabric of the structure. Few advantages were gained from any of the experiments, and in any case the whole method was superseded in the early nineteenth century when techniques in iron founding – developed by the armourers of the Napoleonic Wars (57) – enabled air-tight pipes and stoves to be built that could produce and circulate either steam or hot water. In the manure beds themselves, various other substances were tried. Bark from the tanner's yard was the most important for it gave a good and very long-lasting heat, though it was less widely available than horse dung. The fallen leaves of autumn were also used though the heat was poor and soon finished. They were often used as an additive to more efficient fuels. Cow manure, nowadays the most widely available, produced (and produces) a very high heat very swiftly, but one which then rapidly falls away. In any case, every country household likely to have a full-scale kitchen garden would have had at least a few horses. It was generally felt that even an establishment with just four horses could, if the owner's taste required, produce a pineapple or two every week of the year (69). What a pity that modern modes of transport have few comparable by-products.

Once the water or steam heating systems had become general (and many can still be seen in old conservatories and municipal greenhouses), the main changes became confined to the means of providing heat for the system. Wood and coal were replaced by gas and paraffin, and then by oil. The actual design of the greenhouse has changed little since the great days of the kitchen garden. At the end of the eighteenth century, and well into the nineteenth, there were heated debates about the correct angle of the roof to ensure minimal reflection of the sun's heat. Various compromises were worked out, the roof slope sometimes being determined by the time of year in which the crops growing beneath needed maximum heat from the sun. For instance, vines, needing heat early and late in the year, were sometimes put in steep-roofed houses to catch the low-shining sun of early spring and late autumn. Peaches, maturing during the summer, were grown in houses with much less steeply pitched roofs, to catch the high summer sun. In the early nineteenth century, following J. C. Loudon's development of cast-iron and semi-flexible glazing bars, curved roofs were often used to make glasshouses suitable for all levels of the sun. Glazing was correspondingly complex. For a while it was possible for the informed gardener to say, from a glance at a greenhouse, whether it was intended for pineapples, vines or peaches. Such 'fine tuning' of the gardening system apparently yielded slight advantages, for by the end of the century greenhouse design seems to have aroused no passions at all.

If most glass and heating systems were, and are, designed to produce luxury fruits or lesser crops out of season, quite a number of techniques were once adopted for retarding the ripening of certain plants. For instance, different wall-fruits were grown at various locations in the kitchen garden, those on the sunnier walls ripening first. Currants were commonly treated in this way, especially redcurrants and gooseberries, for they were needed for sauces for game and fish throughout the year. Apples and pears were less frequently treated in the same way. Bush-grown fruits, especially cherries, and some vegetables, particularly artichokes, sometimes had tents of muslin built around them before they ripened. The muslin was kept continually damp, and so the space inside was kept cool by evaporation of the water (78). Similar devices seem to have been used by enthusiastic collectors of tulips to keep those flowers in pristine condition as long as possible. A sketch by John Evelyn shows a rather grand square tent, with a tuft of plumes at each corner like a seventeenth-century bed. In gardens where there was only room for a single range of glass for pineapples, some plants had their ripening retarded by storing fruiting plants in the sheds commonly attached to the outside of the north wall of the garden. Two weeks or so before the properly ripened fruit was needed, the plants were put back under glass. The pineapples then ripened without any diminution of their flavour (90).

For the tree fruits, all the developments in heating and glass, even of the walled gardens themselves, would have been of no use without the techniques of tree pruning used to keep the plant to the required shape and in fruiting condition. The discipline, or even Art, of pruning fruit trees is an ancient one, well understood by the Romans and having an even more ancient Middle Eastern history. The Romans must have introduced such techniques to this country, and they seem to have survived the retreat of the Empire. There are numerous late medieval illustrations showing gardeners pruning vines to arbours, and fruit trees to a shape suitable for bearing. When British gardeners of the Renaissance brought in new types of fruit from other parts of Europe, they must also have brought in other pruning techniques in use there. Certainly by that date, interest in pruning and grafting was sufficiently advanced to support the appearance of a book devoted to the practice: Leonard Mascall's *The booke of Arte and maner, howe to plante and grafte all sortes of trees* of 1569. Fairly sophisticated methods were widely familiar by 1618, for Lawson refers to apricots, cherries and peaches being grown as wall-fruit, and anyone who has tried to keep any of these within bounds will know that quite a degree of skill (and willpower) is needed.

In the early seventeenth century, wealthy owners were still experimenting with fruit on walls of different aspects (54), though the kitchen gardens of lesser owners were still hedged, not walled. In them, pruning techniques were still important, for arbours and bowers were commonly covered with fruit (apples were especially favoured in Britain), trained in fairly precise ways. The main walks of the gardens were often bordered by frameworks of lath to which gooseberries or grander fruits were trained, a feature retained in the kitchen gardens of the eighteenth century and still to be found in cottage gardens at the end of the nineteenth.

By the mid-seventeenth century, the use of walls and pruning methods had reached such a pitch that John Rea could write: 'And although our Countrey cannot boast the benignity of that beautiful Planet that meliorates their fruit in Italy, France and Spain; yet by reflection from good walls, well gravelled walks, the choice of fit kinds, and positions to each particular, we may plentifully partake, and yearly enjoy the benefit, of many delicious fruits.'

Well into the eighteenth century, the wall trees were secured to unheated walls by soft twine or strips of cloth tied to nails hammered into the mortar. Thus sixteenth- and seventeenth-century forms of pruned fruit trees were much less formal than they later became. Informality especially suits peaches and nectarines, where long replacement shoots need tying in every year. It is less suitable for other fruits, for the entire tree needed renailing and retying every year, an immense job. Later on, the walls were fitted with taut horizontal wires to which the trees were trained. This enabled the gardener to make those very precise espaliers and fans that, when well managed, are such a pleasure to look at, even if requiring great patience and self-discipline to create. The trellis frames bordering the garden's main walks were also replaced by wire stretched between posts, and many old walled gardens still have ancient trees growing and fruiting long after the rails have rotted or rusted away. The framework, incidentally, whether of wood or metal, was painted dark green or rusty red. Similar structures are still useful in the garden as a screen to enclose its various parts or to shut out an unwanted view. They need less work than a privet hedge and combine good looks with productivity.

All fruit, whether growing as espaliers or in more natural forms, was dependent on the secondary art of grafting. While this has now been brought to a very high degree of sophistication, so that the vigour of the fruiting plant can be controlled in a remarkably precise way, dwarfing stocks were in use in the sixteenth and seventeenth centuries. While it was realized in ancient times that grafting was often the only way of perpetuating a good variety (though in some, cuttings root easily), it was also thought that the sort of stock used deeply influenced the quality of the fruit produced by the scion. Some unions verged on the eccentric. Googe wrote in the last years of the sixteenth century: 'If you graffe your Peare upon a Mulberie, you shall have red Peares: the Apple is Graffed upon all Peare stocks, and Crab sets, Willow and Poplar: being Graffed upon the Quince, it bringeth forth the fruits which the Greekes call "Melimella": it is also Graffed upon the Plomtree, but being Graffed upon the Plaine tree, it bringeth forth red Apples.' He perhaps did not know what sort of fruit the willow/apple or poplar/apple grafts produced. Such confusion was ancient and widespread, many of the ideas current in those times being derived from Roman beliefs.

However, with the increasingly scientific and experimental attitudes held by seventeenth-century horticulturalists, much of the nonsense fell away. Useful stocks, especially the 'paradise' apple, were imported in large quantities from the Continent. Serious observation of fruit varieties and their behaviour began, and also the selection of good types from what was already available.

Even the most ancient fruit trees and vegetables were attacked by insects and diseases. However little understanding there may have been of the nature of either, early garden books are full of fascinating remedies. Only a few of them can have had much effect.

Of course modern breeding techniques have progressed hand in hand with the development of modern fungicides and insecti-

# Inſtruments for Graffing.

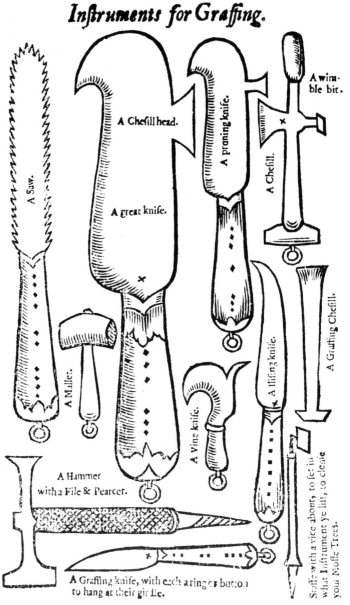

A Saw.

A Cheſill head.

A great knife.

A Maller.

A praning knife.

A Cheſill.

A wimble bit.

A Vine knife.

A liſing knife.

A Grafting Cheſill.

A Hammer with a File & Pearcer.

A Graffing knife, with each a ring or button to hang at their girſle.

Stuffe with a vice about, to ſet in what Inſtrument ye liſt, to cleaſe you Moſſie Trees.

By the sixteenth century, the passion for grafting fruit trees had given rise to many specialized instruments

cides. Consequently plant breeders have, in many crops, tended to ignore the resistance of new varieties to pests and diseases, as any attack could be corrected by new chemicals (though the recent awareness of just how poisonous some of these chemicals are has given a new emphasis to much plant breeding). Before the evolution of these chemicals, a surprising number of ancient crop varieties contained within themselves high degrees of immunity to pests and diseases. Even so, pests and diseases did ruin crops, and at least for insect attack a whole armoury of preventatives was in use. The nature of plant disease was scarcely understood even by the end of the eighteenth century, and so few remedies were used for fungal or viral attack.

Ancient cures persisted long after the introduction of the tobacco plant in the sixteenth century, and solutions made from walnut leaves, wormwood, henbane and elder (the most important) were used throughout that century and the following one. Another concoction to kill pests was the ash of vine stems mixed with water and brushed onto the infected plants (36). For severe infections, garlic stems were burnt near the attacked plant, and the smoke was supposed to destroy the evil-doers. Against caterpillars, or at least the sort of grubs that damage plants below soil level, seeds were soaked in houseleek juice or planted in soot (this last method was also used as a hopeful remedy for finger-and-toe disease in brassica crops). Dill-water, as well as curing colic in babies, stunned caterpillars, enabling their quick despatch. Ants were destroyed by sprinkling their nests with asafoetida mixed with oil, or a few were caught and burnt, for it was believed that the fumes of their scorched comrades would drive the colony away (36).

One of the cures for aphids, suitably called 'garden fleas', was unusual in that it was not derived from any of the plants of the kitchen or herb garden. Crayfish (how nice to have enough to use in this manner) were allowed to rot in warm water for ten days, and the resultant foul juice was sprinkled on the plants. It must have driven gardeners as well as greenfly away. When pineapples became widely grown in the eighteenth century, scale insects became equally widespread. All the usual juices were used in attempts to get rid of them. However, the most famous cure was also found beyond the walls of the garden. Mercury was pounded up with soft soap, and sometimes urine, diluted with water, and the plants were soaked in the resultant fluid. Hopefully, mercury did not lodge in the crevices of the fruit. Although it was then realized that mercury is not in the least soluble in water (94), the

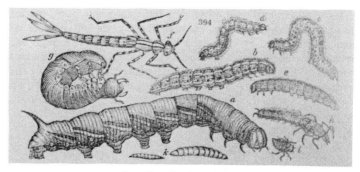

Late Georgian insect pests

cure did seem to work. Perhaps the soap was sufficient. Things were easier for other crops, where nicotine from tobacco leaves was efficient. An infusion of the green leaves was made, some soap added and the fluid put on with a brush or syringe. Smoke from dried leaves was also used, small bellows being made for the purpose. Snuff was almost as effective. As labour was cheap, especially that of the very young and the fairly old, larger insects were easily cleared by hand. The wall fruit was sometimes brushed down with light brooms or sprayed with hot water. In either case, grubs and caterpillars were easily picked up after treatment. Larger still, mice were poisoned by mixing 'beares foot' (*Helleborus foetidus*) with grated cheese and flour. Moles were driven out of their tunnels by pushing down a nut or two, filled with burning chaff, rosin and sulphur.

Birds, one of the curses of modern kitchen gardens, have always been a nuisance. At least in earlier times, the gardener had the satisfaction of being able to eat them. Gervase Markham wrote of such things in 1676:

See you here a whole Army of mischiefs banded in troops against the most fruitful trees the earth bears? assailing your good labours. Good things have most enemies. A skilful Fruiterer must put to his helping hand, and disband, and put them to flight.

For the first rank of beasts, besides your out-strong fence, you must have a fair and swift Grey-hound, a Stone-bow, Gun, and if need require, an Apple with a hook for a Deer, and an Hare-pipe for an Hare.

Your Cherries, and other Berries, when they be ripe, will draw all the Black-birds, Thrustles, and Mag-pies, to your Orchard. The Bul-finch is a devourer of your fruit in the bud, I have had whole Trees shall'd out with them in Winter times.

The best remedy here is a Stone-bow, a Piece, especially if you have a musket, or sparrow-hawk in winter, to make the Black-bird stoop into a bush or hedge.

For the most ingenious pest of all, man-traps were a common piece of kitchen garden equipment until finally outlawed. Even the liberal J. C. Loudon merely suggests (57) the use of the new 'humane' traps, which made a clean break in the leg bone, not crushing it to fragments and making it impossible to set. Subtler, and earlier, Markham wrote: 'Justice and liberality will put away evil neighbours, or evil neighbourhood. And then (if God bless and give success to your labours), I see not what hurt your orchard can sustain.'

# Breeding and Conservation

Primitive man, expert botanist that he was (and remains, in places), was well aware of the connection between plants, their seed and the resultant seedlings. He will also have noticed, both in his own species and in most others, that progeny and parents often look slightly different in spite of the intimate connection between them. Of crop plants, selection of variants showing some advantage over parents or siblings may have started long before formal agriculture began and, in essence, still continues. While we now try to manipulate the genetic system that ensures the continual productions of variants within each species (and call it plant 'breeding'), earlier 'selecting' was a more random affair. While no doubt in the very earliest phases of crop development the selection was entirely passive, with the gardener merely waiting for new types to appear, everyone will be familiar with the urge to plant the seed of a particularly enjoyed fruit, and I can see no reason to assume that 'primitive' gardeners felt differently. Of course, seedlings, particularly of fruit trees, are quite often less good to eat than their parents; only rare ones are better. Nowadays few of us have either garden space or time to spare to let our seedlings develop and show us what they can produce. In earlier times, these difficulties applied less often.

In some crops, especially among the vegetables, there is a tendency to self-pollination. As this generally ensures a high level of seed production, such forms have often been more or less automatically selected, soon becoming unable to produce variants. Such varieties become uniform, and changeless, and while such properties are valuable today, it is not clear how much value they would have had for early gardeners. At a time when most gardeners saved their own seed from year to year, at least there would not have been problems with crop deterioration or transformation. For crops in which self-pollination is rare, there does not seem to have been any understanding of the act of pollination until the eighteenth century. Sixteenth- and seventeenth-century gardening books often have references to the gradual decline of brassica crops grown from saved seed, and the need to buy it in from a foreign source every second year or so. The deterioration (or transformation, as it was sometimes seen) was probably the result of bees working over the various plots of brassica crops in flower and happily distributing the genetic material contained in the pollen.

Consequently, although some crops contain some very ancient varieties, most do not. In the majority of crops, particularly vegetables, maintenance of varieties was fairly haphazard until the nineteenth century, and so the number of them within each species was much smaller than is the case today. However, the diversity of character in many crops, especially the ancient ones like peas, broad beans and cabbages, was often much wider than today. Regrettably, many groups of varieties within the main vegetable crops seem to have vanished forever.

The situation amongst the fruit crops is rather better. Trees are long lived, and in any case interest in new fruit varieties has always been better documented than that in new vegetable cultivars. This is certainly because fruit varieties were bulked up and distributed as grafted plants or cuttings, and as all the plants of one variety were in fact part of one plant, they were both uniform and generally clearly distinguishable from other types of the same crop. There also seems to have been little interest in vegetable varieties as objects for status and show (though of course certain crops such as artichokes and asparagus were regarded as such). With fruit varieties, the situation seems to have been different, at least from the beginning of the sixteenth century. At that time, many new types were brought in from abroad. In the following century, with the increasingly scientific and experimental attitudes held by seventeenth-century horticulturalists, serious observation of fruit varieties and their behaviour began. Seeds were sown in large numbers in the pursuit of improved forms, and many new sorts were brought into commerce. Gentlemen gardeners began to collect them, and new sorts of apple, cherry and peach were planted in the formal gardens in front of town house and country seat as much for show as for the delights of the dessert. A surprising number of varieties taken up during this seventeenth-century wave of interest can still be found in commerce, and forgotten ones no doubt still exist in ancient orchards and gardens. Many of them were particularly suited to local growing conditions or gastronomic habits.

In the early eighteenth century, the nature of the sexual method of reproduction in plants began to be observed, though it was not made much use of until the closing years of the century. Serious breeding work began in strawberries and various other crops, and improvements were made easily and with speed. The nineteenth century saw a huge increase in the understanding of the sexual mechanism, and in the techniques used to exploit it. The twentieth century has seen the rise of the science of genetics and its addition to the plant breeders' armoury. Many new varieties have been so successful that in some crops only a handful are now commonly grown and are expected to suit every garden in Britain. The old diversity has vanished. The small number of varieties available does, of course, have considerable commercial advantages. Because of the structure of the market, the breeder of a new variety, if it is successful, can be sure of a large demand and a corresponding reward. It helps the middlemen in the transaction, because they do not have to build up and hold huge numbers of varieties with only a small sale for each one. To some extent, it helps the gardener who can buy material more cheaply and also needs less information to choose between ten varieties than he does to choose between two hundred.

One major disadvantage is in the gradual reduction of what is known as the 'gene pool'. Take apples, for instance; of the handful of widely grown apples, it must naturally seem to most breeders that the easiest way to produce even better varieties is to use some of that handful as the parents of new types. Breeding is an expensive process (for several reasons), and such a conservative approach reduces the risk of wasting money. Consequently, interest focuses on a few cultivars, and the myriads of other varieties, whatever their flavour, hardiness or keeping qualities, become forgotten. They eventually die out and are lost forever. The qualities which they contained are lost as well and so may never be available to either breeder or grower again.

It is entirely understandable that any private gardener with a small garden can only afford a little space for any fruit tree or odd vegetable. He, or she, is naturally unwilling to take the risk of planting some ancient and half-forgotten local variety; something well known and risk-free is needed.

The state has now been reached where many owners of small gardens, whether in town or country, who have both time and enthusiasm to grow some fruit and vegetables, grow the same varieties that can be more efficiently produced by the farmer (they still taste nicer from the garden, even so) and which can be bought in the nearest greengrocer's. It seems to me that small gardens should be producing what cannot be bought: sorrel, absolutely fresh artichokes, sugar peas, white cucumbers, perfect asparagus, properly ripened apricots, morellos, nectarines and the rest. Certainly, for the gardener or cook who is prepared to be adventurous, the kitchen garden can yield an abundance of interest, beauty and culinary delight. Any gardener who does have some space that can be put at risk for a few years would find it well worth hunting out local or specialist nurseries, seed suppliers or local gardeners, who can yield something that is out of the ordinary, as well as out of the past. Not only does that keep the gene pool at a reasonable level, it can also provide some delicious eating.

It is, though, becoming much easier to find old, new or forgotten kitchen garden plants. For the vegetables, several seed firms now supply many interesting plants, and it is always worth experimenting with something new to you. Quite a number of crop 'groups' (like white cucumbers or striped-pod beans) which were grown in this country in the seventeenth and eighteenth centuries can still be found in the rest of Europe. The Food and Agriculture Organization (FAO), based in Rome, issues a list of all major seed companies worldwide. A surprising number of the companies are perfectly willing to supply catalogues and seed to anyone interested. There are, though, legal restrictions placed on the importation of seed of some crops, especially lettuces and tomatoes, so it is worth checking with your local agricultural advisory office.

As it is now illegal to sell varieties whose names do not appear on the *National List of Varieties*, and as only varieties for which someone is willing to pay for maintenance (and who therefore needs to make a substantial profit from them) are included, many good varieties with small sales have vanished from commerce. Some of the best of these can now be found only in private gardens or in some of the new (and also private) 'vegetable sanctuaries' set up under the aegis of the Henry Doubleday

A fine, walled pomegranate orchard from Austen's *A Treatise of Fruit Trees*, 1753

Foundation. As the sanctuaries cannot sell seed, they 'lend' it out to gardeners who are able to produce a good new generation of seed and return some of it to the sanctuary.

Seed banks have also been set up at various agricultural institutes for the preservation of vanishing varieties, though the banks are primarily resources for the plant breeder rather than the gourmet.

Interesting old fruit varieties can also be hard to find. It is worth checking with the nurseries in your locality, though the majority of them will be buying in their stock and only in well-known varieties. However, several long-established British nurseries hold wide ranges of half-forgotten cultivars, especially of apples and pears, and a number of new nurseries are specializing in rare soft fruits. There are several important national collections of fruit types, and although none of them will supply material directly to the amateur gardener, they do supply a few specialist nurseries.

Help is therefore at hand for some of the old plants that remain. Most of the biggest projects are government funded and are designed mainly to help the plant breeder. However, far more needs doing, and the impetus must come from the millions of ordinary gardeners who could, if they wanted more delectable gardens, easily ensure that all the rich possibilities of the kitchen garden were preserved forever. Perhaps once again we could have gardens as splendid and delightful as that described by William Lawson in 1618. He writes:

> For whereas every other pleasure commonly fills some one of our senses, and that only with delight; this makes all our senses swim in pleasure, and that with infinite variety; joyned with no less commodity. . . . When you behold in divers corners . . . *Mounts* of stone or wood . . . [or] in some corner (or more) a time Dial or Clock, and some Antick works; and especially silver sounding Musick, mixt instruments, and Voices, gracing the rest: How will you be Wrapt with Delight. . . .
>
> Large Walks, broad and long, close and open, like the *Tempe* groves at Thessaly, raised with gravel and sand, having seats and banks of Camomile, all this delights the mind, and brings health to the Body.
>
> View now with delight the works of your own hands, your fruit trees of all sorts, loaden with sweet blossoms, and fruits of all tastes, operations, and colours: your trees standing in comely order, which way soever you look.
>
> For your borders on every side hanging, and dropping with Feberries, Raspberries, Barberries, Currans, and the roots of your trees powdered with Strawberries, Red, White, and Green, what a pleasure this is!

# THE PLANTS

# Almond

*Prunus dulcis* (MILLER) D. A. WEBB

*Origin:* central and western Asia

A lovely tree, native to the central and western parts of Asia (93), with wild types still being found in south-eastern Russia and Afghanistan (46). It seems to have spread rather slowly westwards. There are many biblical references to it. Theophrastus thought it very unusual in that it was the only tree that produced its flowers before the leaves (peaches and nectarines may not have reached Greece in the fourth century BC). In Rome, two hundred years later, Cato was still calling almonds 'Greek nuts' and says that they were highly regarded (66). They cannot yet have been cultivated there, although the Italian climate is ideal for them, and the country has been producing substantial crops since the eighteenth century (66). They seem to have been cultivated by the time Pliny the Elder was writing in the first century AD, for he says that an infusion of the roots of the bitter almond tree was used as a sort of skin tonic (80). A similar use for almond oil persists today (97). Bitter almonds were widely used by the Romans: Plutarch relates that they were used as a preventative of drunkenness. The dose was five bitter almonds for every cup of wine (76), though as the nuts are poisonous the cure might have been more dangerous than the effects of alcohol.

The Romans must have imported the nuts into Britain, though there seems to be no record of their cultivation until the sixteenth century (74). The nuts were an important article of trade long before that, for both culinary and medicinal uses. The trees have never been a particularly successful crop in Britain, though the redoubtable Samuel Hartlib reports a good crop from his brother's free-standing trees by 1653 (38). The trees do not easily go dormant and in our variable winters produce flowers at the least hint of warmth, so that both they and the young fruits are frequently killed by frost. The most reliable way of growing them has generally been as espaliers on a south-facing wall. Suitably looked after, crops can be obtained at least as far north as Fife, where the terraced gardens at Aberdour Castle produced ripe fruit every couple of years in the late seventeenth century (91).

Today the crop is widely distributed all around the Mediterranean, as well as being extensively grown in China and Japan. The species is remarkably variable, and in many places where it is grown as a crop, even the smallest landowner may have his own unique type. Although the almond reached Europe before the closely related peach and apricot, the fact that the plants are self-incompatible is sometimes suggested as evidence that it has been more recently domesticated (46).

For the cook, the almond has always had considerable potential, and one that was once much wider than it now is. Marzipan is an ancient and still admired sweetmeat, though the almond milk once used as a stock in which to cook medieval and Tudor meat is no longer met with (though it can still be found, if rarely, on the Continent). Perhaps the highest peak of the almond's culinary usefulness was in our eighteenth- and nineteenth-century desserts. Innumerable blancmanges, puddings, cakes and pastries were both flavoured and decorated by them; the delicious hedgehog pudding (a thick almond custard) was covered with almond spines (15), and almond and lemon jelly was equally good – a good quantity of ground almond was infused in the hot liquid and then strained out before the lemon jelly was poured into its mould (13). Curiously, in spite of all this, almonds were not regarded as being nutritious (66).

Medicinally they were thought good for 'gravel', kidney stones, coughs and inflammation of the lungs (26). Even in the nineteenth century bitter almonds were still used as a vermifuge and to clear obstructions of liver and spleen (66). The leaves were useful too, at least in the sixteenth century, when they were applied to the brow, mixed with oil of roses and vinegar or 'with great Profite laide to with hony uppon corrupt and naughtie spreading sores and the bitings of mad dogs' (26), though a similar mixture was also used to 'cleanse the skin and face from all spots, pimples and lenticles' (26).

# Apple

*Malus domestica* BORKHAUSEN

*Origin:* the Caucasus and Turkestan

The apple, probably our most important fruit tree, has been cultivated since prehistoric times and was admired enough to be offered as a lure to Eve (but see Quince). Its origin is complex, probably involving hybridization between a number of related *Malus* species (93). The place of origin, or at least of widest diversity of types, is in the Caucasus and Turkestan (46), though many apparent wildlings are found from Turkey to India (93).

In Roman times, orchards were very profitable; over twenty different sorts of apple were grown (76), and at least some of these must have been distributed throughout the Empire. It was realized early that superior sorts do not often come true from seed, and the necessary grafting techniques were well known to Roman gardeners and were probably known very much earlier.

In Britain, the apple was an extremely early arrival, and cultivation continued after the collapse of the Roman Empire. The crop developed over many centuries and gave rise to huge numbers of local varieties, many of which survived into the seventeenth century and were of medieval or earlier origin (only a few are still known to survive). With such a range of colour and flavour, their diversity has always appealed to the collector; forty-eight varieties were listed as growing in the Tradescants' garden in 1634, Parkinson (75) described fifty-seven varieties (excluding sweetings and crabs), and Ray listed seventy-eight important varieties in 1688. Interest in seedlings soon developed, and selection of new varieties began in earnest in the seventeenth century. Soon there were many new sorts of jennets, pippins, pearmains and russets (67). Serious breeding work started in the late eighteenth century (76, 46), by which time a knowledge of the sexual mechanism of plant hybridization was widely accepted. Quite a number of seventeenth- and eighteenth-century apples can still be found in catalogues and are worth trying if you have sufficient room. By the early nineteenth century the list of available apples numbered many hundreds, and even though the number listed today is considerably fewer, anyone trying to select a few trees for the garden will still find the choice bewildering.

The early lists of apples always paid considerable attention to crab and cider varieties. The crab apple, now generally classed as part of the native flora though many trees will be descendants of eating types, was very useful (see Crab apple). Cider, supposedly a Norman invention (76), was a commonly consumed beverage in most parts of the country until the end of the eighteenth century. In Somerset it was common until recent times to include quantities of cider as part of the contracted payments for farm labourers. Its production needed special varieties of apple, sweet but generally too hard to eat. 'Gennet Moyle' was often held to be one of the best varieties, giving a cider with a very delicate perfume. It took twenty-two bushels of fruit to make one hogshead of cider, the apples being shaken or stripped from the trees in early autumn, and often left lying in the orchard to ripen further, until finally carted off to the cider presses (11).

Crab and cider apple trees were often part of the kitchen garden hedge in the sixteenth century (28) and were relegated to the hedgerows once masonry walls became common. Where cider was very popular, the trees were grown in orchards, but only the finest dessert apples were ever admitted to the kitchen garden proper. There, at least after the mid-seventeenth century, they were espaliered along parts of the east and west walls, and often along wire frames bordering the main walks of the garden. The south-facing wall was usually reserved for more exotic fruit.

Of the really ancient varieties, only 'Golden Pippin' and 'Nonpareil' are now at all often seen, both dating to before 1600. The first of the pippin types seem to have been imported from Europe in the early sixteenth century, possibly by Leonard Mascall, a royal fruiterer, though they were still rare even in the middle of the seventeenth century. The Ribston pippin probably dates from the end of that century (92), although the famous and widely grown 'Cox's Orange Pippin' was only bred in the 1830s, by a retired brewer at Colnbrook (92).

Of other famous names, the 'Bramley Seedling', as widely popular now as in Victorian times, probably originated in the early nineteenth century and was sown by a Miss Brailsford, not a Mr Bramley (92). 'Golden Delicious' and its red counterpart are modern American varieties (46).

The market for new apple varieties is now worldwide. Just because the market is so huge and knowledge of the apple's myriad possibilities rather restricted, most modern breeding is between varieties that are already widely popular. Much of the important genetic diversity shown by the older and increasingly rare varieties is being lost. If you have room for some of the unusual ones, do try them; some delicious flavours await you.

Of course, apples have also always been popular because the cultivars all ripen at different times of the year, being available from July to April or May. Before apples were imported, or refrigerated stores were built, late ripening apples (and pears) were the only fresh fruit available through the winter and early spring. Storage was only a slight problem; even quite modest establishments had an apple house or shed attached to a north-facing wall. Sometimes the attics of the main house were utilized. In the sixteenth and seventeenth centuries, apples were most often stored on open shelves, and indeed this remained the most common method into the nineteenth century. However, in the eighteenth century other ways were tried, from storing them in airtight barrels and separated by dry sand to wrapping them in hay, though various writers said that the odour of the hay tainted them (66). Today, most apples are individually wrapped in paper and stored several layers deep in shallow boxes. This reduces the dehydration that must have greatly reduced the storage life of apples set out on open shelves, and also stops one rotting apple from infecting its neighbours.

For apples that had begun to wrinkle and become unfit for dessert, there was an extensive cuisine extending far beyond apple pie and baked apples. Pickled and spiced (delicious), they were served with roast beef, and some early eighteenth-century recipes tried to imitate pickled mango, a long process involving re-boiling the pickle every alternate day for three weeks. There were innumerable apple sauces for fish, pork and game; old eating-apples were parboiled to turn the flesh pink (only a few modern varieties do this) and then finished off by stewing in cream (15). Others were sliced and added to pancakes and puddings; golden pippins were stewed in syrup until they became quite translucent (and still whole) and then flavoured with lemon juice and grated peel (13). The most delicious of all is the old English dish called 'Black Caps', found in many seventeenth- and eighteenth-century cook-books. It is the way we finish off most of the apples grown in my garden. The fruit is halved and cored and placed cut side down in a large dish. Lemon juice is dribbled over each half, then a generous scattering of grated lemon peel, and finally a teaspoon of white sugar. The idea is to get as much peel and sugar as possible to stick to the top of the apple half. Some recipes suggest sprinkling with orange flower or rose water, but if the apples are good, this offers no advantage. The apples are then baked or put under the grill. In either case, when cooked, the sugar should have begun to caramelize, and the skins to blacken.

Not surprisingly for such an ancient fruit, the apple has found a number of non-culinary uses. 'Pomatum' was, at least in the sixteenth century, a pulp of apples and pig fat, scented with rose water and used as a cosmetic to smooth the skin (34). The leaves were 'good to be laide upon the beginnings of phegmons (that is simple tumours or swellings), and are good to be laide upon wounds to keep them from evil heat and postumation' (26). The bark was used to give a yellow dye (66), and the wood was used for cog wheels and 'turned' work (66). It was a valuable and fragrant firewood (76).

# Apricot

*Prunus armeniaca* LINNAEUS

*Origin:* central Asia and western China

An extremely ancient and variable crop that originated farther east than its Latin name suggests and can still be found wild in western China and central Asia (46, 93). All are extremely tolerant of cold, but the season of flowering is very variable, all the forms grown in the West being early. These types seem to have filtered gradually westwards following the eastern invasions of Alexander the Great, only reaching Rome after the Roman-Persian wars of the first century BC. Trees grown then seem only to have been of two varieties. Pliny the Elder reported that the first fruits of the season fetched a dernier apiece and that, whatever the season, they were thought good for invalids (80).

The Romans distributed the fruit throughout Europe (93), and it is hard to believe that they did not bring such a delicious fruit with them to Britain. However, whether or not it was a reintroduction, one of Henry VIII's gardeners brought trees from Italy in 1524 (76). Less than a hundred years later, espaliers are recorded as growing at Hampton Court (87), so the best way of managing

An old and delicious variety of apricot: 'Moor Park'

that plant seems to have been well understood. By 1634 five varieties were growing in the Tradescants' garden (3); Sir Thomas Hanmer grew four on sheltered south- and east-facing walls. Both Parkinson and Rea list six varieties, and by the early eighteenth century Miller is listing seven sorts. The number increased throughout that century, by the end of which the variety 'Moor Park' (named after a famous seventeenth-century garden), was widely grown and remains so today.

By the middle of the nineteenth century the trees were usually grown against east- or west-facing walls (19); the south-facing ones were thought to ripen the fruit too quickly (66) and were reserved for peaches and nectarines (19). For some reason apricots seem rarely grown today, though they are exceptionally hardy and vigorous (46) and produce abundantly outdoors well up to the Firth of Forth and beyond. In fact, they are quite alarmingly vigorous and need heavy pruning to keep them under control. I have seen one as an espalier against the walls of a Scottish castle, and the tree was at least forty feet tall.

Thinnings of the young fruit were stewed in syrup and used in tarts and pies (76), though Cobbett thought that they were inferior to young gooseberries. The mature fruit, apart from being pickled or chutneyed (superb), was used to make apricot 'chips'. It is a commonly found recipe for their preservation; the halved and stoned fruit were steeped in hot and heavy syrup for a whole day and then dried in the sun (13). Probably more pleasant was the recipe 'to preserve Apricots in Jelly', another standard method, but using apples to make the liquor set firm – neither peaches nor apricots have much pectin (15).

Outside the kitchen, the young shoots were used to produce a golden-cinnamon coloured dye (66), or the leaves were boiled with vinegar and used as a hair restorer, in tertian fevers, or fresh leaves were laid on children's navels as a vermifuge (26).

# Artichoke

*Cynara scolymus* LINNAEUS

*Origin:* Mediterranean region

An important, splendid and useful plant, grown since ancient times. Probably a native of the Mediterranean area, it was admired by the Greeks, and Pliny the Elder says that it commanded higher prices in Rome than any other vegetable. Such was the demand that artichokes were imported from North Africa, and commoners were prohibited from eating them – a prohibition perhaps having several motives (77). Ever since then, artichokes have been thought a rather grand crop, even though they grow so easily. Even in nineteenth-century Scotland, only prosperous gentlemen grew them and would have regarded any lesser man growing artichokes as impertinent (69).

The Romans probably distributed the plant throughout the Empire, though the earliest reference to them growing in England dates from 1551 (101); they were certainly widely grown by 1596. Parkinson says (74) that the plants grew so well here that many were exported, some even to Italy. By 1687 it was thought 'One of the most excellent Fruits of the Kitchen-garden' (108).

Such was the enthusiasm for it, that it was often the centre of the gardener's attention. Because the plants produce two flushes of flower heads each year, one in early summer and the other in early autumn, the first flush was smoothed out so that artichokes were available steadily throughout the summer; muslin tents were built over the plants, and the cloth was kept damp to keep the temperature inside as low as possible (78).

In the seventeenth century only Evelyn (30) seems to have suggested the Continental practice of eating the young flower heads raw. He ate them quartered, washed down with a glass of wine. Only the very young heads of some varieties can be so treated. More generally, they were boiled (as commonly today) or fried until crisp, flavoured with parsley and dressed with orange juice – excellent (30). The Romans preserved the 'fonds' for winter use, using either vinegar or honey (77). Eighteenth-century cooks used similar methods or dried them, in which case they needed soaking for two days before eating (13), or parboiled them and then potted them up in melted butter (68).

It was once common to use the plant in other ways. Sometimes, the young stalks of the flower heads were eaten in their own right (and are good, though they rapidly become stringy as the flower matures). More frequently, the young leaf bunches, whether produced in spring or after the plants were cut down following the first flush of flowering (68), were blanched. Called 'chards' or 'custons' (68), they were then pickled (and are good) or boiled as a vegetable. There seems to have been some difference of opinion as to whether they were better than cardoons (12). I think not. For the youngish flower heads, of all the sauces suggested to go with them, I still think that the best is an ordinary butter sauce, sharpened with just a dash of vinegar. If you have enough of them just to use the 'fonds', there are dozens of possibilities available. Two nice early eighteenth-century ones are artichoke pie – layers of 'fonds', egg yolks, butter, flavoured with a little mace, morels and truffles if available, and all moistened with a little stock and white wine, and baked in a puff pastry case (1) – or artichoke broth. In this, the stock from a boiled chicken is used to make a lettuce and spinach soup. At the last moment a few quartered 'fonds' are added, as well as the scrapings from the artichoke scales. The mixture, again with a little vinegar, is poured round the bird. Lady Castlehill (15) does not say exactly how the dish was eaten; presumably the carcase was carved after the soup had gone down.

Artichoke plants once had many medicinal and other uses.

Since Roman times the plants were thought to be aphrodisiac (21, 26, 28), a belief that lasted here well into the seventeenth century. Estienne and Liebault even suggested them as a powder, to be applied for 'Weaknesse of the generative Parts'. The Romans also used the juice of the head before it flowers as a cure for baldness, and the roots were eaten to increase alcohol tolerance (77). Both were used to ensure male children for mothers. Lyte's translation of Dodoens' herbal, says, among other things, that 'they engender noughtie humours, especially being eaten raw and unprepared . . . the rote is good against the ranke smell of the arme pittes, if after taking cleare away of the pith, the same rote is boiled in wine and dronken. For it sendeth forth plentie of stinking urine, whereby the ranke and rammish savour of all the body is amended.'

In eighteenth-century England the florets were used as a substitute for rennet (66), and the plants were also used to produce a yellow dye. Extracts are still used in digestive tonics and in some apéritifs and are sometimes suggested by herbalists for jaundice, anaemia and liver damage (97).

There are dozens of varieties, differing in colour, size, meatiness and the shape and sharpness of the scales. It was once thought that smooth artichokes were grown by breaking the spine off the seed before planting (28). Certainly, growing the plants from seed does produce a good range of types, and it is an easy matter thereafter to select ones which you find most useful. It is often suggested that the plants be replaced every few years (not a difficult matter), though plants will happily produce crops for fifteen or twenty years.

# Asparagus

### *Asparagus officinalis* LINNAEUS

*Origin:* Europe and Asia

A native of Europe and Asia, it seems to have been known as a vegetable to the ancient Greeks – though they may have eaten the spiny buds of another species, *A. acutifolius* (51). If not by the

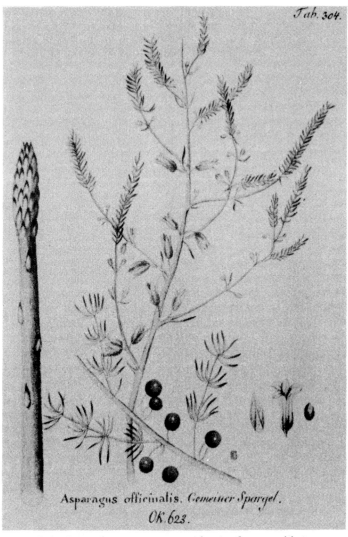

*Tab. 304.*

Asparagus officinalis. *Gemeiner Spargel.*

*OK. 623.*

Early nineteenth-century asparagus, showing flowers and fruit

Greeks, it was certainly domesticated by the Romans, who grew it in trenches to blanch the young stems and achieved such spear weights that there were only three of them to the Roman pound (51), about 11½ ounces. The main centre of cultivation was at Ravenna (80).

The Romans may have introduced the cultivated sorts to Britain, but thereafter it seems not to have been extensively cultivated until the sixteenth century and then, as now, was served at the beginning of a meal. They were generally stewed in broth, and thereafter served with oil and vinegar (34). Estienne and Liebault quote the curious belief that asparagus plants could be obtained by burying a ram's horn with holes drilled in it, a superstition that seems to have originated in ancient Greece (58). Even by the end of the seventeenth century, Worlidge (107) was writing that 'some curious persons put Rams-horns at the bottom of the Trench, and hold for certain, that they have a kind of Sympathy with Asparagus which makes them prosper the better'. Of course, horns have plenty of nitrogen.

Whatever the superstition, by the seventeenth century the cuisine associated with asparagus was splendidly various. Evelyn preferred his asparagus less heavily boiled than was then general, and also preferred the English varieties to the larger and less well flavoured Dutch ones. Young spears were often chopped into short lengths as a substitute for early green peas, and asparagus ragout was becoming popular (77).

However, the eighteenth century was the great age of asparagus. In Scotland it was available all year round (49), as it was no doubt in England, with some of the crop being cut to the ground and heavily manured in July to provide spears for September (77). Other roots were lifted in winter and forced on hot beds (see p. 39; 49), or in melon stoves (90). The quantity of asparagus suggested for small households was quite prodigious; Martyn (66) recommended eight roods (two acres) for a small family. Urban Londoners were supplied from Battersea, where there were 260 acres of the crop in the early nineteenth century.

By the middle of that century there were many varieties (105). There are fewer today, though the varieties have always been poorly defined (93). The 'Argenteuil' types are most popular in Britain; varieties from Holland and Germany are often paler and need more diligent peeling of the lower parts of the spear if the skin's bitter flavour is to be avoided.

For such a curious-looking plant, it seems to have rather few magic or herbal properties. Roman beekeepers believed that the insects would not sting them if they rubbed themselves with a liniment of oil and asparagus (77). Similar beliefs persisted into the sixteenth century, for Dodoens suggested boiling the roots in wine and using the liquor to protect one from venomous beasts.

Considering how early the plant was grown, it is surprising, too, how rarely it is seen in today's gardens. Seed from good plants germinates easily and will yield the first crop in three years. Even a row or two of plants will give an occasional 'bonne bouche' for a small family. One of the nicest ways of making use of a small quantity is a sauce for a boiled chicken. The spears are chopped into half-inch lengths, parboiled and then stewed in butter until tender. Plenty of cream is added, and the sauce heated again until it thickens. Only five or six spears are necessary, and the results transform the fowl. The above is a good eighteenth-century recipe from Martha Bradley.

The crop is fairly pest-proof (asparagus beetle can be a nuisance in some gardens but is easily eradicated) and does not require too much attention, though obviously big spears are obtained by good feeding. The foliage is good-looking and goes a handsome yellow in autumn.

# Asparagus Pea

*Tetragonolobus purpureus* MOENCH (*Lotus tetragonolobus* LINNAEUS)

*Origin:* southern Europe

This charming and delicious plant is a native of southern Europe and was cultivated by Gerard before 1596, though as a decorative, not an esculent. Parkinson called it (74) 'Crimson blossomed or square Podded Vetch'. The flowers certainly are crimson, but with a very dark central patch. Its edible qualities seem to have been discovered soon afterwards, but it seems not to have achieved great popularity. In the 1807 edition of Miller's *Gardener's Dictionary* Martyn says, rather stuffily, that 'it was formerly cultivated as an esculent plant, for the green pods but they are very coarse. This plant is now chiefly cultivated in flower gardens for ornament.'

Perhaps Dr Martyn gathered the pods when they were too mature, for they rapidly become stringy and inedible. In my garden, they remain eatable up to 1½ inches long, though it is usually recommended that they are eaten at an inch long. A good test is to find out how flexible the pods are; if they do not bend easily, they will be too woody to eat.

It is also often said that the plants do best on a poor soil; they certainly grow well, but the yield can be disappointing. It is better to include them in the leguminous part of the rotation. The flavour is so delicate (which does not mean that there is none) that they should be served by themselves, unseasoned, perhaps on toast to mop up the cooking juices (really the only way of cooking them is to stew them in butter in a closed pan until they are tender). One of the objections to the crop is the difficulty of actually gathering the pods, as they are green and leaf-like. The best time to do the job is a little after sundown when the leaves themselves close up and the pods become more easily visible.

It cannot honestly be said that they are especially decorative, certainly not enough to qualify them as a productive part of the flower garden. There seems to have been no herbal interest in them, though the seeds were once roasted as a substitute for coffee (105).

# Aubergine
## (or Egg Plant)

**Solanum melongena** LINNAEUS

*Origin:* central and southern Asia

A plant of ancient cultivation, first domesticated in India or China – the earliest Chinese records date from the fifth century BC (93). The wild plants have spiny and bitter fruit but have given rise to a large number of edible types and a very extensive cuisine.

The first European records are from the sixteenth century, and, as with the tomato, it must first have been regarded with suspi-

Elizabethan aubergines, perhaps a small white type

cion. Early names include 'madde apple' (26) or *'mala insana'*; the distaste is said to have been because the fruits resemble those of the 'male' mandrake (77). The word 'aubergine' is a corruption of an Arabic word (93), and there are records of the plant's cultivation by the Arabs from the fourth century AD. Possibly the plant reached northern Europe via North Africa and Spain. 'Egg plant' refers to the smaller white-fruited varieties that seem to have been most common here when first introduced.

Needing considerable warmth to ripen its fruit, it was scarcely grown here until the use of glasshouses became widespread and cheap. Gerard grew it as a considerable rarity, and it remained uncommon on British tables until the nineteenth century, being confined to wealthy or Jewish households (77). On the Continent, however, it was by then widely grown and eaten as far north as Paris. Four varieties were grown, cooked in much the same ways as they are today. One nice recipe suggests stewing them in wine, with plenty of pepper (26). They were also pickled in honey and vinegar for winter use (77).

It was sometimes described as an aphrodisiac, though it seems to have been rarely used medicinally. No doubt the association with lechery stems in part from the curious shape of some varieties of the fruit. Dodoens says of it, after noting how it should be cooked, 'But it is an unholsome meate, ingendring the body full of evil humours.'

In Britain the plants need to be under cover to fruit well. Greenfly and red spider develop a considerable passion for them, and here we find it difficult to give the crop the attention it needs. Nevertheless, a well-grown plant in full production can be a very handsome sight and well worth attempting.

# Balm

*Melissa officinalis* LINNAEUS

*Origin:* southern Europe

A good, if vigorous, plant for the garden with bright green, golden or variegated leaves and a nice, if unsubtle, lemony smell. Little used in cooking (it is sometimes used as a substitute for lemon but can be a trifle bitter), it has been used for wine – one which Evelyn said was incomparable (30) – as well as for many medicinal uses. Paracelsus (95) hoped to use it as a recipe for the complete restoration of Man. The nearest it got to that was no doubt the wine (Mortimer thought it at least as good as cowslip), though the leaves are used in Benedictine and Chartreuse. A few leaves once found their way into eighteenth-century salads (97), a use which is worth reviving, if in moderation, for although the leaves have a nice taste the texture is very rough.

A native of southern Europe, Gerard said that it was introduced in 1573. It may have been here much earlier for it was
extensively used for medicine in the Greek, Roman and Islamic
worlds. Its main use seems to have been as a cure for melancholia
and hypochondria. The plant was usually taken as tea, the green
leaves being most effective, though in France the young shoots
were made into cakes with sugar, eggs and rosewater and in that
form were given to mothers in childbirth (26, 68).

The plant has always been associated with bees. Pliny the Elder
noted that hives were rubbed with leaves to keep the swarm at
home, a practice still carried out in early nineteenth-century
England (77). The leaves are still supposed to be a good cure for a
bee sting (I have not tried it), and the juice was once used for
'green' wounds (26). The vigorous growth and pleasing smell
ensured that the plant was used to strew Elizabethan floors, and
the scent of lemons must have done much to lighten the heavier
odours of the time.

In the garden the plant can easily swamp its neighbours, and if
it has not been gathered (before the flowers open is the best time)
and dried, a host of seedlings rapidly appears. If you do not want
the leaves for tea or pot-pourri, the plants can be cut to the
ground in the summer and are rapidly furnished with new shoots.

# Barberry

*Berberis vulgaris* LINNAEUS

*Origin:* native

Possibly a native plant, though its wide, if very local, occurrence
may be due to the culinary importance it once had. Both berries
and leaves were used in the kitchen; the berries pickled, and used
as a garnish for all 'white' dishes and a number of others. For
instance, the unpleasant eyeballs of cooked hares, rabbits and
fish were generally replaced by them. The resultant red glare
does not seem to have unnerved sixteenth-, seventeenth- or
eighteenth-century diners. The crystallized berries decorated
some desserts, and fresh ones were used to make jams, jellies and

comfits. All three, while delicious, were thought to have various medicinal uses, being used for gum ulcers, sore throats, dysentery (76) and even gout and rheumatism (97). Herbalists still recommend them as a diuretic and antiseptic (97). Worlidge was clearly right when he wrote, in 1668, 'a common Plant . . . and bears Fruit very useful in Housewifery'.

The leaves are pleasantly acid, and the young ones were added to salads from at least the sixteenth century to the eighteenth (34, 66), and were also used to make a good jelly, one eaten with cold meats. Roots or bark, boiled in lye, made a yellow dye used especially in Poland to colour leather (66, 75), and the bark, boiled in water, was used (as were many yellow substances) in the treatment of jaundice. The most useful culinary variety was one with seedless berries (68) but this is now very rare.

The role of the barberry as the intermediate host in the life cycle of fungal disease of cereals was beginning to be recognized in the early nineteenth century. Both Dr Martyn and Phillips note the deleterious effect the presence of a barberry bush has on nearby wheat, though Duhamel (a contemporary authority on such things) thought the idea bunkum.

By the same date, culinary and medicinal changes ensured that that barberry was falling out of use in any case, and it was to be found more often in the shrubbery than in the kitchen garden. Its disadvantage in the shrubbery is that the flowers smell vile.

# Basil

### *Ocimum basilicum* LINNAEUS

*Origin:* southern Asia and Africa

A very mysterious plant indeed, whose present innocuous, if delicious, use as a flavouring for tomato salads would once have seemed very humdrum if not downright dangerous.

'Basil' is an English shortening of the more widespread name of 'basilikum', meaning king. This has almost certainly meant more than simply that the plant is king of herbs, though with its magnificent savour, it is that (well, savours, in fact, for there are many varieties all with different odours, and even the leaves and flowering top of one plant smell subtly different). It may perhaps have been associated in some way with kingship, for there were once powerful taboos surrounding it, evidenced by its strong association with snakes, worms, scorpions, maggots, headaches and blindness, and it may only have been safe for kings to handle. In 200 BC it was thought hurtful for stomach, eyes and wits (77). Diodorus said that eating it gave rise to insects on the skin. Other ancient beliefs suggested that if powdered basil was put under a stone, it bred serpents, or if it was chewed, it bred maggots in the gut. Even Estienne and Liebault thought that the smell caused headaches and 'sometimes it engendereth in the head little small wormes, like unto scorpions'. The only positive, if equally magical use, was in the reduction of childbirth pangs; the mother had to hold a sprig of it in her hand, together with a swallow's feather (77).

It is difficult to discover if this was its main use in the sixteenth century, though it seems to have been widely grown. Liebault gives some curious horticultural details: 'Some report a marvellous thing . . . it groweth fairer and higher if it be sown with curses and injuries offerred to it.' He also says that, if it is grown in a dry and sunny position, it will eventually change into mountain thyme or cress; not my experience.

Whatever its disadvantages, by the eighteenth century it was widely used in salads and ragouts (68). Various sorts were grown, including types with purple, frilled or savoyed leaves (66, 105). Powdered leaves were sometimes used as snuff, and the old beliefs had been reversed, for it was thought good for headaches. The seeds were still thought good for snakebite (66).

# Beet

*Beta vulgaris* subsp. *vulgaris* LINNAEUS

*Origin:* native; widespread elsewhere

The subspecies includes a number of crops: spinach beet, Swiss chard, sugar beet and mangold. The first two of these are selections used for their leaves, probably the most ancient use (see

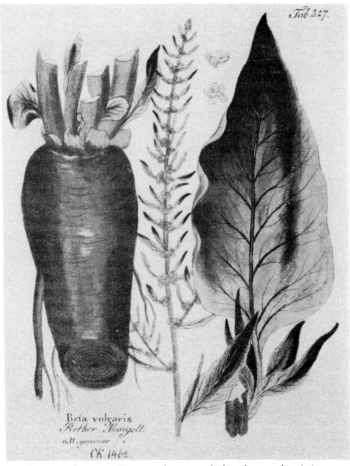

Nineteenth-century European beetroots, before the round varieties
were popular

Swiss Chard). Certainly the crop was well known to the Greeks,
who may have preferred the leaves, although the roots were eaten
with lentils and beans, with mustard to give them flavour (77).
The red-coloured roots of certain beets were used by the Romans
in the second and third centuries AD (93), and the crop was
probably disseminated by them through the Empire. The first
modern record is in a German source of 1557, when the crop is
still called Roman beet (93). Later, Estienne and Liebault say that

the roots were only in occasional use, roasted (still an excellent way of cooking them, especially if you have an oven in constant use, for it takes a long time), and they mention a persistent belief that eating them removed the smell of garlic on the breath. For some reason Elizabethans thought it 'proper' to wipe newly harvested roots, especially the white sorts, with fresh dung before cooking them (36).

The crop soon became valued as a winter salad, garnish and pickle (66). There were a few more elaborate ways of cooking it, including a delicious one of the mid-eighteenth century: baked beetroots are sliced, covered in batter flavoured lightly with cloves, dredged with chopped parsley and breadcrumbs, fried and finally served with slices of Seville orange (13).

In Britain, beets are most admired if they are uniformly deep red and round. There are, though, many more sorts grown elsewhere, including amusing varieties which, when sliced, show concentric bands of red and white. These, as well as the yellow and golden types, I find preferable in flavour as well as in their properties on the plate: they do not leak purple juice over the rest of the contents. They are especially nice when boiled, peeled, diced and then warmed through in plenty of butter with a few drops of good vinegar. The unusual types are just as easy to grow as the ordinary ones, though perhaps they are more beloved by slugs, and have the same degree of cold tolerance. Obviously, they do not make such a dramatically coloured pickle.

# Blackberry
## (or Bramble)

Various species of **Rubus**, including **R. ulmifolius** SCHOTT

*Origin:* native

Once known also as 'bumblekites' or 'scald berries' (66), blackberries have been widely used, most often medicinally, since early times. Widely found in hedgerows, they have been used as part of the kitchen garden hedge at least since the sixteenth century.

However, serious garden cultivation and breeding began much later, in America, and only from 1840 (93).

Pliny suggested using the fruits' juice for swollen tonsils and gum ulcers, and it is still sometimes used as a gargle. Blackberry wine has been admired at least since the seventeenth century and was also used, mixed with raisin wine to fake good claret (76). I have not found any early recipes for blackberry pie; perhaps it was too humble a fruit for many cooks.

However, the rest of the plant was also of considerable and widespread use. Young shoots, peeled, were put in salads and were also thought useful for tightening loose teeth (76). They also produced a black dye widely used for wool, silk and mohair (66). The roots yield an orange dye (97). The pulp of the leaves was used for ringworm and ulcers of the leg (76) and may have also been used for scalds. The whole plants, or rather the lower parts, were once used as grafting stocks for most of the rosaceous fruits, from cherries to medlars (36), in the sixteenth century, though the use seems not to have long persisted.

By the early nineteenth century a number of varieties were grown, including ones with white fruit, with double flowers, without thorns or with heavily dissected foliage (66). Many of these were later hybridized with American species of *Rubus*, especially *R. vitifolius* (93). For average gardens, the most useful cultivar is the pretty 'Oregon', which is cut-leaved, thornless and quite small. 'Himalaya' is also widely available in Britain. In spite of its name, it originated in southern Europe, and it has been in cultivation since 1900 (93). It is almost frighteningly vigorous, producing immense stems every season. It is also very well armed and, though producing quite good fruit, is probably too much of a handful for most small gardens. It has naturalized in America (46).

# Blackcurrant

*Ribes nigrum* LINNAEUS

*Origin:* native

One of a number of native species of *Ribes*, once called the 'squinnancy berry' (46, 76). It seems to have been only a recent introduction to the kitchen garden, having been cultivated for only four or five hundred years (46). Even today most cultivars are little different from the wild species (93). The plant was not known to the Romans and was not even mentioned in Tusser's herbal of 1557, though Estienne and Liebault did suggest it as part of the kitchen garden hedge in 1570. It may, of course, have been in longer use on the Continent than in Britain; certainly the Tradescants found improved sorts there, available in Delft for one shilling per dozen (3). No doubt the new bushes were intended for tarts and puddings, or perhaps wine. However, most of the early uses seem to have been medicinal; the juice was used as a gargle, the jelly for sore throats, and especially for the acute form called 'quinsy'. The juice, concentrated and sweetened, was once called 'Rob' (see Cornelian Cherry) but more often nowadays 'shrub' (66). The leaves were once considered quite as useful as the fruit; they are still occasionally used today as a flavouring for desserts, especially creams and custards. In the eighteenth century they were used for a tea thought to be quite as good as 'green' tea (66), and they are still used today to treat diarrhoea and urinogenital infections (97).

The berry was introduced to America in 1629 (46) and was widely grown until the 1890s, when it was discovered that it acted as intermediate host to fungal diseases. It was then eradicated. In Britain, Thomas Hitt described one variety in 1757; Lindley has two in 1831; Hogg has three in 1875, and there were twenty-six by 1920; many of the nineteenth-century types are still grown. The popular 'Wellington XXX' was bred in 1927 (93).

Blackcurrant is a good bush for the fruit cage, providing jams and jellies for winter teas. As a simple dessert, though, it is especially good softened, sieved, sweetened, warmed up again and poured into small glasses. Very cold cream is then poured carefully on top, so that each spoonful should hold a contrast in temperature as well as in taste and colour.

The plant is not easily managed as a wall-fruit, though espaliers have often been attempted. A few were once planted in the shade of north-facing walls to give a later crop (57).

# Borage

*Borago officinalis* LINNAEUS

*Origin:* southern Europe

Once used to stop melancholy Elizabethans from finally going mad, the plant is now mostly used for its blue flowers; they make a lovely salad garnish.

Not native, it was once thought to hail from Aleppo (77), though it is native to central Europe and most Mediterranean countries (32). From ancient times it has been associated with high spirits and merriment and was once called 'euphrosyron' (77). It was commonly added to cups of wine, though no doubt the effect of the alcohol must have confused the effect of the borage. European and British Renaissance writers followed Classical precedent. Lord Bacon said that it was used 'to repress fuliginous vapours of dusky melancholy, and so to cure madness', and Gerard, after more prosaically extolling its virtues in a salad, says 'sirrupe made of the flowers of borage, comforteth the heart, purgeth melancholie, quieteth the phreneticke or lunaticke person. The leaves eaten raw do engender good bloode, and when boiled in honey and water, they cure hoarseness.'

The plant was still used for cordial water well into the nineteenth century, and most chemists' shops produced their own distillate of leaves and flowers (77). The conserve was used as an expectorant (77). Taken with wine, as a 'cup' or 'cool tankard', Cobbett's recipe (19) used flowers with wine, water and a little nutmeg. Victorian hotel-keepers grew or bought it in large quantities for 'claret cup' (105).

Decorative uses (and it is extremely effective) included scattering it over sixteenth-century roasts (12) – the nasturtium eventually took over this role – and over salads, from about the same date.

The plant grows very easily from seed and is attractive enough to include in the flower border. The leaves are really too coarse for all but the most robust of salads; the flowers are best picked with sepals and stalks; they are easily separated from these a few minutes later, especially if immersed in cold water. It will seed itself happily after its first introduction, and it is a simple matter to 'edit' the seedlings to give the desired effect. Each plant needs plenty of space, easily swamping anything less vigorous growing too close.

# Broad Bean

*Vicia faba* LINNAEUS

*Origin:* probably eastern Mediterranean region

An extremely ancient crop, now widely used for man and beast. The species seems to have been first domesticated in the neolithic period, probably in the eastern Mediterranean region. By the Iron Age, it was widely disseminated throughout Europe (93). There are numerous references to various types in Greek and Roman literature, and by the time of the latter civilization it had much religious and magical significance (77, 93), perhaps not surprising in such an ancient crop. The curious assemblage of beliefs suggests that, by Roman times, their original significance had become garbled. The beans were dedicated to Apollo but were also used in festivals in honour of the wife of Janus. In other rites, cakes of bacon and beans (still a good combination of flavours for secular occasions) were used. In spite of this, over-indulgence in beans was thought to dull the senses and understanding, and to cause bad dreams (due, no doubt, to the flatulence described by Dioscorides) and even sterility. They were commonly eaten at funerals, though they were thought to bring luck, and were mixed with merchandise to bring an easy sale. They were also used in the voting system; white for 'yes', black for 'no' (77).

By Columella's time (the first century AD), beans were not eaten by patricians but perhaps continued to dull the senses of the working class (77). (For other dietary distinctions, see Artichoke.) Such distinctions were still operative in nineteenth-century Britain, Phillips writing that beans were excellent food for the lower classes but unsuitable for what he calls the 'sedentary' ones because they cause flatulence.

The beans' capacity to enrich the soil had already been noticed by Pliny's time, and they were commonly used as green manure, being ploughed in as they were about to flower. They had many other uses: small ones were used until the nineteenth century as fish bait, being cooked, then flavoured with honey and musk. Once the over-curious fish had congregated, they were caught in nets (77). Bean flour was once used as face powder.

Even if you do not especially like the beans, it is almost worth having a few plants simply for the marvellous smell of the flowers. If you have the beans to cook, the pods, usually discarded, can be used to make quite a pleasant soup. Of the large-seeded sort most often used for human consumption, modern breeders try to increase the seed number in each pod, and their disease resistance and uniformity. Because of their success, whole groups of varieties have dropped out of commerce in the last 150 years and the old garden books are filled with forgotten names. Sometimes old varieties can be found in out-of-the-way gardens, being maintained by enthusiasts, though I have not yet discovered if any of the old varieties taste sufficiently different to the ones now available to make me an enthusiast too.

# Broccoli

*Brassica oleracea* var. *italica*  PLENCK

*Origin:* possibly Italy

The crop's name is derived from the Italian for 'shoot', and it has been cultivated in southern Europe since early times (71). It seems to have been introduced into the United Kingdom in the mid-sixteenth century (57), though there are no clear descrip-

Sprouting broccoli of 1819

tions of it until 1660 (93). It may have come from Cyprus, an island also said to have seen the origin of the cauliflower, itself closely related to the broccoli. Switzer, who wrote a slim treatise on broccoli in 1729, thought that wild plants grew on the cliffs near Naples. In the next century, Phillips thought that it was the result of an accidental hybridization between cauliflowers and cabbages; he did not realize that broccoli is probably an intermediate development on the way to cauliflower (different broccolis show different stages in that evolution).

We now grow a rather limited range of broccolis; even in the nineteenth century, the kitchen garden could have had brown, red and cream heading types, as well as green, purple and white sprouting ones. Of the heading types, browns and purples are still grown in other European countries, and occasionally one can find the green and very elegant 'Romanesco' advertised in British catalogues (a similar-sounding variety called 'Roman' can be found in the 1807 edition of the *Gardener's Dictionary*). I find the flavour rather coarse, though Dr Martyn thought it almost as good as asparagus. He suggested cutting the heads with four or five inches of stem, peeling the lower part and eating that as well. In comparing it with asparagus, he is perhaps paying tribute to the memory of Miller who, in the first edition of the book of 1724, calls the plant 'Italian asparagus'. Most of the sprouting broccolis are exceptionally useful plants and reasonably hardy. They must have improved since Switzer's day. He encouraged his to sprout an early crop before Christmas by lopping off the heads, though it is not clear if he wanted flowering shoots or merely tufts of new leaves. He is right about the flavour, though, for the purple sort is better than the white.

The plant called 'perennial cauliflower', of which seed can occasionally be found, is closer to the broccolis in habit, hardiness and generally in flavour. It only looks like a yellowish cauliflower. I have not come across any early references to it, though there are nineteenth-century descriptions of perennial cabbages and kales. The perennial broccoli is perennial in that the old plant can be left in the ground to produce a rather ragged crop the following year (the plants become very large indeed), or the multitude of tiny side shoots can be removed and treated as cuttings. As the plants grown from seed are of variable quality, the latter method is a good way of increasing your stock of well-headed plants. Personally I find the flavour a bit thin, but it is worth having a plant or two as a 'curiosity'.

# Brussels Sprout

*Brassica oleracea* var. *gemmifera* DE CANDOLLE

*Origin:* Belgium

For all its immense popularity now, the crop was not grown in Britain until the early years of the nineteenth century. For many years, too, the plant's capacity for the production of a series of sprouts was not known. The plants were sold leafless, but with the sprouts still attached to the stems, which is decorative but wasteful (69).

The crop may have originated near Brussels and is generally thought to be a sport that appeared about 1750, though there are early records between the thirteenth and the sixteenth century that refer to a 'sproq', though there is no suggestion that these plants had the characteristic cabbage top of the Brussels sprout (93). With such an excellent flavour, and such hardiness, had it been an ancient crop it ought to have reached these shores long before it actually did.

There were only two types in 1885, short and tall (105); today there are hundreds, and the numbers increase steadily each year. Breeding work takes place in all countries where it is popular, and new cultivars are generally especially suited to particular conditions, uses and preferences in sprout size. In the domestic kitchen garden, there is often no advantage in growing expensive and highly bred varieties as most of them are designed for field-scale cultivation and harvesting. The farmer generally needs plants that bring all their sprouts to maturity at the same time, a positive disadvantage to the gardener who prefers to eat his crop direct from the garden, rather than direct from the freezer. All the herbals had vanished by the time the sprout appeared, and it is hard to imagine any magical use. I suggest, though, that you do not try Cobbett's cultural hint (19): 'The large leaves are broken down in the month of August to give the little cabbages room to grow. . . .' Still, the crop was fairly new to him.

# Burnet

Salad burnet: *Sanguisorba minor* subsp. *minor* SCOPOLI
Great burnet: *Sanguisorba officinalis* LINNAEUS

*Origin:* native

Both natives, and both grown in gardens from earliest times, although it is only the salad burnet that is worth experimenting with today. The uses of the two plants often seem to have been confused. The Lyte translation of Dodoens herbal says that, 'The leaves . . . stiped in wine, and dronken, both comfort and rejoice the hart, and are good against the trembling and shaking of the same . . .' (the standard suggestions for salad burnet) but goes on to add what are probably the properties of the great burnet, saying that it is good for those 'spitting and pissing of blood, and the green leaves will staunch a bleeding or inflamed wound'.

Gerard was more cautious: 'It is pleasant to be eaten in salads, in which it is thought to make the heart merry and glad, as also being put into wine, to which it yieldeth a certaine grace in the drinking.' As with borage (q.v.), it is difficult to know how the drinker distinguished between the effects of the salad burnet and the alcohol; certainly, I have never managed. Indeed, so many plants seem to have been used to gladden the heart that one must assume that depression was a common state in the sixteenth and seventeenth centuries.

The *Gardener's Dictionary* of 1807 amplifies on Gerard's description of salad burnet, saying: 'The leaves, when bruised, smell like Cucumber and taste something like the parings of that fruit; they are sometimes put into salads and cool-tankards . . .', though it adds, 'The leaves and seeds are mildly astringent, and have been used in dysenteries and haemorhages', being the properties of *Sanguisorba officinalis*.

It does seem to have been a very common salad herb in the early eighteenth century (68), and though falling out of use by its end, there were schemes to promote one of them as a forage crop. However, it is certainly salad burnet that Cobbett is referring to when he says (19), 'Some people use it in salads, for what reason I know not. . . . It's taste is certainly most disagreeable.'

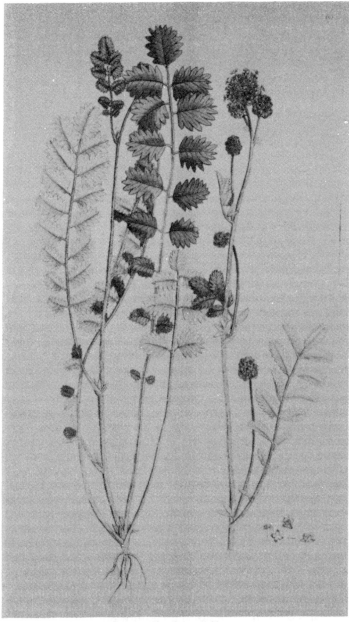

The cucumber-flavoured burnet

# Cabbage
## (including red and white types, Savoys, and Chinese Cabbage)

Cabbages and Savoys: ***Brassica oleracea*** var.
***capitata*** LINNAEUS

Origin: native; widespread elsewhere

Chinese cabbage: ***Brassica chinensis*** JUSLENIUS and ***B.***
***pekinensis*** (LOUREIRO) RUPRECHT

Origin: Far East

The species is probably native, but with cabbages having been so long cultivated, its status is difficult to assess. The crop, perhaps making use of characters from other species, seems to have been domesticated in early times in the eastern Mediterranean region and Asia Minor (93). The divisions between the various *Brassica* types (kales, kohl rabis, cabbages etc), were much less clear in ancient times than they are now, but the Greeks grew a 'kale' in 600 BC, and the Romans had heading cabbages of types recognizable today, as well as a type which was possibly kohl rabi (93).

Attitudes to the cabbage seem to have been ambiguous (Romans debated whether it was good or bad for their eyes and bowels), and not surprisingly coleworts (an old name for the crop) were supposed to have sprung from Jupiter's sweat as he laboured to explain two oracles that contradicted one another (77). Greeks and Romans ate the plants in autumn, but the stalks were left in the ground, presumably with cross-wounds in the top as is still practised today (and mentioned by de Bonnefons in 1651). The fresh growth that sprouts from the cuts was eaten in spring as it is today. The Romans may also have used raw cabbage as yet another protection before, or a cure after, drunkenness, a custom still recommended by Estienne and Liebault in the sixteenth century. Probably the belief that cabbages, vines, origanum and sowbread (cyclamen) will not grow near each other also stems from Classical times. It was still current in the sixteenth century, for it was well known that 'the Vineyards (they say) where Coleworts grow, doe yeeld the worser Wines' (28).

The red cabbage has an early history and is probably as old as the white. There are German records of 1150, and it was certainly grown in Britain by the fourteenth century (93). Estienne and Liebault thought that they were made, not bred, and were obtained by watering ordinary cabbages with red wine lees or by sowing the plants in hot places.

Of the savoy, three types were described in a German herbal of 1543, and Gerard grew several sorts in Britain by 1597. They may actually have originated in Italy, spreading to Germany and France in the fifteenth and sixteenth centuries. In the eighteenth, they were extremely popular. This is surprising, considering the lack of insecticides, for my own, even with them, become havens for overwintering slugs and insects. I must try something of Mortimer's: 'If your Cabbages and Colliflowers are troubled with Caterpillars, mix Salt and Water, and water them therewith and it will kill them.' As no quantities are given, the ambiguity of the sentence may be justified. One recipe for savoy soup starts 'Chuse 5 large savoys . . .'. They were also commonly boiled with duck. Cabbages and their allies were thought to be laxative, a property they were supposed to lose if they were boiled for a long time – two hours was common (13). The earliest plea for less dreary results seems to have been that of Phillips in 1822.

Chinese cabbage is of very recent introduction. Vilmorin-Andrieux, listing the still available 'Pak choi' in 1885, says that new sorts are still being introduced.

Whatever new varieties are produced nowadays, special flavours are never sought. Yet there are many vanished types of cabbage that were considered very special indeed. One of these, its loss bemoaned in 1807, was the musk cabbage (66). It was not winter hardy, so of little use for humble gardeners, though Dr Martyn thought it a 'must' for grander kitchen gardens. The old Dorsetshire Kale, really a primitive cabbage, was vanishing by the same date. Apparently it had a very strong flavour; perhaps it is still growing somewhere. I hope so.

Many gardeners and gourmets disregard the cabbage, perhaps because too many are boiled for too long, even now. However, Googe related that Cato preferred cabbage to all other vegetables, and goes on, '. . . this sort is commonly known, which being the pleasanter in winter, when it is bitter with the frosts, is sod [stewed] with Baken, and used in Porredge. . . . In Germanie, there is one kind of them that they call Lumbardy Colewort, or

Savoy Colwort, and another . . . which the Italians call Nigre-caules. . . .' These last are the dark red sorts that still have the same Italian name.

Apart from the difficulties with vines already mentioned, there were other pieces of magic: seeds, according to Googe, 'appeareth within ten days, except your seedes be old and dry, for old seed will grow to Rapes, as old Rape seed will to Colworts'.

# Capsicum
## (or Sweet Pepper)

*Capsicum annuum* LINNAEUS and *C. frutescens*
LINNAEUS

*Origin:* Central and South America

A large and diverse genus, all the species probably of American origin. All are perennial, even though one is not so named, and few are grown as such. The large fleshy sorts cultivated for table use today were once called 'bell peppers' (66), but there were, and still are, dozens of other species available in many colours, shapes and degrees of hotness. In general the sweet peppers are restricted to temperate zones (and all belong to *C. annuum*); only the hot ones (belonging to both *C. annuum* and *C. frutescens*) are widely grown in the tropics (93).

The first interest in these plants, after the discovery of the Americas, was in the small hot sorts as alternatives to the Asian pepper (*Piper nigrum*). A letter of Peter Martyn's, of 1493, says that Columbus had found peppers more pungent than the ones already known. The Spanish brought the seed to Europe. However, before this sudden expansion of its range, the genus had been extensively used by central and southern American Indians, and seeds of various sorts have been found in excavation sites dated from 5000 BC (93).

Unlike many other American crops, all the peppers found immediate favour in Europe and were soon widely grown in areas with a suitable climate. Sweet, in *Hortus Britannicus*

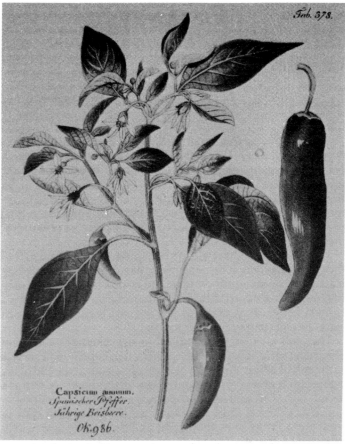

*Tab. 378.*

Capsicum annuum.
*Spanischer Pfeffer.*
*Jährige Beisbeere.*
*Ok. 986.*

A rather hot-looking annual pepper from the nineteenth century

(1827), lists them as having been introduced from India, C. *annuum* in 1548, and C. *frutescens* in 1656, and they might well have reached this country by that circuitous route.

Often a rather tricky crop to grow, requiring remarkably warm conditions to grow outdoors, and under glass, showing considerable affinity with greenfly and red spider. However, well-grown plants yield heavily and, if space can be found for them over the winter, will produce a much earlier crop in subsequent years.

# Caraway

*Carum carvi* LINNAEUS

*Origin:* Europe

Possibly native to this country, though Gerard thought otherwise, saying that it had probably been introduced from Germany.
Native or not, it is of ancient cultivation. It was one of the
principal spices in Roman kitchens (77) – Pliny the Elder thought
that the plant originated in Asia Minor – and had many medicinal
uses, being a cordial and a dispeller of flatulence and indigestion
(97). Dioscorides recommended its use by pale-faced girls to give
them a better colour (66).

Though the seeds have always been the most important part of
the plant, seedlings and young plants have been used in salads at
least since the sixteenth century, and also as a pot-herb in soup
(74, 66). I have not tried the roots, but young ones are supposed
to make better eating than parsnips and have been so used at least
since the eighteenth century (74, 77).

The seeds are used to flavour bread and cakes. The custom of
rewarding farm servants with special cakes containing caraway
at the end of wheat sowing, which was dying out at the end of the
eighteenth century (77), was quite possibly a culinary, as well as a
social, loss. The seed is still used as the principal flavouring of
kummel. It makes quite a pleasant garden plant, with tufts of
fresh green frilly leaves, though the umbels of white flowers that
follow are rather undistinguished.

# Cardoon

*Cynara cardunculus* LINNAEUS

*Origin:* Mediterranean region

Though this is very closely related to the artichoke (q.v.), it is a variant selected for the exceptionally fleshy midribs of the leaves, not for the edible flower buds. It is eaten rather rarely in this country, though it is frequently grown as a handsome foliage plant in grand flower borders, or in those culled by fanatic flower arrangers.

Cardoon may not have been known here until the mid-seventeenth century (99); John Tradescant saw several acres of it being cultivated near Brussels in 1629 but did not know how it was cropped or cooked (66). However, the plant was certainly in cultivation in Scotland by 1683 (84) and a common plant in markets by 1813 (69). Today few greengrocers even know the name. Both Miller and Sweet maintain that its place of origin was Crete.

A winter crop, the midribs of yearling plants are blanched by bunching up the leaves in September (no easy task) and tying with tape or soft twine (anything sharp cuts into the leaves). The bunches are not absolutely frost-proof, and the cut bundles were often stored in cellars. If left in the open, the bunches sometimes survive being frozen but more often rot nastily: a garage or shed would do for the cellar-less. In the kitchen, the most common way of serving them was to cook them in meat, cheese or anchovy sauces (13), the dish usually being browned before serving, using a salamander (an iron lattice heated in the fire and used rather like a modern grill). Otherwise the blanched shoots were, and are, a nice crisp winter salad when eaten raw. The veins on the back of the midrib need removing from all but the innermost of the leaves. One slight disadvantage, cooked or raw, is that each 'heart' is rather large and does not store well once cut open. So the whole thing needs to be used, requiring a corresponding number of mouths to feed. The vast root is also fleshy and tender and has been said to be good if cooked carefully (108). I have not tried it. As with artichokes, the florets were sometimes used as a substitute for rennet. The flower head itself will cook too but has a

A Victorian bunch of the 'Prickly Tours' cardoon

much poorer flavour than the artichoke and almost no 'fond'.

Though the plant can be produced from offsets formed if the main plant is cut down in early summer (105), the most usual way is by seed. This has generally to be imported, for in Britain the plants flower too late to give good seed. In the early eighteenth century, they were often transported to the greenhouse after flowering and seeded satisfactorily (68). On the whole, the cardoon is a good plant for any part of the garden. It looks spectacular amongst other vegetables and does not suffer those untidy periods that artichokes have between bouts of flowering. Cardoons also flower spectacularly, if happily established, producing six-foot-high candelabra of purple thistles.

# Carrot

*Daucus carota* subsp. *sativus* (HOFFMAN) THELL

Origin: Mediterranean region

The orange-coloured carrot, like many other sensible things, is an eighteenth-century invention. It is now, in Europe at least, the dominant type, though white and yellow types are occasionally seen as rarities. Once though, the most popular types were purple or violet, still widely grown in Asia Minor, India and the Far East.

The crop has been grown since earliest times. As there are many wild forms all round the Mediterranean and in Iran and the Balkans, domestication may have taken place throughout the area (93). In ancient times there was debate about where the best forms came from: Pliny the Elder thought from Crete, Theophrastus thought from Sparta. Googe quotes a story to the effect that the Emperor Tiberius had his carrots specially brought from the 'Castell of Gelduba, standing upon the Rhine', though as Googe includes a number of species under 'carret', Tiberius may have been thinking of something else (see Parsnip).

In Roman and early medieval times carrots were probably as branched as the wild types. The present-day conical root shape seems to have originated in Asia Minor in the tenth or eleventh century (93). Its added convenience as a pot-herb ensured its rapid dissemination. It reached Arab-occupied Spain in the twelfth century, north-west Europe by the fourteenth, and England in the fifteenth (93). Gerard says that only some types were used as pot-herbs (the others may have been medicinal). He mentions only one yellow variety; the purple ones were still the most popular being very mild flavoured, although they cook to a nasty brownish colour. In the early eighteenth century, red types were still preferred to yellow and orange (68). However, by the mid-century most of the current groups of varieties had been developed in Holland and rapidly ousted all the other sorts, though the white and violet ones were still fairly common in France in the early nineteenth century (77). All of them were, and are, biennial, thus ensuring the build-up of a good root. The primitive purple ones behave in northern gardens as annuals, and so need to be grown extremely fast if much of a root is to be had before the plants run to flower.

Of the herbalist's uses, carrot seed was used for many of the complaints also cured by other members of the umbellifer family. Where snake bite was common, a dram of seed taken in wine was supposed to effect a cure. Perhaps a related use was as a cure for fits. A poultice of carrot roots was used to relieve 'the pain and stench of foul and cancerous ulcers' (66). A similar pulp, apparently of overwhelming attraction to crickets, was mixed with arsenic for their destruction.

The amusing Elizabethan and early Stuart fashion for decorating hats, sleeves and dresses with flowers, fruit, feathers or leaves, also extended to carrot tops (see also Strawberry). The tops were most esteemed when they were colouring up for autumn (74) and were thought a worthy substitute for feathers. The fashion being suitable for gentlewomen, carrots may have been more of a kitchen garden curiosity than might be thought.

It was early recognized that carrots have a high sugar content, and they were widely used in sweet dishes of all sorts well into the Victorian period. Carrot cake is one of the few survivors of a once extensive cuisine, though a dessert decorated with finely grated roots is still occasionally seen. During the Second World War, sliced carrots were used in sweet pies and flans, though that use does not seem to have survived the conflict. The sugar content was once also used to produce alcohol, and one acre of carrots could be used to produce 168 gallons of spirit (66).

# Cauliflower

*Brassica oleracea* var. *botrytis* LINNAEUS

*Origin:* eastern Mediterranean region

'Cauliflower' is a term that is horticulturally restricted to summer or autumn flowering plants, generally not winter hardy and consequently being sown in early spring. In general the most prized colours are white and cream, though purple and red types were once common in Britain and can occasionally still be seen on the Continent. 'Winter cauliflowers', being cold-tolerant and biennial, in fact class as broccoli.

The cauliflower was known to the Romans and much admired (77). Gerard called it the 'Cole flowery' and also liked it. It seems not to have been widely grown before the end of the seventeenth century (71), not appearing in London markets until 1680 (66), though even in Scotland, seed was regularly imported from Crete in 1684 (84). Cyprus was sometimes accredited with the actual origin of the plant (77). By the end of the eighteenth century it was very highly regarded, great trouble being taken to produce it early and late. Dr Johnson is said to have remarked 'Of all the flowers in the garden, I like the cauliflower.'

The crop seems to have been much improved after 1700; certainly British-produced plants were much better than their European equivalents, and part of the crop was exported to Holland and Germany (66). Late sown and winter tender types were often kept going through the winter by covering them with mats when conditions were bad (68). The culinary uses have remained fairly static since early times, the heads being used in salads, boiled and served with gravy or white sauce, and also pickled.

# Celery
## (including Celeriac and Smallage)

*Apium graveolens* LINNAEUS

*Origin:* Europe

Wild celery is a native of Britain and other temperate Eurasian countries (93). It has been cultivated since earliest times, though of course its derivatives are of more recent origin (105). The plant was probably first used by the ancient Greeks for medicinal purposes and was probably first domesticated in the Mediterranean region.

Smallage may perhaps have been an early domesticated form, leafier than the species and used as a seasoning for salads and as a pot-herb. It survived as 'soup celery' well into the present century (105). True celery, or 'sellery' (derived from the Latin name), with a thickened and succulent leaf stem, seems to have evolved in Italy in the sixteenth or seventeenth century. Evelyn (30) noted it as a recent and important addition to the salad. Later it was admired 'for its high and grateful Taste . . . [and] is ever plac'd in the middle of the grand Sallet at Great Men's Tables', though Mortimer went on to add a word of caution: 'Have a care of a small red Worm that is often lurking in these stalks.' Miller tried growing smallage under exceptionally good conditions to see if he could create celery, but failed, so assumed that celery was a new species (66).

Celery was only widely grown towards the end of the eighteenth century, and by the middle of the nineteenth there were green, white and reddish sorts available, as well as ones with heavily frilled leaves (105). Forms with solid leaf stalks, now the most popular, were thought to have a less fine flavour than hollow-stalked sorts (19).

Celeriac, a variety with leathery leaves and stalks, is grown for its turnip-shaped root. It seems to be an eighteenth- or early nineteenth-century variant, described in 1885 as not yet being widely grown (105). A number of other related edible species were selected for enlarged roots at about the same period; the celeriac has been the most successful.

Celery and smallage were used as anti-scorbutics well into the nineteenth century (66) and were also thought good for digestion and the stomach generally, perhaps being part of the reason for the plants' success. The conserve was used to alleviate chest pains (77).

As with many recent crops, the associated cuisine is rather slight. Almost since its introduction celery has been an important salad plant or, if cooked, it has been boiled or braised and served with a white or cream sauce. In the nineteenth century it was used in almost every stew (77).

Celeriac makes a pleasant, if sweet, cream soup and is good when added towards the end of the cooking of beef stews. It can be baked, chipped or mashed (it is really excellent if a half quantity by weight is added to the potatoes put on to boil, and the mash is excellent with all sorts of game). To serve it by itself, the roots should be cooked before peeling to keep in as much of the flavour as possible. After cooling under the cold tap, they can be peeled, diced and warmed up again in butter. The roots are excellent, too, if raw and finely grated, used as part of a winter *crudité*. They need dressing with lemon juice to stop them going brown.

I find it difficult to get the roots to grow as large as the ones commonly seen in Continental markets, but the quality is just as good.

# Cherry

Sweet cherry: ***Prunus avium*** LINNAEUS
Sour cherry: ***P. cerasus*** LINNAEUS
Duke cherry: ***P. gonduini*** (POITEAU and TURPIN) REHDER

*Origin of cultivated types:* Greece and Turkey

Of the species, only the first is native to Britain, though it has an extensive distribution, reaching western Asia. The cultivated cherries probably arose in Greece or Turkey, only a few centuries before Theophrastus mentions them in about the third century

A lovely early nineteenth-century plate of the 'May Duke' cherry

BC. They seem to have been much valued by Mithridates, King of Pontus, a ruler who was also a skilful physician. To pass on his great knowledge, he wrote (or at least gave his name to) a treatise on botany (76), and his name eventually became used for any substance believed to counteract poisons. His virtues could not, however, preserve his kingdom from another man whose name later became associated with great luxury. The Roman general Lucullus, during his campaign against Mithridates, supposedly found a cherry tree at Cerasus (now Giresun) in Turkey. The tree was one of the treasures displayed at the subsequent 'triumph' in Rome (66, 76).

A romantic story certainly, and it is known that cherry varieties spread rapidly through the Roman Empire from 68 BC onwards (93). Pliny mentions eight kinds, both red and black, in Rome, and there were certainly more. Many, no doubt, were grown in Britain. After the fall of the Empire, most kinds seem to have been lost, and a German herbal of 1491 lists only two types, sweet and sour (93). Whether they vanished from Britain is not known; the cherry orchards of Kent are traditionally believed to be very ancient. Nevertheless, Henry VIII's fruiterer, Richard Harris, is credited with reintroducing the cherry to this country (76), but it is more likely that he brought in better varieties.

The Tradescant garden catalogue of 1634 lists fifteen varieties, and Ray listed twenty-four in 1688, though later, Miller, in 1724, thought only twenty-one worth eating. The variety sometimes met with today under the name 'Noble' was called, in the eighteenth century, 'Tradescant's' cherry and had actually been imported by John Tradescant the Elder from Belgium as 'the boores Cherye' for 12 shillings (3).

The decorative aspects of the cherry were realized very early and, in the absence of many of the flowering trees which we take for granted today, much more appreciated. Evelyn (31) had them planted in an oval at his house. By then, serious selection of new varieties had been under way for a hundred years or so (46), and some interesting cherries were grown that have unaccountably dropped out of use. For instance, in the seventeenth century, 'May Duke' and 'Kentish' were the first cherries to ripen each season, the first of these in the month of its name. Both are still available. 'Kentish' is a type of morello, possibly very ancient. The morellos pollinate themselves and will come true from seed, contributing to the longevity of all the varieties in the group. The various 'Duke' types are hybrids between morello and sweet cherries, sharing the qualities of both and having the self-fertility of the morello. I do not know why morellos and Dukes are not more often grown; perhaps the nursery catalogues are at fault by consigning both to the ranks of cooking cherries, though personally I find a dish of ripe morellos a more perfect close to a meal than a dish of sweet cherries. The equally ancient mazzard cherries can also still be found with a bit of hunting. Googe erroneously suggested that all these early types were simply obtained by grafting a late type on a vine stock.

Cherries will fit onto walls only with some difficulty. They were often found in kitchen gardens loosely tied against the brick or stone, but otherwise left 'rude and unseemly' (49). The 'May Duke' mentioned above was one of the commonest varieties, against a south wall for early fruit, and a north one for late. Other sorts of cherry were sometimes retarded by building a cloth tent over them and keeping the structure damp, so cooling the air inside (78). However, this was perhaps not so common, as I have come across only one source for this idea, in a book composed entirely of curious ideas. It ranges from 'Sundrie new and artificial ways for the keeping of fruits and flowers in their fresh hue, after they are gathered from their stalkes and branches', through 'How to carry gold in a most secret manner' (as fake bullets covered in lead), and 'How to steal bees', to the entirely myste-rious 'A Piece whereby to perform some extraordinary service'. Nevertheless, muslin tents were commonly used in the flower garden to protect seventeenth-century tulips from over-hot sun-shine.

In eighteenth- and nineteenth-century cherry orchards the trees were often underplanted with strawberries and currants (a lovely sight, surely), even though Dr Martyn (66) considered that the drip from cherry leaves is harmful to many plants.

Small trees were often grown in pots, a practice common into the early years of this century. It enabled vigour to be controlled, the trees to be taken indoors with the dessert still on the branch, and also for the plants to be forced. This is easy to do with cherries, provided that they have had a dormant period. Grand eighteenth-century gardens frequently produced cherries almost all year round (69). For gardens that could not, the fruit was often dried for winter puddings, as well as being crystallized or bathed in brandy (76). Cherry wine was once very popular, as was the liqueur. In the seventeenth century they were sometimes kept in more or less suspended animation by hanging them under bell-jars standing in a pan of water (78), though how this worked, and for how long, I am not sure.

Of the cherry's other uses, the wood was highly valued by joiners, being especially good for turning. It was commonly used to make chairs and could easily be stained to resemble maho-gany.

# Chervil

*Anthriscus cerefolium* (LINNAEUS) HOFFMAN

*Origin:* eastern Europe, Russia and Asia Minor

A native of eastern Europe, central and southern Russia, and Asia Minor to the Urals, it seems to have been grown in Britain as a salad and pot-herb since very early times. Its value probably accounts for its very widespread naturalization. Gerard and Parkinson grew it, and in late seventeenth-century kitchen gardens it was sown for salading beneath espalier fruit trees against the walls, or between rows of young melon plants (12). The roots of mature chervil plants were also eaten, usually with oil and vinegar (34). Later, fleshy rooted sorts were developed and were still available in the nineteenth century (105), though now they seem to have vanished. There were also sorts with very frilly leaves, a useful development that enabled the plant to be clearly distinguished from its poisonous and close relatives (105). In the early eighteenth century there was also a 'musked' type grown that had especially aromatic leaves (68), but this seems to have vanished by the following century. Even the wide cultivation of ordinary chervil was beginning to diminish here by the early nineteenth century, and it is now scarcely seen, though is sometimes used as a pleasant flavouring of sauces for fish. In old gardens like mine, root fly can make it almost impossible to grow well.

Medicinally, it was yet another plant that the Romans believed lifted the spirits, a hope that persisted until the sixteenth century, when apart from giving 'good taste to meates', it was also 'good for people that be dull, old and without courage, for it rejoiceth and comforteth them, and increaseth their strength' (26).

# Chicory

*Cichorium intybus* LINNAEUS

*Origin:* Europe, central Russia, western Asia and North
Africa

Native to much of Europe, central Russia, western Asia and North Africa, it has been cultivated since Greek and Roman times (93). Pliny says that 'cichorium' is a Greek adaptation of the Egyptian word for the plant, so domestication was probably even earlier. It seems always to have been used as a salad (though there were once medicinal uses), but as the green leaves are bitter, they have been blanched at least since Roman times, and

presumably long before. In seventeenth-century Britain, Parkinson piled sand over his, though garden soil is perfectly adequate (74).

Not surprisingly for such an ancient crop, there are many types, all perennial, though they are all usually discarded after the first cropping season. The Witloof types, producing those expensive clusters of narrow white leaves, have been known at least since the late eighteenth century (70) and became a widely popular crop from the middle of the following one. They are extremely easy to grow, and there is no reason why everyone with a garden should not have them. The plants are generally forced indoors for a winter crop, though the ones blanched outdoors for eating in March have a much finer flavour. There are some very handsome red-leaved varieties, now found in Italy but once used here to decorate both salads and roasts. The heads were popular when cooked, at least from the eighteenth century onwards, and are especially good braised with plenty of butter and a sliced tomato (13).

Other varieties of chicory produce loose and leafy heads, some more or less self-blanching. 'Sugar Loaf' is an attractive green variety freely available here, which is moderately hardy, though I find that the outer leaves get very battered in the worst weather. There are also some quite spectacular varieties that have leaves splashed and streaked with red or mahogany-brown. They can be blanched by covering with soil or an earthenware pot; all make excellent winter eating.

The large-rooted varieties are also used to make a rather bitter substitute for coffee and seem to have been so used since the wars with Napoleon, when our blockade of French shores cut that nation from its supplies of that important beverage (70).

The attractive flowers of the chicory (pink ones are sometimes used in the herbaceous border)

# Chives

## Allium schoenoprasum LINNAEUS

*Origin:* native

Of the huge genus *Allium*, with about six hundred species, at least forty are used as culinary plants (93). Chives are native to this country though the distribution extends to the Far East and also North America (32).

The garden cultivation of the plant is not recorded earlier than the sixteenth century (93), though it may have been gathered for use from wild populations. In the eighteenth century it was as much in demand as it is today for soups and spring salads (77), though it seems to have fallen out of favour at least in the early part of the nineteenth (66).

An attractive plant, it was once used as an edging for the major beds in kitchen gardens, as an alternative to box, parsley or strawberries. It is fairly well suited to this use, as it does not spread and is uniform in height. It looks untidy once the flower heads begin to fade, and it is worth trimming them off. Trimming also prevents the unwanted production of huge quantities of seed. There are a number of forms, differing usually in size rather than flavour, and one rather rare sort has wavy leaves. The plants are generally propagated by division, if need be, though a very small patch is sufficient for most kitchens (19). If used as an edging, a single seed head will furnish many yards of seedlings.

In the kitchen, few dishes are entirely dependent on chives for their main character, though many are considerably improved. They are especially good added to mayonnaise, giving it a more delicate flavour than if garlic is used and, if added during the last few minutes of blending, a lovely pale green colour. It is just right for serving with freshly cooked beetroots or some really good tomatoes.

# Clary

*Salvia sclarea* LINNAEUS

*Origin:* southern Europe

Though the annual and decorative plant commonly called clary in the seed catalogues is *Salvia horminium,* it is useless in the kitchen. The true clary is more rarely met with, almost as decorative and biennial. The thickly felted leaves were used for fritters in eighteenth-century desserts (13) and occasionally (for the stout toothed) in salads (68). However, the most exciting use relates to the flowers and was well known in the sixteenth century. Estienne and Liebault wrote that clary 'in wine, makes men carnal and cheerful', and Dodoens wrote that 'it stirreth up bodily lust'. By the eighteenth century, however, everything had become more polite, and clary wine was no longer regarded as an aphrodisiac, though much admired for its flavour. The respectable Dr Martyn (66) thought it had a taste similar to grape wine made from the widely grown Frontiniac vine (q.v.). Evelyn thought (30) that clary-flavoured cream was a lovely dessert.

The seeds, when soaked, yield large quantities of mucilage, and this was used to get grit out of the eye (97), or the seeds were mashed with honey to 'recover splinters' (26).

The plant was first mentioned as a British garden plant by Turner in his *A new herball* of 1551. Today, the plant is the source of the muscatel oil used as a perfume and flavouring. It is a handsome garden plant and should be more widely grown.

# Coriander

*Coriandrum sativum* LINNAEUS

*Origin:* eastern Mediterranean region

Once widely cultivated for medicinal and culinary properties, it is occasionally grown in Britain today as a flavouring for pickles, chutney, curry and gin. Probably a native of the eastern Mediterranean region, it is reputed to have been introduced by the Romans (it was much used in their kitchens) and is now very widely naturalized. Seed was being purchased for the gardens of Hampton Court in 1515 (87), and it was grown on a field scale in the south of England in the eighteenth century, with Ipswich as the main centre of production (66).

Though the green leaves have a very disagreeable smell (but dry they can be used in pot-pourri), the ripe fruits have a pleasant taste and aroma. Unripe, they were used for scrofula, the king's evil, and St Anthony's fire, though there were risks. 'Green Coriander, taken into the body, causes one to ware hoarse, and to fall into a frenzie, and doth much dull the understanding, that it seemeth the partie were dronke . . .', and the book, Dodoens' *A niewe Herball . . .*, goes on to insist that apothecaries should only sell it in its prepared form, dried and roasted.

Seeds, or rather fruits, encrusted with sugar, were sold as sweets or comfits to scent the breath (probably often necessary), as a digestive (still used in gripe water) and as a vermifuge (66). In the eighteenth century, coriander was used in many meat recipes, especially in the basting liquors for roasting meat (still worth trying), or used to give a pleasant flavour to the otherwise unpleasant extract of senna (66).

Coriander flowers and fruit in the eighteenth century

# Cornelian Cherry

**Cornus mas** LINNAEUS

*Origin:* central and southern Europe

Now rarely encountered, except in one of its decorative forms, the tree was once popular for its fruit. A native of central and southern Europe, it was certainly in cultivation in Britain by the late sixteenth century, reaching Scotland by the late seventeenth (91). It was sufficiently important to be trained as an espalier on south- or east-facing walls of seventeenth-century gardens (85), where it probably fruited far more successfully than when grown as a standard – it is generally in flower in February, and so most flowers drop off, frosted, without fruiting (66).

The fruit, not to me an especially inspiring flavour, was used to make tarts and cordials, 'rob de Cornis' being sold in shops for the latter purpose at the end of the eighteenth century (66). By that time, the small tree was being relegated to the 'wilderness', where it remains.

# Crab Apple

**Malus sylvestris** MILLER (*Malus communis* subsp. *silvestris* (MILLER) GAMS)

*Origin:* native

Attractive trees, often with more strongly scented flowers than those of the eating apple, they will only rarely have been grown in the kitchen garden proper. More often they were grown in the 'slips' or in the nearby hedgerows (28). Though the fruit is scarcely edible fresh, it played a valuable part in the household economy until the end of the eighteenth century.

The fruit was used in tarts and pies and gave additional flavour to apple jams and jellies (it makes a quite sumptuous jelly on its own, especially suitable for winter breakfasts) or to cider. For this latter purpose the fruits were stored until December and used to strengthen the flavour of 'cider washings'. It gave a rather bitter cider that was thought suitable for day-labourers (11).

The fruits were also pulped in a cider press to give verjuice (unripe grapes were another source). This was used as a substitute for vinegar or lemon juice, especially to sharpen sauces and dressings and sometimes to tenderize meat, being put in the marinade. It was also dabbed on sprains to relieve the swelling (66).

There are many varieties, most now grown only for their decorative qualities. 'John Downie' is the one most often grown for its attractive fruit and is widely available. It is excellent.

# Cucumber
## (including Gherkin)

Cucumber: *Cucumis sativus* LINNAEUS

*Origin:* central Asia

Gherkin: *C. anguria* LINNAEUS

*Origin:* central America

Though two species are involved, many small cucumbers are treated in exactly the same way as the proper, and West Indian, gherkin. It seems best to treat them as one entry.

*C. sativus* is the only Asian representative of an otherwise entirely African genus. It has been cultivated in India since at least 1000 BC (14), and it is there that the widest range of diversity is found. It reached the West early, and many types were well known to Greek and Roman cooks. In Rome their cultivation was brought to a high pitch in the first century AD, being grown in baskets and moved from warm place to warm place as the sun moved through the heavens, a practice still being carried out in Scotland in the 1730s (49). Later Roman cucumbers were grown in frames or special houses, glazed with specularia (possibly a form of mica) or perhaps oiled cloth (55). Tiberius liked them so much that he ate them every day of the year (80). Many sorts may have retained the bitterness of primitive varieties, for they were generally boiled first, then peeled and served with oil, vinegar and honey (77). Though nowadays they are almost always used only as a salad, they were widely used in soups and stews and as a cooked vegetable well into the nineteenth century.

Some Georgian recipes were rather bizarre; one had large numbers of cucumbers stuffed with partly cooked pigeons, which had been cleaned normally but had had the heads left on, feathers and all. The trick was to get the heads looking as if they were attached to the cucumber. The whole lot was then cooked to a finish in broth, and the heads garnished with barberries (q.v.) (81). However, other dishes were less dreadful to look at, and some of the mutton and cucumber, or ham and cucumber, ragouts are delicious (15). Fully ripened cucumbers also make a splendid vegetable if peeled, seeded, roughly diced and stewed in a little water and butter until soft (about twenty minutes). The juices can be thickened using a roux, or adding plenty of thick cream and warming up. It is delicious with fish, especially the richer-flavoured ones.

Cucumbers were probably grown in Britain from the time of the Roman occupation and were certainly known to Edward III. They may have been reintroduced, following their loss, during the reign of Henry VIII. As with many ancient crops they were the subject of numerous superstitions and taboos and had supposed medicinal properties.

In Rome, wild cucumbers were used against scorpion bites, dropsy, quinsy (a sudden and disastrous swelling of the throat), dimness of the eyes and ringworm, as well as scaring away mice and other vermin (perhaps Theophrastus and Pliny had the long and snake-like ones in mind for this). Wives wishing for children wore them tied around their waists, or they were carried by midwives and thrown away hastily as soon as the child was born (77). Even in the sixteenth century, it was thought that cucumbers were frightened of thunderstorms, beneath which they withered and died. They were also thought to grow with the moon and shrivel as it waned. Tricky plants, they also hated oil and would not grow if tended by someone who regularly handled the stuff (28). Dangers lay in eating them, too, for apart from the flatulence still experienced by some people, 'the immeasurable use thereof, filleth the vaines with cold noughtie humours, the which (because they may not be converted with good blood), do at length bring forth long and great agues and other diseases' (26). There were the usual magic transformations that would have made splendid nonsense of today's seeds regulations. For instance, Estienne and Liebault warned gardeners to be careful 'that your seed be not olde, for if it be three years olde, it will bring forth Radishes'.

Being such an important commercial crop today, it is not surprising that new varieties are constantly appearing, to add to the already vast number of cultivars. Size, straightness, disease resistance, skin characters and shelf life are among the main breeding characteristics. However, in 1629 only seven types were known to Parkinson. Pickled cucumbers and gherkins were a common ingredient in sauces during Jacobean winters, though the pickles were often imported (66). Two hundred years later there were many more, including the white-skinned Italian sorts known to Evelyn and still to be found in that country (they do well here and have an excellent flavour). However, only two types seem to have been commonly grown, for even by 1707 Mortimer only mentions the 'large Horse cucumber' (an alarming name) and the 'small white prickly'. Vilmorin-Andrieux listed many more varieties in 1885, saying that the curly sorts were only rarely grown in Britain (I cannot imagine that they were still used for scaring mice) and equally rarely cooked.

With a bit of searching, some interesting varieties can still be found, from the monstrous and slight-flavoured 'Zeppelin' to the tiny, round and pale-skinned 'Crystal Apple'. This last has a rather good flavour, though it can be difficult to fruit, and the male flowers need constant removal.

Most gardeners harvest cucumbers while immature, to use in salads. For cooking, it is much better to follow the sixteenth-century practice and leave the fruit on the plant until much riper. They usually begin to mottle in brown and yellow, and the flavour develops a pleasant richness which adds greatly to the dish. Properly ripe cucumbers will also store excellently, preferably hung in nets like marrows. They will usually keep until February or March.

Any small cucumber can be pickled. It is always tempting to leave them until they are too large, but then they are also too watery and the pickle is poorly flavoured and does not last. We have not tried one recipe of 1714 (1) which suggests drying out the large cucumbers for ten days in heavy brine and then heating up the drained vegetable in vinegar every other day for three weeks. I think my enthusiasm would wane. In general, the outdoor prickly type of cucumbers are best for pickling, though I am not sure if they have quite the flavour of the *C. anguria* types.

# Damson

*Prunus domestica* subsp. *insititia* (LINNAEUS) C. K. SCHNEIDER (*P. insititia* LINNAEUS; *P. domestica* subsp. *italica* (BORKHAUSEN) HEGI)

*Origin:* eastern Europe and western Asia

Variously placed as a plum, or as a species in its own right, the plant probably arose in eastern Europe or western Asia and may have been domesticated before the plum (46). The earliest name for it is the 'Damascene plum' (damson being a shortening of that), and it is supposed to have been brought from Damascus to Italy in 114 BC (76). After its translation from Syria, it seemed not to grow especially well in Rome, and damsons can still be finicky about whether they will or will not fruit.

The fruit was much used for wines, conserves – often using one part of fruit to three parts of sugar (66) – and jellies (delicious). In the walled garden, espaliers were usually placed on east-, west- or north-facing walls; walls with too much sun brought the trees into flower very early, making it difficult to get them then to set fruit. Even so, in my garden, on an easterly wall, the flowers are out long before any insect is around to pollinate them. Things may have once been better; Cobbett (19) notes that damsons and bullaces were very prolific.

In the sixteenth century, one sort, called 'Sebestens' (perhaps 'Sebastian's'), was used specially as a cure for catarrh and 'rheums of the lungs' (26). Some eighteenth-century illustrations of Sebestens plum show an exotic fruit entirely unrelated to *P. domestica*.

An early nineteenth-century damson called the 'Shropshire', still available
and of excellent flavour

# Dill

***Anethum graveolens*** LINNAEUS

*Origin:* southern Europe

A charming plant too little used in the British cuisine. A native of southern Europe, it was certainly in cultivation here by 1570 (99), at which time it had very extensive medicinal applications. Leaves, seeds and the oil obtained from them were widely used in flatulencies (66) (still used for young children), to increase the quantity of a mother's milk, and for various difficulties of the womb, as well as 'rifts of the fundament' and hiccups (26). The seeds boiled in oil 'provoketh carnal lust' but if taken in too large quantities diminished the sight, as well as the seed of generation (26).

Nowadays it is sometimes used in perfumery (97) and for flavouring pickled gherkins and fish. It also goes marvellously in celery or courgette soups. The leaves, in very small quantities, make a fine flavouring for a salad.

# Elder

***Sambucus nigra*** LINNAEUS

*Origin:* native

One of those interesting plants whose use was once central to rural economy, now justly regarded as a noxious garden weed. Native to most of Europe, western Asia and North Africa, it has been used in dozens of ways since earliest times. Greying Romans used the juice of the berries to keep their hair black, and a good black dye made from the green bark was used well into the eighteenth century (76). Leaves were used as a purgative and emetic (76), and switches of young branches were used to whip fruit trees and other kitchen crops to stock attack by greenfly and caterpillars; an infusion was made from the leaves for the same purpose (66). Even by 1807, Dr Martyn could write: 'the whole plant has a narcotic smell, and it is not prudent to sleep under its shade'. Moles seem not to have done, for elder leaves were commonly pushed into mole hills to move the animals on. The leaves were also pounded with beef tallow to ease the pain of hot swellings and tumours.

The young green shoots of spring were pickled for salads and known as 'English bamboo' by the eighteenth century (13) and were a substitute for the pickled true bamboo shoots even then being imported from India and China. The method of pickling was to peel the shoots (especially large if the elder has been cut back), soak them in brine for twenty-four hours, then put them in a pickle of one part wine vinegar, one part beer vinegar, flavoured gently with pickling spices (13, 30).

The inner bark of the branches, apart from the dye, was used as a cure for dropsy, 'glandular obstructions' (66), against choler, as a purge – the action was said to be very violent (26) and as a sheep dip (65). The wood had a remarkable and wide range of uses. It found its way into the musical instruments of the Romans (76) and became eighteenth-century butchers' skewers, tops for fishing rods, needles for weaving nets and often a substitute for the boxwood used in fine turned work for furniture or 'treen' (76).

Of course, nowadays it is the flowers and fruit that are used in the kitchen, if too rarely. The flowers give a quite marvellous flavour to gooseberry jam and jelly and make good wine and occasionally vinegar. The berries make excellent wine and jam. However, once elderflower tea was used as a laxative; the dried flowers were used for erysipelas and other skin disorders (76) and were pickled for salads and used to flavour custards and creams (delicious). The berries were made into a jelly thought good for sore throats and catarrh (66) – elderberry jam is rarely seen in Britain, though common elsewhere, or they were used to give a fine flavour and colour to raisin or sugar wine. Elderberry wine itself was thought by those with refined palates (not mine) to be nauseous, though it was a common beverage for cottagers (66, 76).

Elders appear in the garden without invitation and have not been deliberately cultivated since the seventeenth century. However, in the sixteenth century, before many ordinary kitchen gardens were walled, it was one of the main constituents of the garden hedge (28).

# Endive

*Cichorium endivia* LINNAEUS

*Origin:* eastern Mediterranean region

Native to the Mediterranean region – though it is sometimes credited with an Indian origin (99, 105), it was probably brought into cultivation fairly early (see Chicory). The Romans, according to Pliny the Elder, used several sorts as salad and pot-herbs, and there are still very large numbers of cultivars to be found in Italy. The date of its introduction to Britain is not known precisely, though has been given as 1548 (99). It seems likely to have been in use much earlier. Certainly, Barnaby Googe was well aware of its need to be sown late and watered plenteously, and of the methods of blanching it (he suggested tying the leaves up in bunches or putting the whole plant under a crock), by 1578.

Perhaps the difficulties of cultivation stopped it becoming more popular; by the early eighteenth century there seem to have been only three varieties available in Britain (69). Even that, though, is a wider range than generally available today, which is surprising in view of the refreshing flavour and excellent keeping qualities that the plants have.

Apart from salading, endives were frequently boiled and buttered (105) and are excellent. There were few medicinal properties, though they were thought to 'comfort the weake and feeble stomack' (26) and to help gouty limbs and sore eyes.

Early eighteenth-century endive, less curled than today's types

# Fennel

*Foeniculum vulgare* MILLER

*Origin:* Europe

A most attractive plant, possibly native to Britain (32) and certainly to the Mediterranean region – it was extensively used in Roman kitchens (66). It has been cultivated since the earliest times and is widely naturalized. It has many forms, only a few of which are cultivated here, and in common with other ancient crops is associated with magic and medical lore.

The sorts eaten are 'sweet fennel', the seeds of the bitter kind being used to flavour liqueurs (105). The sweet ones were once thought to have originated in the Azores, though in the sixteenth century sweet fennel was created magically by soaking seed of the bitter kind in honey (28). Of the numerous selections of the sweet ones, seeds, leaves, swollen leaf bases, stems and roots can all be used in the kitchen. The lovely feathery leaves are the most commonly used part of the plant in Britain, finely chopped to flavour salads (or whole, as decoration, in seventeenth-century ones), to flavour sauces for fish or to wrap fish in when the fish (especially mackerel) is to be baked. Initially, I was always left with fish covered in a filigree of charcoal until I discovered that the leaves should be soaked before tying around the fish (13). The leaves can also be used in pickles, especially pickled meats, and as a flavouring in many soups.

The young flower bunches, as well as the young leaf tufts, were also used fresh in seventeenth-century salads (29), though the florets have a rather sharp taste closer to aniseed than fennel. Evelyn, who used them in his salads, said that only the Italians ate the blanched leaf stalks. He was referring to what we now call 'Florence' fennel, or 'Finocchio', where the bases of the leaf stalks are fleshy, clasping one another to form a 'bulb'. Similar forms of fennel were only just beginning to be grown in Britain by the start of the eighteenth century (66, 105), and they can still be tricky things to grow. Seed was brought in from Leghorn for the Duke of Chandos' stupendous (and vanished) garden at Canons (9). No doubt his gardeners knew that dryness, or sowing too early, makes the plants bolt long before producing a proper 'bulb', though there now seem to be strains which are less susceptible to day-length and drought factors. In any case, it is not easy to produce growths the size of those that are imported, so it is best to eat your own when two or three inches across. They are good fresh but delicious partly cooked in a little water and finished off in plenty of butter. Partially bolted plants are just as edible but do not look so good in the dish. Fully bolted ones have stalks like fibreboard. If you do not want flower heads for decoration or seed, cut the plants from the root at ground level, and the root will go on to produce several small and delicious 'bulbs' later in the season. Some Italian varieties (which I have not managed to trace), were grown as catch crops, forming no bulb but bolting when very small and tender. The plants were broken into pieces for a salad (105).

Fennel roots, long, white and fanged, cook well in winter. They have been used in this way at least since the seventeenth century (84). In some strains, or at some stages, the roots are tender all the way through. In others the central core remains woody and has to be cut out. The flavour of the edible part is excellent.

Fennel has associations with serpents, scorpions and eyes. Snakes were believed to like eating it before casting their skins, and Pliny related that snakes wounded the plant with their fangs, then rubbed their eyes in the juices. Eating the leaves was supposed to strengthen human sight, and the seeds were taken in wine to cure scorpion stings (66, 77). Dodoens recommends a tisane of the leaves for 'wamblings' of the gut and kidney pains. He also says that it 'filleth women's breasts or dugs with milke', will cure the 'wild fire, and all hote swellings' and even 'boyled in wine or pound with oyle, is very good for the yard, or secret part of man, to be either bathed or stewed, or rubbed and annointed with the same'. In 1807 Dr Martyn writes that roots, cooked, were 'supposed by some to be equivalent in virtue to the Ginseng', though whether for the same reasons, he does not say.

# Fig

*Ficus carica* LINNAEUS

*Origin:* Middle East

Ancient, mysterious and delicious, the fig should be far more widely grown than it is. If you plant one you will have in your garden something that grew in the earliest gardens of all. In Britain it seems to have been grown first by the Romans (63); the fruit was used in various meat dishes in medieval times, and new varieties were imported during the Renaissance – it was once believed that these varieties were the first introduction of the fig to Britain (76, 99). Trees planted in the sixteenth century survived for at least three hundred years in many places, including Lambeth, Mitcham – the tree said to have been planted by Cranmer (66) – and Rea's garden at Winchester. There is a magnificent and vast seventeenth-century example engulfing part of the Old Royal Observatory at Greenwich, and although most ancient examples are near London, figs fruit excellently against walls well up to the Firth of Forth and beyond.

The earliest references to the fig are in Sumerian records of 2500 BC, and of course there are biblical references to it as one of the plants of the Garden of Eden. The probable site of domestication was in southern Arabia, where wild types are still found. However, one Greek legend suggests southern Turkey was the site, for the town of Sykea (Soğuksu Liman) was named after the titan Sykeus whose mother helpfully turned him into a fig tree at that location, when he was being too closely pursued by Zeus during the war between the gods and the titans. The Athenians, though, claimed the fig as their discovery, it having been revealed to them as one of the fruits of autumn by the goddess Demeter. Perhaps it was the Athenians who first grew them in Attica, for they were forbidden to export them to other city states. There must, however, have been a black market in the fruit, for informers on fruit sales were called '*sykophanta*' or 'discoverers of figs' (93) – 'fig' is still, in Greece, a term of abuse. The fig also seems to have been sacred to Dionysos; at his festivals a phallus carved from fig wood was carried (46), and the tree still has phallic associations in India.

Figs must have escaped to Italy, for Romulus and Remus were nursed beneath one, by a she-wolf and a woodpecker. Some Roman representations of Saturn show him with a crown of new figs, and wrestlers and champions were fed on them (76). Pliny the Elder knew twenty-nine different varieties, some apparently still in cultivation (93), and no doubt a few of them reached these shores. In spite of their medieval uses, they are not mentioned in Tusser's *Five Hundred Points of Good Husbandry* of 1573, though they do appear in Turner's *A new herball* of 1551. Whatever had happened to our figs, they were taken to the New World by Columbus in 1492 and were established in the West Indies and Peru by the sixteenth century, were in Mexico by the seventeenth and reached California in 1769 (46). New sorts were still coming to Britain, Tradescant buying white-fruited ones in Holland in 1611 to plant at Hatfield. Five varieties had reached Scotland by 1732 and were protected from late frosts by having matting hung over them (49). Where the gardens had terraces (common in seventeenth-century Scotland, where houses were still being built on steep and defensible sites), figs were often planted between the wall's buttresses.

Quite a few types are available here. 'Brown Turkey' is probably the most useful (it does not need to have its roots restricted) and, though delicious, has a rather mild flavour. Anyone with a heated greenhouse or sunroom should try some of the more glamorous sorts. None of the figs grown in Britain needs pollination by the wasp that is necessary for the fruiting of the Smyrna types. Outdoors here, only one crop is usual, developed from tiny fig buds that have overwintered. Under glass, especially if heat is available, it is possible to have a second crop from the buds produced in the current year. Of pests, red spider can be a nuisance, and woodlice happily climb the stems and can ruin ripe fruit. Nevertheless, it is a delicious and easily grown fruit should there be space. It is worth skinning the figs (easy to do from the opening), as some people find it produces a curious tingling sensation on the lips. Many varieties do well in pots and can be forced, then brought indoors for decoration.

Apart from their well-known mildly laxative properties, figs have long been known to have a tenderizing effect on meat – hence their use in many medieval recipes. It was even thought that carcases hung up in a fig tree were similarly affected (76), though perhaps summer warmth helped a little. The tree yields an oil of very high quality once much used by lock and gunsmiths. More unusually, and worth remembering if you have a large crop, is that 'Those that feede much upon Figs become lousie and full of vermine', though Dodoens may have been referring to dried figs. Fresh figs were also given to children with measles or smallpox as they were thought to cause sweating (perhaps because of their high sugar content) which drove out 'corrupt and stinking humours'. The meat tenderizing properties may have been behind the fig's use for bruises, for it was thought to dissolve the congealed blood beneath the skin and also alleviate the pain. Even more useful, figs pounded with salt, rue and nuts made a mithridate or counter-poison. Pounded with wormwood and wine, they cured dropsies, or taken with mustard seed, tintinabulation. The milk from wounded stems was mopped up with a piece of cloth and laid on a sore tooth, and a pulp of the leaves cured the 'king's evil' if one was unable to visit Court (26).

# Filbert
## (or Cob-nut, or Hazel)

*Corylus avellana* LINNAEUS and *C. maxima* MILLER

*Origin:* native; widespread elsewhere

Two very closely related species, interfertile, and so with many intermediate types, but the filbert differs from the cob or hazel in having an outer covering that is longer than the nut, and that closes in around its apex. Though the filbert is extremely variable, there are few named varieties in commerce.

It seems likely that the nuts are an extremely ancient food source in southern Europe and Asia, for they are deeply associated with magic and superstition and once had many medical uses. It was one of the five sacred nourishments in ancient China (46). In the West, Virgil says the plant was more honoured than either vine, myrtle or bay (46). The nut was emblematic of a fruitful marriage and, farther north in Europe, it protected houses against witches and lightning and was used for wands and divining-rods, as well as rods of authority (46). In the seventeenth century it was still used for cudgels (66). The plant was sacred, perhaps not surprisingly, to Thor.

Redouté's magnificent illustration of *Corylus maxima*

The first types cultivated by the Romans may have come from Turkey, for the early name was '*nux pontica*'. It became '*nux avellina*' later, when cultivation had become established, probably at Avellino in Sicily (66). As well as being eaten for delight, they were used with vinegar and wormwood seed as a cure for jaundice, and a cream made from the nuts was used for malfunctions of the bladder (66, 76).

The Romans brought various improved types to these shores, where wildlings were already in use. In fact, the wildlings remained in use, for the nuts were being collected and sent to the

London markets into the early nineteenth century (66). Kent was one of the best-known places for their cultivation, and the filbert plantations there, as with the cherry, may be of Roman origin. Whatever early filberts or wildlings were like, by the late seventeenth century at least the average tree 'yields a most excellent fruit, not much inferior to the best and sweetest Almonds' (107). Curiously, the widespread variety called 'Kentish Cob' was only introduced to Britain in 1812, by a Mr A. R. Lambert (hence the confusing synonym 'Lambert's Filbert'). It is, though, a very ancient German variety (46).

For nuts, the plants are best grown as bushes and kept pruned in the manner of gooseberries. Twelve-foot centres are the best spacing. They also fruit well if grown as espaliers on a north-facing wall, keeping company with the morellos (68). In the seventeenth century, wall plants were heavily pruned to increase nut size (83). Pollen of one plant is commonly shed before the female catkins are receptive, so it is a good idea to plant two varieties to ensure a good crop.

Hazel or filbert wood, apart from the magical uses already mentioned, was used for hoops, hurdles, wattle and springs for bird traps (66), as well as poles, spars, rake handles, fishing rods and fuel ties (68). Chips from the wood were used to clear wine (66, 68) or even as a source of yeast when no brewing yeast was to be had (switches of leaves were whisked through the liquid).

# French Bean
## (or Kidney Bean)

**Phaseolus vulgaris** LINNAEUS

*Origin:* South, Central and North America

Radio carbon dates of 8000 BC have been obtained for these beans at archaeological sites in Peru, and they were cultivated in North America by 5000 BC. Probably reaching Europe in the early sixteenth century they were soon widely grown (93). They may have been most successful in Italy, for early English and French names call them 'Roman' beans. Gerard grew and ate them, calling them also 'sperage' beans, 'long peason' or even 'garden smilax'. He seems not to have grown the dwarf types, as his French beans clambered up poles or over 'arbors of banquetting places'. Runner beans were similarly grown, though as decoration (q.v.). Parkinson (73) says that they were esteemed by the rich, for their flavour, but also because they were thought not to be the cause of flatulence (see Broad Bean). By 1681 Worlidge could still write: 'it is a plant lately brought into use among us, and not yet sufficiently known; the greatest impediment [is] to be devoured by Snails, Worms etc.' By that date, too, all of Gerard's names for the bean were still current.

There do not seem to have been very many varieties available; even by the early eighteenth century only a handful were known, though by then they included bush types. By the 1880s vast numbers had come into commerce, including many very rarely seen here today (105). A pity this, for some of the types still grown on the Continent have excellent flavours.

Bush sorts were forced under glass, almost as soon as they were introduced, and were a common crop between melons in the melon house (90). However, Mortimer thought that forced beans were inferior in flavour to outdoor ones, though this is not my experience. With a bit of hunting, some spectacular pod types can be found, some nearly two feet in length, others coloured violet, yellow or scarlet, plain or streaked. There are also many variations in seed design and decoration; variations in flavour do exist but are less marked. The types grown for dry seed are not often planted here, for in them the inner membrane of the pod quickly becomes too tough to cook.

In the nineteenth century, cultivation must have been of a remarkably high standard; Cobbett (19) maintains that plants were commonly in flower only ten days after germination. In market gardens they were often intercropped with brassicas, still quite a good idea if you are short of garden space.

Altogether a lovely vegetable, and well worth trying under glass if you have it, and it is not already crammed with other things. The climbing forms are obviously the most economical of space. An early spring sowing will be in pod by the end of April; a late summer sowing will still be giving you pickings at the end of November. Parkinson's method of cooking them is still the best (boiled until just tender, then finished off in butter), with perhaps the addition of a few leaves of one of the savories (q.v.).

# Garlic
## (and Rocambole)

Garlic: **Allium sativum** LINNAEUS

*Origin:* possibly central Asia

Rocambole: **A. scorodoprasum** LINNAEUS

*Origin:* native

Garlic, a venerable and venerated plant, is essential flavouring for whole sections of the cuisine, yet is detested by many. It was once used as a cure for dropsy, for rheumatism (pounded with honey and rubbed on the joint) and as a vermifuge. As garlic syrup (an infusion in vinegar and sweetened with honey) it was sold in the nineteenth century for disorders of the breast (66).

The species is known only in cultivation, though Vavilov maintains that the centre of evolution is in central Asia. It is difficult to see how that evolution took place (or the formation of so many different varieties), as the plants very rarely flower, and even the seed heads are composed mainly of bulbils, not seedpods (93). Egyptian records of garlic exist from 3200 BC – it was a sacred plant (80); there are ancient Chinese records (93) and various Greek ones. The Greeks seem to have regarded it with disgust and believed that those who had eaten it were profaned; criminals were made to eat it for several days to cleanse them of their crime (77).

There are many Roman records, and Pliny the Elder mentions several distinct cultivars. Early on, following Greek precedent, upper-class Romans refused to taste garlic. However, game-cocks, soldiers and workmen were fed on it to encourage energy and aggression. By late Roman times garlic was established in the kitchens of all classes (77).

Since the earliest times, too, there have been numerous recipes for sweetening the breath following a garlic-scented meal. Those usually suggested in sixteenth-, seventeenth- and eighteenth-century garden and cook-books (chewing a raw bean, parsley or baked beetroot) all follow Roman methods, the beetroot recipe deriving from Menander.

Chaucer mentions garlic, though the first herbal reference is in Tusser, and it seems likely that it has been cultivated or naturalized since Roman times. In any case, it was an important medicinal preventative against the plague in medieval times, a clove being held in the mouth. Perhaps it worked by reducing close personal contact. Garlic is widely used today and is easily grown by anyone with a vegetable patch. It needs as long a growth season as possible, and it helps to get the cloves planted very early. Various pests like eating the roots, and a watch should be kept. The plant is sometimes said to reduce greenfly infestation in nearby plants; I cannot say that I have noticed any effect.

The rocambole, now no longer used in British kitchens though it was popular up to the end of the eighteenth century, was long thought to be a type of wild garlic, also having clusters of bulblets or 'cloves'. However, it belongs to a native species, the flavour being less pungent than that of garlic. It was cultivated by Gerard before 1596 and is still used in America.

# Gooseberry

*Ribes uva-crispa* LINNAEUS

*Origin:* native

Also once called 'feaberry bush', 'feabes' (34) and 'carberry' (66), the less picturesque word had ousted all the others by the mid-nineteenth century. The word 'gooseberry' is derived from old French, and some of the early English derivatives, like 'grosier' and 'groser bush', are scarcely different to the original. As is suggested by the number of vernacular names, the plant is native, though improved domesticated forms may have been selected in northern Europe. They were known to the Greeks and Romans, and the fruiterer to Edward I was importing French bushes to England between 1276 and 1292 (46), though by 1551 Turner can write that the British cultivars are superior to European ones (101). The crop is very easily bred, frequently throw-

A nineteenth-century plate, when gooseberries were far more
popular than today

ing up new characteristics, producing plenty of seed and coming
quickly to maturity. Mortimer mentions six types in 1707, Mawe
mentions twenty-three types in 1767, but following the formation of 'gooseberry clubs' in the north of England in the early
nineteenth century, three hundred cultivars were in commerce by
1821, and over seven hundred by 1831 (46). All these were of
sweet varieties; the tart ones entered commerce in a major way
only after the abolition of Sugar Tax in 1874 (93), though
presumably they had been grown in early kitchen gardens for the
sauces in which they substitute for verjuice.

Gerard writes of the gooseberry: 'These plants do grow in our London gardens, and elsewhere, in great abundance. The fruit is used in divers sauces for meat: They are used in brothes instead of verjuice, which maketh the broth not only pleasant to taste, but is greatly profitable to such as are troubled with a hot burning ague.' During the reign of Elizabeth, gooseberries were also used in salads, as a substitute for lettuce, but these must have been the sweet sort (76). Markham describes their use as a stuffing or sauce for a green goose.

Some of the fruit must have been spectacular to look at; by 1629, red, green, yellow, white and waxy blue sorts were grown (93). Early in the next century, black and even striped ones were available (68). However, by 1833 Cobbett dismisses all the new varieties as all skin and no flesh and regrets that the best type, small, black and smooth (perhaps that mentioned by Mortimer), 'is now only seen in the gardens of our farmhouses'. All the exotic types now seem to have vanished without trace. A shame that, for I would like to have tried a decorative seventeenth-century idea in which several differently coloured sorts were grafted together to provide a spectacular-looking bush (83).

Because gooseberries are quite prickly shrubs, they were used as part of the kitchen garden hedge in the sixteenth century (28). The use persisted even when kitchen gardens had stone or brick walls, for while apple espaliers often lined the main path on the north-south axis, gooseberry bushes, pruned or natural, often lined the main east-west path. In tiny gardens they were often trained to trellis work as a background to the flower border (76). When trained against walls, they were often planted on a north-facing one or between young fruit trees on any of the others. The gooseberries, swift to come into production, were stripped out when the grander wall-fruit needed the space.

While we now regard them as an early summer fruit, the berries were once frequently left on the bushes until November, and so tarts, pies and sauces were available fresh throughout the summer and autumn. The sauce was used, by the eighteenth century, for mackerel (delicious) and for goose and pork. For tarts, the smallest berries were harvested first, which was thought to encourage the remainder to grow larger and so to make a better fresh dessert (76). Towards the end of the season, gooseberries were preserved in brine, jellied or jammed.

The main curse of the gooseberry, apart from hungry birds, is mildew. This can devastate the crop and needs catching very early if the bushes are to thrive. It is only a recent problem though, for it was introduced from America in 1905 (93) and decimated commercial production. American gooseberries are immune to the disease but are small berried and as yet are not frequently found in Britain. So the crop is now less used than it was when Worlidge could write 'but this Fruit taken in its right time, yields so delicate a Wine that you cannot solace yourself with a finer Summer Repast'. He thought too, that 'Gooseberries being through ripe, taste the most like Grapes of any of our English Fruits; and . . . will yield in Distillery, the best Brandy of any of our Fruits, and very near as good as the best French Brandy.'

# Grapefruit

*Citrus paradisi* MACFADYEN

*Origin:* West Indies

The grapefruit originated in the West Indies in the eighteenth century and is probably derived from, and certainly related to, the pummelo (*C. grandis*) or pumplemus (*pompelmoes* in Dutch, *pamplemousse* in French) or shaddock (46). Like the latter, the grapefruit has clusters of fruit (hence the modern name), with a greenish yellow skin and sweetish or downright sour flesh. The flowers have a marvellous smell; a single one will perfume an entire greenhouse.

Though the shaddock was cultivated by Miller in 1739, the grapefruit itself did not become a popular fruit until the twentieth century. It missed the great age of British citrus growing, possibly because, as Dr Martyn wrote, it was thought to be a degenerate shaddock and to be irrelevant to the garden. Nowadays, trees are occasionally to be found in British greenhouses, grown for amusement rather than as a crop. They are fairly hardy, and mine survived for several years, bedded out in an unheated greenhouse. Immature wood is lost in hard winters, and the fruit does not often ripen. Seedlings take many years to reach flowering size, and it is best to obtain material from an already mature tree. Cuttings root with ease. Alternatively, shoots can be grafted onto suitably sized seedlings.

# Greengage

*Prunus domestica* subsp. *insititia* (LINNAEUS) C. K.
SCHNEIDER (*P. domestica* subsp. *italica* (BORKHAUSEN)
HEGI)

*Origin:* Turkey

Though now usually listed with the plums, the greengages were once thought more wholesome, and many still find them more delicious. What may be wild plants can still be found in Asia Minor, so they may have been early introductions to Italy. The wife of François I of France imported them from that country in the sixteenth century, and at least one variety was given her name, 'Reine Claude' (92). Lord Cromwell brought several to Britain for Henry VIII, including the ancient and still grown Perdrigan (76) – it is not, so far as I know, in commerce, but nineteenth-century trees still exist.

The name for the group seems to be only of eighteenth-century origin. The Gage family were said to have imported a batch of fruit trees from the Chartreuse monastery at Paris. When the trees arrived at Hengrave Hall, one tree was unlabelled. It proved to have especially good fruit, and the gardener called the tree 'Greengage'. The variety still bearing that name is therefore perhaps French, and perhaps very old. It is sometimes thought to be but a synonym of 'Reine Claude' (76).

Almost all the gages were grown as wall-fruit, usually east- or west-facing, but sometimes the choicest were given the benefit of the south-facing one. They were also grown in pots and occasionally forced (83).

The ancient greengage 'Reine Claude', by Redouté

# Hop

*Humulus lupulus* LINNAEUS

*Origin:* native; widespread elsewhere

Native to Britain, as well as southern Europe and western Asia, it has probably been used here as a vegetable and medicinal plant since earliest times. Pliny the Elder says that the ancients made no use of the flowers except as decoration (for which they are still very effective if you have room for a plant or two), though by his own times (the first century AD), the young shoots were eaten as a spring vegetable (77). This use, though surprising today, persisted in Britain well into the nineteenth century, Cobbett writing (19) that hop shoots are 'as delightful a vegetable as ever was put on a table, not yielding, during about the three weeks that it is in season, to the asparagus itself'. The shoots, harvested in April, are cut when about four to five inches long and bunched like asparagus. They are then boiled gently for about thirty minutes and served with butter (19). Martha Bradley, a lady with great culinary taste, thought that they were excellent, and even Cobbett himself was not easily pleased. It is difficult to know why the plant has dropped out of use here, though when the vines mature, they do take up a lot of space; the growth rate is prodigious – up to 25 centimetres a day (93).

Medicinally, hops have been thought good for 'stoppings of the liver', 'corruption of the blood', scabs and scurvies (26), prostate troubles, nervous indigestion (97) and of course insomnia, as well as 'correcting the viscidity of the lymph' and 'cleaning the kidneys' (66). For the sleepless, hop pillows, still advertised in the Press, have been used at least since the sixteenth century and may actually work (I have not tried them), for the resins on the cones are mildly sedative (91).

The same resins also inhibit the multiplication of bacteria, and it is this property that was the original reason for adding them to ale. However, the hops gave the drink their own special flavour and so turned the 'ale' to 'beer'. This transformation seems to have happened in Britain early in the sixteenth century, following either Henry VIII's expedition to Tournai (77) or the arrival here of Flemish immigrants – surely the most likely (93). Beer had established itself much earlier in other parts of Europe, though it is not clear from all early references to hop cultivation what the reason for the cultivation was; the earliest is in the Finnish saga of *Kalevala,* and there are other European references from the ninth century (93). Certainly, cultivation was widespread by the thirteenth century, suggesting a major market for the product. By 1574 hop production was sufficiently important to support the appearance of Reginald Scot's *A perfite platforme of a hoppe garden,* by which time there were no legal barriers to using hops for beer (it had once been believed dangerous).

Apart from their use in beer, as an asparagus substitute and as a cure for a vast number of ailments, hops served other functions. They were used as a source of a yellow dye for wool, and the stems were 'retted' like flax and made into a coarse cloth, used for sacking (66). Unretted stems were also used in basket work, and an oil is still extracted from the cones, to be used in perfumery (97).

Though better varieties are propagated by cuttings or division of the 'stool', the plant is easily obtained from seed. Though the young plants grow rapidly, several seasons are necessary before a reasonable crop of young shoots can be obtained. Heavy cropping of these also helps to reduce the vigour of the whole plant, necessary if the kitchen garden is to grow anything else.

# Horseradish

*Armoracia rusticana* P. GAERTNER, B. MEYER and J. C. D. SCHREBER

*Origin:* eastern Europe and Turkey

The plant is native to eastern Europe and Turkey and seems to have been used medicinally and as a condiment since earliest times. It is referred to by Dioscorides and was much used by the Romans. It may have been introduced here by them. Certainly it is widely naturalized. The plant rarely produces seed, and with its ability to produce new plants from the tiniest scrap of root it scarcely needs to. The various types are therefore all clones (93), and some are very ancient.

Gerard describes how the sauce was made in Germany, so perhaps it was not in common use in Elizabethan England. It was used, incidentally, for fish, not meat. Such a use continued into the seventeenth century and is mentioned by Parkinson (74). Having a vastly more powerful flavour than all the other radishes (q.v.), it was regarded as a more powerful medicine. It seems, though, never to have achieved the vast range of uses that the radishes did, being used mainly to cure melancholia and as a vermifuge.

It is not a very useful garden plant, unless you have plenty of space. A single root rapidly produces a far bigger crop than any present-day kitchen can ever use. If you then need the space for something else, the plant is impossible to eradicate.

# Hyssop

*Hyssopus officinalis* LINNAEUS

*Origin:* southern Europe

A charming and pungently aromatic small shrub, usually seen in its blue-flowered and flat-leafed form. A common variant has white flowers, but others exist with red or pink flowers and variously frilled and divided leaves. Once often grown in the kitchen garden as a border to the beds, it had a vast range of medicinal uses, and though still used by the herbalists, it is occasionally used for flavouring salads and soup and meat dishes.

Native to southern Europe, the earliest British record of its use dates from 1548. Such a range of uses was described in early herbals that it seems to have been cultivated in Britain long before that date. The Romans used it as a purgative (mixed with figs) and as an emetic (mixed with honey) or for snakebite, as a poultice (77). Pliny the Elder describes its use as an expectorant (the Lyte/Dodoens herbal uses the picturesque phrase 'A purge for clammy fleume'). It is still sometimes used for this purpose (97), though unless your kitchen garden is well organized, the recipe is not easy to assemble in its nineteenth-century version: five sprigs of hyssop, two of rue, boiled up with three figs (77). A very similar recipe was used in nineteenth-century Britain for 'stoppings of the breast' and colds. Apart from making a hyssop gargle for all sorts of awful-sounding ailments of mouth and throat, the vinegar was used for toothache, to dissolve clotted blood beneath the skin, '. . . and all blacke and blew marks that come of stripes or beating'. The skin was washed in hyssop water for itch, scurf and 'foul manginess' (26).

The plant flowers freely, the bees like it, and it produces seed in abundance. If you can find a special type, cuttings root easily in April and May.

# Jerusalem Artichoke

*Helianthus tuberosus* LINNAEUS

*Origin:* North America

'This plant has beans at the root, like a potato, which to the great misfortune of the human race, is everywhere but too well known.' Thus complains William Cobbett in 1833, expressing a widespread and long-held feeling, for the plants, widely grown in the late sixteenth and early seventeenth century, soon dropped from common use. This is surprising, both because the roots are good (in moderation) and because only a few decades before the plant became unpopular, Parkinson said the plant was a great dainty, and fit for a Queen.

These 'artichokes' are natives of North America and probably reached Europe in the sixteenth century. Early names included 'Canada potatoes' and 'French potatoes', as well as the one used now. 'Jerusalem' is probably a corruption of the Italian 'Girasole' referring to the flowers turning towards the sun. This is not often seen in northern countries, for there the plants very rarely flower.

Early methods of cooking were to bake them in pies – rich and sweet ones, too, that included bone marrow, dates, ginger, raisins and sack (74), to boil and peel them, finishing them off in plenty of butter and a little white wine (and excellent, too). Vilmorin-

Andrieux, describing the rather few varieties in 1885, suggests that the best way of cooking them is simply to bake them. This certainly does increase the flavour, but also their tendency to cause flatulence. However, a light and creamy soup, flavoured with almonds or hazelnuts, is the most delicious way of eating them, and the plants are worth growing for that dish alone.

In the garden it is better to give them a permanent patch of their own than to try to make them part of the rotation. Even in a light soil it is almost impossible to harvest the entire plant, and the smallest piece left in the ground seems to produce another stem. They are sometimes suggested as a windbreak in the vegetable garden, though they are not high enough to protect anything from a draught until August, and they are easily blown over by autumn gales (needing support from strings stretched between poles). An awkward plant in many ways, though one which is worth a row or two.

# Kale

*Brassica oleracea* var. *acephala* DE CANDOLLE

*Origin:* possibly eastern Mediterranean region

The kales, of the whole cabbage group, are the most closely related to wild types and have been cultivated since earliest times (71). Kales were grown widely by the Greeks, and with present-day types being named by their place of origin (everywhere from Scotland to Siberia), it seems likely that they are also an ancient crop away from the Mediterranean region.

The most cold-tolerant of all the brassicas, it is generally only the frilled-leaf types that are grown for human consumption in northern and western Europe, and even those need frosting fairly heavily before the leaves cook at all tenderly. For an unknown reason, Estienne and Liebault say that the tops and side shoots should not be eaten, but anyone who follows that sixteenth-century advice misses by far the best part of the crop. The side shoots, in February and March, eat better than the best sprouting broccoli, with a lovely mild and sweet flavour. Perhaps warmer

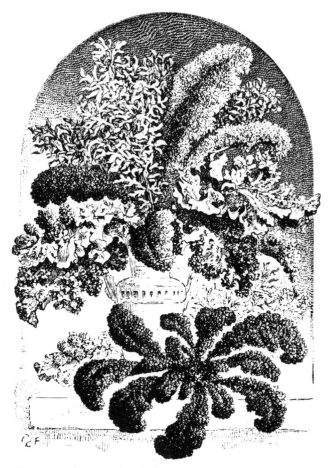

Victorian gardeners used many decorative kales, some still available,
in their bedding schemes

gardens than mine would produce less good results; certainly
Cobbett, in his *English Gardener*, thought it was a coarse thing
and that, as savoy cabbages are almost as hardy, they should be
grown in preference to kale.

Various oddities were once grown, including several non-
flowering perennial sorts (57) which produced clusters of shoots
from the stem base that were treated as cuttings. These, and the
still available perennial 'cauliflower' (actually a broccoli), were

thought of as cottagers' plants (57), saving them the cost of seed or the difficulty of producing their own. The variegated and horribly colourful kales also still available were used to decorate Victorian dinner tables (105), not the garden itself.

# Kohl Rabi

*Brassica olearacea* var. *gongylodes* LINNAEUS

*Origin:* central and southern Europe

A vegetable rarely grown in Britain, which accounts for its lack of an English name, though it is sometimes called 'turnip rooted cabbage'. Kohl rabi is not mentioned by Sweet or Miller or even in Loudon's *Encyclopaedia of Gardening* of 1827, though the vegetable was by then widely grown in German-speaking countries. The crop may have originated in Germany, although the Romans grew a plant that sounds very like a kohl rabi. If so, it is surprising that there is only one name in use. There are a large number of cultivars, though the swollen stems are only of two colours: pale green or purple. The green sorts are supposed to have the most delicate flavour, though personally I think that the purple ones make better eating.

In British gardens they are a useful catch crop, best grown in the more fertile part of the rotation. They need fast growing for best results, though with some of the better cultivars even slow-grown plants can yield a good vegetable. Though the roots do get very woody, and a tough kohl rabi is something to be reckoned with, it is important to remember to peel thickly enough, most of the fibres being in the outer part of the stem. They are easily cut away; experience will soon show the necessary depth. The plants are best harvested between golf- and tennis-ball sizes, peeled, lightly boiled and finished off with a knob of butter. A few drops of wine vinegar give an already agreeable dish an extra lift.

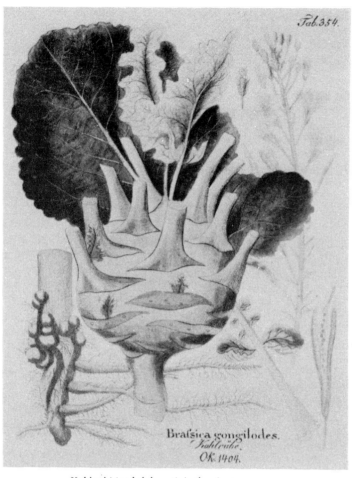

Kohl rabi (and clubroot), in the nineteentcentury

# Lamb's Lettuce
## (or Corn Salad)

*Valerianella locusta* (LINNAEUS) LATERRADE (*V. olitoria* (LINNAEUS) POLLICH)

*Origin:* native; widespread elsewhere

A native, and one once widely used in Britain and on the Continent as a winter salading. In Europe, several varieties are still in commerce, some with frilled, or flat and round, leaves. As far as I have discovered, there is little difference in the flavour. The plants are rarely grown as a crop in their own right, but as useful things to sow between rows of more valuable crops (105).

Before winter lettuces were widely grown, lamb's lettuce was the main winter leaf salad. Great use was made of it in the seventeenth century (84), when it was served with cold boiled beetroot or celery. It was often allowed to self-seed amongst crops (68), though a well-grown and uneaten plant can become quite large, as well as producing alarming quantities of seed. Seedlings can be found over most of my garden.

Lamb's lettuce began to fall out of favour in the eighteenth century (66) (see Lettuce), and in the nineteenth, Cobbett wrote (19): '. . . it is, indeed, a *weed*, and can be of no real use where lettuces are to be had. . . .' Perhaps so, but winter lettuces can be tricky, whereas lamb's lettuce needs no trouble at all. It is crisp and juicy, and the flavour is really very nice, and I cannot think why Miller thought that one of the reasons it was then falling out of use was the strength of its taste. The only real difficulty is that the plants do need careful washing, and the separation of fresh leaves from old ones and roots takes time. However, all that can be done indoors. Lastly, some of the European varieties I have tried are susceptible to mildew, though British ones seem not to be.

In spite of its ancient usage, the plant seems to have had no medicinal properties.

# Lavender

*Lavandula angustifolia* MILLER (*L. Spica* LINNAEUS *nomen ambiguum*), and other species

*Origin:* southern Europe

Though not a culinary plant, lavenders have been grown in British kitchen gardens at least since the mid-fifteenth century. The type once commonly called *Lavandula spica* can be found in numerous varieties, some very old (Gerard mentions several). The plants were used as borders to the vegetable beds (66, 68) for the pleasure of their smell, for their use in the laundry, for scenting the linen chest and for pot-pourris, as well as for many medicinal uses.

Lavender was the chief 'cephalic' drug, and spirits of lavender were used to treat palsies, vertigo, tremors (66), apoplexies and convulsions (28), as well as helping to remove dead children from the womb (26). Leaves or lavender ointment were used to stimulate paralysed limbs.

In the early nineteenth century desserts were sometimes served at table sitting on a bed of lavender flowers (77).

# Leek

*Allium porrum* LINNAEUS (*A. ampeloprasum* var. *porrum* (LINNAEUS) GAY)

*Origin:* possibly eastern Mediterranean region

Almost certainly derived from the wild leek (*Allium ampeloprasum*), the latter being a native of Britain, as well as of the whole Mediterranean region. The earliest records of leek cultivation are Egyptian and date from 3200 BC (93), and Vavilov suggests an

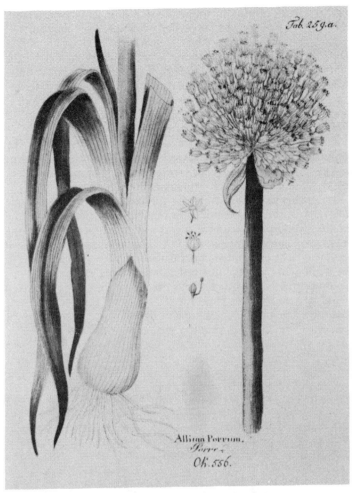

A leek, from Vietz's *Icones Plantarum* of 1819

east Mediterranean origin for cultivated types. Even in the first century AD, Pliny thought that the best leeks came from Egypt. They were much admired by the Romans, and Nero himself ate them several days a month to 'clear his voice', and though brave (he ate them raw, dressed only with oil), he could not avoid the derisive nickname '*porrophagus*' (77), 'leek eater'.

Though both Aiton and Sweet thought that leeks were a

mid-sixteenth-century introduction to Britain from Switzerland, there are numerous and far earlier references (93), medical and poetic (they are mentioned by Chaucer). The association with St David's Day may commemorate a sixth-century victory by the Welsh against the Saxons, though it is difficult to know quite what sort of plants these very early sources intended to describe. Leeks were once much more various in form than they are today, some being used for their leafage, like the modern 'kurrat' of India, and others being grown for bulbs and offsets (even in Victorian times, flowering leeks were commonly left in the ground to produce a crop of fat leek side-bulbs, to be used both as a vegetable and as a source of further plants; they make excellent eating). Some forms were propagated entirely by bulbs (93).

It is rather surprising that leeks survived at all, for many magic tales about their husbandry are remarkably deleterious to the plants' growth. For instance, it was widely believed that to make leeks grow large, a melon seed (28), cucumber seed or rape seed (36) was to be embedded into the plant's crown. The hole was to be made with 'a peece of Reede, or any thing except Iron . . .'. Another widely quoted method of attaining the same end was to 'bind up a pinch of seed into a foul linen cloth' (28), or 'you must hollow a Treatle of Goates dung' (36) and plant the malodorous packets. The idea was that the seedlings would coalesce into a single vigorous plant. Certainly, fouled linen or goat's dung should have given any seedling powerful enough to germinate a very high nitrogen level. Other techniques were to pull the young seedlings half out of the ground, to give them more room to grow downwards, or to plant them on a tile, so that the plant produced very fat stems as it could not grow long and narrow ones. The present-day gardeners' tip is to take off the ends of the leaves. This has been current at least since the sixteenth century and has recently been shown to have no foundation. At the other end of the plant, Cobbett (19) says that when planting out the young leeks, the roots should be trimmed to an inch long, though he does not say why.

A lovely crop, not only for soups and stews but as a fine vegetable and an exceptional 'starter' for meals in winter and early spring. For this, the white parts are steamed until just tender, drained and served with a good vinaigrette and plenty of chopped parsley. It puts one in mind of the asparagus still dormant in the chilly soil.

Most other members of the genus seem to have had far wider medicinal usage than the leek ever achieved. A hot poultice of leek greenery was used to relieve the pain of haemorrhoids (28, 34), the roast stems were a hopeful antidote to mushroom poisoning (74), and they were also thought good for removing bad phlegm from the lungs (74) and for nosebleeds (28).

# Lemon

*Citrus limon* (LINNAEUS) BURMAN FIL.

*Origin:* India

Those marvellous potted lemon trees that line the terraces and steps of ancient Italian gardens have for many centuries been the envy of gardeners from less favoured climates. As interest in Italian culture spread through the rest of Europe in the fifteenth and sixteenth centuries, various sorts of citrus followed the new style of architecture and the new literature, as the northern rich began to imitate their Italian counterparts. While much of the interest in Italy was to do with its relationship to ancient Rome, the various sorts of citrus must have been admired for their particular virtues, not for historical precedent. Though the Romans knew the fruit, they do not seem to have been able to grow the plants; it may be that the sorts first to reach Italy were less hardy than the sorts which established themselves later. The Romans had to content themselves by hanging the fruit among their clothes to perfume them (76).

The lemon's place of origin seems to be in central and eastern India (93), whence it must have spread slowly westwards, for Palladius is credited with its introduction to Italy from Medea in the fourth century AD. Hardier sorts had arrived a thousand years later, and there are references to their culture in Europe from the twelfth and thirteenth centuries (93); but their growth was hardly widespread until the sixteenth. At the end of that century Dodoens writes that, 'These fruites do now grow in Italy, Spaine, and some places of France.' They were grown in London from at least the early seventeenth century (57, 76) and had reached Oxford by 1648 (66). Large numbers of cultivars were soon being introduced, many directly from the East, and this gave a truer picture of the diversity of types than our modern and crude distinctions. Googe is giving a fair description when he writes, in 1578, 'Such of them as are yellow, and of a golden colour, they commonly call Oranges: such as are of a greenish pale yellow, they call Cotrols or Citrulls: those that are long fashioned like a Egge, if they be yellow, are called Citrons, if they be green, Lemons: if they be very great and round like Pompeons, they call them Pomecitrons. . . .' By that time French, German and Spanish gardeners were growing them in tubs that were moved indoors in winter, though in this country they were mostly being moved to unlighted cellars.

By 1683 fifty sorts of lemon were being grown in Italy, though only four of these had reached Holland by that date. Commelin, who wrote the first book devoted exclusively to the culture of citrus fruits, once picked eighty fruits from a single tree of his in one day: an enviable feat for any northern gardener. A hundred years later every garden with a greenhouse or a proper orangery grew lemons, both for the delight of their scented flowers and for the equal delights of the fruit. Some, including the rare 'Hand of Bhudda', grown in Holland in the seventeenth century and in Britain in the early years of the nineteenth, were believed to have other delights still: another name for the plant was 'Cloiser Apple', which had, according to Commelin, 'pointes sticking out and dinted corners, representing the Fashion of a Man's Members, others of a Woman . . . this kind is desired here by many lovers, and is found in many gardens. . . .'

Lemon juice was an early cure for scurvy, Sir James Lancaster feeding his sailors on it in 1601. Otherwise it was used to whiten the skin. Lemon brandy and lemonade were early confections (76), and even lemon barley water is older than the Victorian butlers who are supposed to serve it (see Sorrel). Commelin thought it 'the most pleasant and cooling drink that can be desired' (22). Evelyn liked the pickled peel in salads (30) – the lemon was rare enough then that none of it could be wasted, and numerous eighteenth-century recipes for lemon cream can be found. One, of 1714 (1), uses the juice of a lemon to four egg whites, the yolks of two eggs, sugar and a pint of water. The mixture is stirred and heated until thick.

In the garden, lemon trees are actually quite tough and can easily be overwintered indoors in a reasonably light room or corridor. In summer they grow for me much better under glass than they do when I attempt to imitate Italy and put them out in the garden. The leaves smell delicious when crushed, though different varieties have different smells. The flowers are marvellous. Seed saved from the fruit can take ten years to flower; it is better to obtain plants that are cuttings or grafts from an already mature tree. A few nurseries still sell such things.

# Lettuce
## (and Celtuce)

Lettuce: *Lactuca sativa* LINNAEUS

*Origin:* eastern Mediterranean region

Celtuce: *L. sativa* var. *augustana* IRISH EX BREMER

*Origin:* Far East

If your lettuces are of poor flavour and are not heading as you would like them to, steep the seeds in rosewater to cure the first problem, or trample on the young seedlings to cure the latter. These suggestions of 1570 (28) might alarm the modern gardener, who should in any case be growing 'Webbs Wonderful', a lettuce that could never need either cure.

The second of Estienne and Liebault's suggestions is the more interesting; heading lettuces seem to be a fairly modern selection, for the earliest references to them date from 1543 (93). Earlier sorts, mostly of the 'cos' type, are extremely ancient. Some are painted on the walls of Egyptian tombs (93), and there are many references to them in Greek and Roman literature. In the latter, Pliny refers to sorts from Egypt, Sicily, Cappadocia and elsewhere. In the early part of the Roman period they were eaten at the end of a meal (possibly because of their sleep-inducing properties), but late Romans ate them at the beginning as an hors d'œuvre – a practice still followed in Elizabethan England (34) and today on the Continent. The Romans were so fond of lettuces that it is hard to imagine that they did not grow them in Britain. However, Gerard described only eight types in 1597, and even by

1822 there only seem to have been thirty (77). Today there are hundreds.

Most of the modern varieties have been bred for disease resistance, speed of growth and shelf life. Few are selected for flavour, and these are either slow to mature or do not travel. It is worth exploring the different types; too many gardeners are content with the butterhead group. There are some good flavours to be found, and some interesting-looking plants too, with frilled or strap-shaped leaves, speckled, streaked or suffused with red or brown. Sadly, some groups seem forever lost, and gardens will never contain the delights of Passion lettuces, Georges, Imperials and Bright Genoas (68).

Whether the first of these sorts refers to the religious festival of that name or to the generalized feeling is not known. Lettuces had a reputation for cooling ardour, and laudanum is an extract from lettuce stems (the content is highest in bolted lettuces and can be dangerous), a substance known to the Romans. Even lettuce soup can have a quietening effect on a dinner party, so beware. Phillips (77) thought a diet of lettuces more suitable to celibates than settlers, and Googe (while suggesting putting a stone on top of the plants to stop them bolting), suggested that they reduced lechery. However, they were allowed some positive qualities, Dodoens saying that they 'engendreth better bloode, and causeth better digestion than the other woort or potherbe, especially being boiled and not eaten rawe'. Lettuce juice was used as gargle (28) and as a mild laxative. One of the many good ways of cooking them, if you have a glut, is to braise them with pigeon breasts (the breasts are skewered or tied between halved lettuce hearts and braised in white wine).

The celtuce, or asparagus lettuce, is an eastern selection of the lettuce with especially large, crisp and succulent stems. It is described by Vilmorin-Andrieux in 1885, but seems not to have been grown much before that date. It is often recommended as a dual-use vegetable, but the leaves can be a bit leathery to use as a salad and, cooked, have a taste that is bland to say the least. The stem, peeled and sliced, is very juicy indeed, with a pleasant if elusive flavour. It is nice, too, stir fried.

# Liquorice

*Glycyrrhiza glabra* LINNAEUS

*Origin:* eastern Mediterranean region

An ancient flavouring and medicinal plant, well known to the ancient Greeks. Possibly introduced here by the Romans, but the earliest record dates from the first year of Elizabeth I's reign. Turner described it in 1562, and Gerard grew plenty in his garden. It seems to have dropped out of use as a kitchen garden plant rather early, becoming grown on a field scale, especially near Godalming and Pontefract.

English liquorice was supposed to be better than that produced by any other country (82), and large quantities were once exported. 'Pontefract cakes' were an imitation of those described by Dodoens as being made in Dutch abbeys, flavoured with ginger and spices and taken for coughs and colds, hoarseness and catarrh. All these functions, described by Pliny in the first century AD, are still attributed to liquorice pills.

# Loganberry

*Rubus x loganobaccus* L. H. BAILEY

*Origin:* North America

A modern crop, originating in California, which is probably a cross between some sort of blackberry and a raspberry. The plants crop heavily, though the flavour of the fruit is perhaps inferior to that of a good example of either parent.

An early eighteenth-century plant of liquorice

# Lovage

Lovage: *Levisticum officinale* KOCH

*Origin:* southern Europe

Scots Lovage: *Ligusticum scoticum* LINNAEUS

*Origin:* native

Lovage is a native of southern Europe and was certainly growing in Britain by 1596. However, it had by that date a wide range of medicinal uses, which suggests that it had been in cultivation long before. It was recommended as a vermifuge (21) and as a cure for excessive belching and indigestion (26); lovage water was used as a cordial (58), to remove freckles from the face, as well as spots (26). The leaves, taken in wine, were used to speed childbirth (66), or as a salad, to induce menstruation.

The leaf stalks were once candied like angelica, and the leaves and leaf stalks were, and are, used as a flavouring in soups or in cucumber dishes. The taste is pleasant enough, but the smell of the leaves is powerful and awful and clings with determination to the fingers. Dr Martyn wrote (66): 'The odour of this plant is very strong and peculiarly ungrateful; its taste is warm and aromatic.' Very polite. The plant, when old, can grow very large and is quite handsome. It is fine in the flower garden if you do not have to touch it, and even there one plant is enough.

The Scots lovage, of similar flavour, is a native. Called 'skemis' or 'skunis', it used to be eaten in times of scarcity.

# Maize

## (or Sweetcorn, or Corn on the Cob)

***Zea mays*** LINNAEUS

*Origin:* Central America

Though the plant was introduced to Europe in the early sixteenth century (93) and was soon widely grown in the warmer parts of the Continent, especially Italy and southern Germany (66), it was scarcely grown in British kitchen gardens until the present century. This was in spite of Martyn's and Cobbett's advocacy – Cobbett was of course familiar with its virtues from his American sojourn. The lack of interest in the culinary possibilities of sweetcorn may have been because in the countries where it was grown it was a food for the poorest classes. Also, the short-stemmed and early maturing varieties suitable to our climate were not available in the seventeenth and eighteenth centuries. In those days interest seems to have been restricted to the brightly coloured varieties then, as now, used primarily for decoration (34).

Whatever the crop's reception in Europe, in the Americas it already had an ancient and distinguished past. Excavations in Mexico show that it was extensively cultivated in 5000 BC, though the cobs were small by present-day standards. Early types were probably all 'pop' corns. By 1000 BC, cob size was approaching that of today's smaller varieties (93). The coloured sorts (blue, scarlet, brown and near-black) predominated in South America; the first sorts introduced to Europe were probably from the Caribbean area, where the yellow ones were the most common.

A great deal of breeding work is being carried out in the crop, in the Americas as well as in Europe, and the pursuit of short-summer forms will perhaps soon ensure that all British gardeners can enjoy the fresh vegetable (far better newly harvested than either plastic wrapped or from the freezer). Meanwhile, it is always a slightly risky crop out of doors, though it does well under a plastic tunnel or under glass, provided that the atmosphere during flowering is kept sufficiently dry to allow the anthers to open, and sufficiently on the move to allow the pollen to reach the 'silk'. Some of the new white seeded types developed in America are delicious and worth trying, if you can find them.

# Marigold

*Calendula officinalis* LINNAEUS

> *Origin:* probably central or southern Europe

Cultivated in kitchen gardens 'time out of mind' (66), and of unknown origin (32), it seems to have dropped out of use in the late nineteenth century. A shame, that, for a few plants add a delightful splash of colour to the rows of greenery, and the flowers still have their uses.

Cobbett wrote in the *English Gardener* in 1833 that the petals were 'excellent in broths, soups and stews'. They give all of them a fine colour, though I can never detect any addition to the flavour. Earlier, they enjoyed an extensive medical reputation. Like many plants, marigolds had the rather general property of 'comforting the heart and spirits' (66) and were used against plague (chewed or taken by drinking an infusion in vinegar). The syrup, or the smoke from dried petals, was said to induce menstruation (28), to suppress it (66), to speed the production of the after-birth (28) and to cure toothache (28), jaundice (28, 77) – a horrible cure too, for the petals had to be mashed up with earthworms and drunk, smallpox, measles, warts and scrofula. Flowers were rubbed on bee and wasp stings to reduce the swelling (66). Modern herbalists still use marigold preparations for duodenal ulcers, as well as for external ones and inflamed lymph nodes (97).

In the kitchen the petals, used in moderation, give a pleasant decorative quality to a summer salad. The flowers still make a reasonable tea – it was once thought good for agues (66), and fresh flowers make a spectacular garnish to a roast chicken.

Whatever the wild progenitor, the plants seem to have originated in central and southern Europe and to have been introduced here by the Romans. Various colour forms have been known at least since the sixteenth century, so the sorts nowadays marketed as 'Art Shades' are the ones to go for if you do not like the ordinary orange sort. Old names were 'Golds' or 'Ruddes' (66).

# Marjoram

Most often *Origanum marjorana* LINNAEUS (*Marjorana hortensis* MOENCH), but other species sometimes used

*Origin:* southern Europe

With parsley, one of the most useful herbs in the garden, and no winter kitchen should be without a number of bunches hanging from the beams or from a hook on the cupboard door. Good with all sorts of meats, grilled or stewed, and essential for many Italian dishes. It was once even more widely used.

The Elizabethans used it in many of their dishes, and its introduction is probably earlier than the mid-sixteenth-century date often given. They used it even more widely for medicine, whether for stings, rheumatism, dropsy or tumours under the ears (28). It was commonly used as an embrocation, for 'the Oyle made thereof is very warming, and comfortable to the joynts which are stiffe, and the Sinews which are hard, to mollifie, supple, and stretch them forth. . . .' (21). It was also used in the sixteenth century, as it is now, as a perfume for cosmetics. At the end of a long list of properties, William Coles says, 'lastly, it is to be used in all odoriferous Waters, Powders etc., and is a chief Ingredient in most of the Powders that Barbers use, in whose shops I have seen great store of this Herb hanged up' (21).

The oil was also used in the same way as clove oil still is, to stop teeth aching, and the powdered leaves were used as a snuff which 'draweth down humours from the Head, mundifieth the Braine, causeth to sneeze, and is very good for them that have lost their smelling' (26). It was also used for 'sneezing disorders' (77), perhaps hay fever.

The flowering tops of the plant, which have a more interesting

Common marjoram

savour than the purely leafy parts, were once used to dye woollen cloth a purple colour, and linens a reddish brown (66).

Marjoram is perennial in very mild locations but is most often grown as an annual. Today's seed gives only normal and green plants; once many different leaf types were available, frilled, jagged and even variegated in various colours (66). While these were all in gardens in the eighteenth century, they now seem to have vanished.

# Marrow
## (or Vegetable Marrow, or Courgette)

*Cucurbita pepo* LINNAEUS, though it sometimes includes other species

*Origin:* Central America

The marrow, as grown in Britain, whether as whoppers for the summer flower show or as courgettes for the kitchen, generally belongs to C. *pepo*. In American usage, marrows can sometimes belong to some of the other cultivated species (see entry for Pumpkin and Squash).

As with pumpkins and squashes, the centre of origin for the marrow is Central America. Excavations there suggest that they have been in use for at least a thousand years (106), and many types are now used all over the Americas. It is difficult to know when the word 'marrow' achieved its present usage. When mentioned in early eighteenth-century cook-books, 'marrow' always refers to bone marrow. Nineteenth-century cook-books use the phrase 'vegetable marrow', the garden product supposedly having a similar taste to the animal one. The use of bone marrow to enrich the table (desserts, as well as the more expected meat dishes) seems to have vanished by the twentieth century, freeing the word for its present general use. Gardening books of the nineteenth century also refer to 'vegetable marrow', and Loudon (57) believed them to be recently introduced from Persia. Seed might well have been introduced from the East, but it must have reached there via Spanish or Portuguese sources in the sixteenth or seventeenth centuries.

Varieties of early introduction were in shades of yellow and tan (the former coming back into use) and were smaller than our current monsters, though cooked in similar ways. The inevitable white sauce has a long history. The use of the immature fruit as 'courgettes' or 'zucchini' dates only from the recent British interest in food from the rest of Europe. It is certainly by far the best way of eating them, though mature marrows store well when hung in nets (they bruise and rot if placed on a shelf) and provide a moderately useful vegetable for winter eating. They are best when halved, parboiled and then slowly baked after stuffing with onions, tomatoes, parsley and oil.

# Medlar

*Mespilus germanica* LINNAEUS

*Origin:* southern Europe and Turkey

A really charming medium-sized tree, and although native of southern Europe and Asia Minor, it grows well in most parts of Britain. Even if Cobbett thought it 'only one degree better than a rotten apple' (19), the curiously flavoured fruit makes an interesting dessert for November dinners, and a really delicious jelly for the rest of the year.

The medlar is now widely distributed in Europe, though it seems to have been unknown to the early Romans (or perhaps of no interest to them), and even Pliny's description of some sorts might well apply to the service tree, q.v. (36). However, every Renaissance writer knew it, and by then there were a number of medicinal uses though no magical ones; for instance, the seeds were dried and powdered, and used to help 'gravel' and kidney stones (107).

Estienne and Liebault suggested the medlar as part of the kitchen garden hedge (it is still a common hedgerow plant in parts of Europe). In the seventeenth century, because of its handsome appearance, a free-standing tree or two might be planted in the kitchen garden proper (the tree has large pale flowers in spring and a very picturesque shape, and the leaves colour magnificently in autumn). It was also much used as an espalier, though I have not seen one treated in this way. The fruits were harvested when hard if they were to be kept into midwinter, otherwise they were left on the tree until ripe (or 'bletted'). They were occasionally preserved in wine or pickled in vinegar (36).

Though 'mellowed fruit is often served amongst other sorts of fruit at the table, and eaten with pleasure by those who have no need of Physicke' (21), they were used for various digestive and intestinal difficulties, and also 'to stay their [pregnant women's] longings for unusual meats etc., as also very effective for them that are apt to miscarry, and make them joyful Mothers' (21). Leaves were chopped and applied to a bleeding wound to staunch it (21). In the sixteenth century, the wood was used to make the spokes of wheels (it is fairly springy), and the twigs to make carters' whips (36). The tree seems to have passed out of use at the end of the seventeenth century, perhaps with some regret; 'yet they have been long standing; they are pleasing to the palate' was Worlidge's comment in 1677.

# Melon

**Cucumis melo** LINNAEUS

*Origin:* probably Africa

Evelyn (29) calls the melon 'the noblest production of the garden', which in some ways it still is, needing heat, hand pollination and constant protection from pests and diseases. The first taste of a good home-grown fruit makes most of the trouble worthwhile.

There are more than forty species of *Cucumis* in Africa, and the edible *C. melo* probably originated there. It seems to have arrived in Asia late, for there is no Sanskrit word for it, though there is a Tamil one (106). Melons may have reached Rome as one of the spoils of the war against Mithridates (see Cherry) (76), though de Candolle thought that they were unknown in the Roman Empire. They were nevertheless an early introduction to Italy, the most

A magnificent 'Black Rock' melon from Hooker's *Drawings of Fruits* (1817)

popular sort still being called 'canteloup' after a location near Rome (76).

Italian melon seed was being ordered for the gardens at Hampton Court by 1515 (87), so perhaps some sort of frames and hotbeds existed there by then. Such things were not widespread until much later; Estienne and Liebault could write in 1570 that melons were not much grown in France as they did not 'do' (they must have had a northern audience in mind), and Gerard himself did not grow them. Even Evelyn, writing in 1699, could remember the time when melons were extremely expensive, because hotbed technology was not widely understood. However, Parkinson described such things in 1629, and by t' end of the century almost everyone with several horses (to provide dung for heating) grew melons. The seed was sown in February at full moon (68), and harvesting started a few months later. The crop took some while to reach Scotland, and Reid still thought that melons were a waste of time in the 1690s. Forty years later, another Scots writer, James Justice, was full of enthusiasm and grew musk melons and canteloups, importing the seed from France (49).

Yields were astonishing. Highly nourished and well cared for plants sometimes gave up to twenty fruit; nowadays, it is usual to have five or six without too much fuss. It is surprising that any of the seed ever germinated, for they were subject to all sorts of bizarre treatments (designed to improve the fruit's flavour) before planting. De Bonnefons suggested steeping them in vinegar for two days. Another technique was to soak them in milk or wine and sugar (68). The final fruit seems to have had few magical or medicinal properties, though the flesh was used to soothe sore eyes, and Phillips maintained that the roots were used in Roman wash-balls and in pan scourers (76). A slice of melon put in the kettle was supposed to bring it faster to the boil (28), perhaps the origin of some of the melon-based sauces of French nineteenth-century cuisine.

Only the last edition of the *Gardener's Dictionary* says that, 'under certain circumstances [the melon] is apt to disagree. . . .' One of the certain circumstances is over-ripeness, when the fruit can have a disastrous and long-lasting effect on the innards. A melon 'over the top' does taste a bit odd and has a very powerful smell, but do not let that put you off allowing them to ripen properly or be tempted to eat them too young. This is always tempting, as the plants take such a lot of looking after (red spider multiplies at great speed, and various fungal diseases affect melons too) that harvesting the fruit sometimes seems to be something like a rescue. In the seventeenth century, the fruits were harvested with a few leaves attached, and before sunrise (12). The fruits were ripened off for a few days indoors (28). In dry summers it was quite a common practice to keep the plants moist by watering them by means of a 'wick' of cloth with one end placed in a pot of water and the other by the roots of the plant (28).

# Mint
## (including Peppermint and Pennyroyal)

Mint: *Mentha spicata* LINNAEUS
Peppermint: *M. x piperita* LINNAEUS (*M. nigricans* MILLER)
Pennyroyal: *M. pulegium* LINNAEUS (*Pulegium vulgare* MILLER)

*Origin:* central and southern Europe

Of the large number of garden mints, most are hybrids between *M. spicata* and the numerous other species.

A large number of *Mentha* species and hybrids are grown in the kitchen and herb garden, though the various spearmints (*Mentha spicata*) are the ones most usually grown as a flavouring. Some gourmets prefer the apple-mint (*M. x rotundifolia*). The pennyroyal is widely grown but now hardly ever used in the kitchen.

All the mints have been widely used since ancient times, though probably more for real or supposed medicinal properties than as a condiment. Pennyroyal was the most admired, being used to dampen hysteria, speed the menopause (66), disperse fleas (28) and flies – the Romans hung bunches of it in their rooms (69) – and purify dirty water for drinking. Pigs, when they were fed on 'pudding', liked it flavoured with pennyroyal (69).

Spearmint, used for sauces on lamb since earliest times and as a flavouring for pea soup for as long, was thought the most useful by Pliny. He said that it was good for the memory, acted as a vermifuge, stopped milk going off in the hot Roman summer and had the same effect on cheese (28, 77). Although peppermint had, and has, a wider range of medicinal uses, especially for dyspepsia, retchings and spasms of the stomach (66), both it and spearmint were used for the bites of mad dogs (pounded with salt), in pomegranate juice for the 'hiquets', for headaches and breasts sore with milk, in a poultice of parched barley meal for swellings and tumours and as a strewing herb for feasts and church festivals

(26). The Romans often rubbed it on their tables before a meal, perhaps to ensure the participants' good digestion, as well as to preserve a fresh smell (77).

Among the mints are some excellent garden plants, with some lovely smells; eau-de-Cologne is good, as is orange (Evelyn thought that shoot tips of this were excellent in salads, though they are quite pungent), as well as pineapple and ginger. A good way of growing them is in large earthenware pots, placed wherever you are likely to stop and have time to sniff them. The tiny creeping mint *M. requienii* is a good plant for the joints between paving stones or cobbles, giving a lovely smell of mint when trodden on even in the depths of winter.

# Mulberry

*Morus nigra* LINNAEUS (The white mulberry, *M. alba*, is rarely grown for its sweet and insipid fruit)

*Origin*: Turkey

A fruit of exquisite, if elusive, taste that comes from a handsome tree, sometimes used for avenues, often as 'specimens' on the lawn and occasionally as a wall-fruit in the kitchen garden (it is easily trained and spur pruned).

*M. nigra* is a native of Asia Minor and early moved west to Greece and Rome. Pliny quotes the old saying that it is the wisest of trees, being the last to unfurl its leaves and so always avoiding the cold weather. He also says that they grow so fast thereafter that the buds can be heard to burst – not a noise that I can claim to have heard.

Mulberry leaves were used medicinally by the Romans for diseases of mouth, trachea and lungs (76). By the seventeenth century the bark of the roots was used to expel both tapeworms and roundworms from the gut, as a cathartic and as a dye. A decoction of leaves and roots was held in the mouth for toothache, and if that was too much of a nuisance, and one had the foresight, the roots could be scarified in autumn and oozed a gum that had the same effect (26).

An early nineteenth-century French plate of the black mulberry

The first trees in Britain were thought to be growing at Syon in 1548. However, they were fairly common by the time Gerard was writing, later in the century, and their culture was further encouraged by James VI and I in the early years of the seventeenth century. However, he was far more interested in the white mulberry and in the silkworms that would feed in its leaves (they only reluctantly eat the leaves of *M. nigra*). In the early eighteenth century a single white mulberry tree could be let out for £1 a year, just for its leaves. The dull fruit was fed to poultry (68).

Cobbett suggested that the black mulberry should not stand in the kitchen garden because it 'should have grass beneath to receive the falling fruit, which is never so good when gathered from the tree'. True, if the birds are sufficiently generous to allow any to drop. Free-standing trees are difficult to protect, though it is a fairly easy matter to net one trained against a wall. Two nineteenth-century espaliers at Holkham Hall covered walls nearly a hundred feet long and sixteen feet high and fruited abundantly. They were only thirty years old (76). Other gardeners were forcing potted trees at the same date.

Mulberry juice mixed with cider was thought one of the most delicious native wines, and the jam and jelly are still good. Altogether a good plant, and one far too rarely planted. Incidentally, however wise the ancients thought the tree, it keeps its leaves well into winter, dropping them only with the first heavy frosts.

# Mushroom

*Agaricus bisporus* (LANGE) PILÁT

*Origin:* native

This is the only commonly cultivated species in Britain, though some adventurous seed merchants offer various Oriental ones. Indeed, in the United Kingdom the mushroom is the only species treated as edible (the rich also eat truffles), though a number of other fungi are eaten and enjoyed elsewhere in Europe. From the seventeenth century to the end of the nineteenth most stable-yards had a shady corner given over to a mushroom bed. More organized households had the beds built in a spare outhouse, where the conditions provided a more equable climate for the mushrooms than the open air. King George IV had his mushroom house at Kensington (77). Mushrooms were generally available from September to April.

Knowledge of the edible wild species had never been widespread in Britain, and the prejudice against them even extended to the cultivated one; Evelyn thought the whole thing was too dangerous and advised that all mushrooms should be kept out of the kitchen. Even Cobbett, who seems to have been allergic (he always came out in a rash after eating them), concluded 'that there must be something poisonous in [them] . . . and, therefore, I do not advise anyone to cultivate these things'. In spite of these strictures, mushrooms were much used in stews and sauces and especially for mushroom ketchup, a favourite sauce on eighteenth- and nineteenth-century tables, now displaced by its tomato equivalent.

In the past the only other fungus in general use in British kitchens was the truffle, and occasionally the morel. Some cookbooks, no doubt influenced by French cuisine, suggested the use of both in surprising quantities, and to copy some of these dishes would ruin most modern cooks. The fungi seem to have been imported.

# Nasturtium

*Tropaeolum majus* LINNAEUS
(though *T. minus* LINNAEUS was once in use)

*Origin:* Central America

Quite a useful plant in the kitchen garden, bringing to it a splash of colour which can also be added to the salad bowl. The leaves add quite a good spicy taste to the same dish (best if not overdone), and its resemblance to some of the cresses accounts for both the present-day name of 'nasturtium' (the Latin name for cress) and the older one of 'Indian cress'.

'Indian' in this case refers to those of Peru. The plants are yet another example of the vast range of new introductions from the Americas that occurred in the sixteenth and seventeenth centuries. Gerard got seeds for his Holborn garden (of *T. minus*) from the botanical garden at Paris and included the plant in the first edition of the Herbal. In the next century Parkinson also liked it, but surprisingly the plant then seems to have been lost to cultivation. *T. majus* was introduced to Britain by the 1680s (77), soon after its first appearance in Europe, and quickly replaced the earlier species. Various colour forms were known, as well as the double flowered sorts that can still be grown today. They were said to have a better perfume but a less pleasant taste. The leaves of the single sorts were sold in vegetable markets, those in Edinburgh being priced at one shilling a pint in 1813 (69).

Because the flower colour is both brilliant and translucent, they were chosen, from an early date, to look splendid by candlelight. They were used for garnishing dishes, especially the larger roasts (66, 77), and are still worth using today. The flowers need careful inspection as earwigs like the spurs as a daytime bolt-hole. The green seeds can be pickled and make a good substitute for capers, having been used as such since the eighteenth century. The true caper was generally imported and was thus expensive, though the bush was occasionally cultivated in the orangery. In common with many of the other American crops, nasturtiums have few medicinal uses. They are sometimes used as an antimycotic or antibacterial agent or in infections of the urinogenital tract (95).

# Nectarine

***Prunus persica*** var. ***nucipersica*** (BORKHAUSEN) C. K. SCHNEIDER

*Origin:* probably China

A gorgeous fruit, a smooth-skinned and firmer-fleshed variant of the peach, but also less hardy and with a more complex and aromatic taste. If glasshouse space is available but limited, peaches should be grown on an outside wall, keeping the nectarines under protection. Probably the nectar-like taste gives the tree its name.

Nectarines seem to have been grown in Britain at least since the sixteenth century. However, though they were well known to the Romans, their writers did not distinguish between peaches and nectarines, except to note the firmer flesh.

Gerard grew them at Holborn by 1597, and Sir Thomas Hanmer grew six varieties in 1659. Two of these came true from seed, something that peaches generally refuse to do. Rea notes, in 1665, that reproduction of material by seed was fairly common,

A Victorian magazine plate of a nectarine

but that as the seedlings do not transplant well (not something I have yet tried), most plants were grafted. In Scotland four varieties were in cultivation by the 1730s (49). Of those available today, the one called 'Early Rivers' celebrates a famous British nurseryman and nursery garden. The fruit of the tree is delicious.

The nectarine had only one medicinal use that I have come across: an infusion of the flowers was used as a children's laxative.

# Onion
## (including Tree, Egyptian and Potato Onions)

*Allium cepa* LINNAEUS

*Origin:* central Asia

Curiously, though the onion nowadays plays a fundamental part in a large section of our cuisine, and though it is a very ancient plant – it probably originated in Afghanistan but spread westwards, being known to the Greeks, Egyptians and Romans (93), until the seventeenth century it was thought to have some distinctly unpleasant properties and was much used medicinally well into the nineteenth.

Gerard wrote: 'The onion being eaten, yea, though it be boiled, causeth headaches; hurteth the eies, and maketh a man dim-sighted, dulleth the sences, engendereth windiness, and provoketh overmuch sleepe, especially being eaten raw.' All very unfortunate if you suffered from 'dropsy, white spots and running ears', for all of which it was the principal cure (28), or 'reines, bladder stones and strangury' (21). In a more civilized age, it was used for difficulties of the urinary tract, as an expectorant, for asthma or for hard tumours (66). With such a huge span of uses, it is surprising that it was hardly a cottage garden plant until the early nineteenth century but was only to be found in the gardens of a wealthier class of person (69).

Little magic seems to have accumulated around onions, in spite of the crop's age. Most of it is to do with husbandry; Pliny suggests planting them among savory for maximum yield (77), and there may have been some connection with the moon, for even in the sixteenth century Lord Bacon was observing the moon's phase for planting and setting (8).

As the phrase 'to know one's onions' suggests, the species is extremely variable. Some are propagated without using seed, the plants either producing clusters of side bulbs that grow beneath soil level (the potato onion, probably introduced from the east Mediterranean region in the early nineteenth century) or having reduced flower heads that are largely given over to producing several bulbils that can be rooted and grown on (the tree, or Egyptian onion introduced here in the eighteenth century) (57). In the seed-propagated varieties there is a large range of bulb shapes and skin colours, almost all of them known to the Greeks and Romans. It is worth growing as many types as you can, to find out which best suits your garden and your kitchen. Bulb size is not important unless you want to show them in the local flower show; varieties with small bulbs generally have a good flavour and often keep well. The red-skinned forms have the advantage of looking good too.

Onion seed has a fairly short life and usually needs buying every year. It is also of better quality when produced in countries with a warmer climate than Britain's. At least since the seventeenth century both seeds and bulbs have been imported from Spain, with Holland, France and Italy supplying lesser quantities of both. The planting of onion 'sets' has been a sure way of getting large and early bulbs since at least the early nineteenth century (66). If you are sowing seed, I do not think that there is much point in following Mortimer's suggestion of 1707; to get large bulbs, he tells the gardener to tread the seedlings into the ground as soon as they appear.

'Scalions' (the word is occasionally found in early cook-books and herbals) may refer either to the green tops of ordinary onions or to the so-called Welsh onion (q.v.). They were thought to 'serve for no other thing but to provoke and stirre folke to the act of carnal copulation, and to have a good appetite' (28).

# Orange
## (including Seville Orange, Mandarin and Tangerine)

Sweet orange: *Citrus sinensis* (LINNAEUS) OSBECK

*Origin:* eastern India

Seville orange: *C. aurantium* BLANCO

*Origin:* eastern India

Mandarin: *C. reticulata* BLANCO

*Origin:* China

Tangerine: *C. deliciosa* TENORE

*Origin:* China

Always a status crop for northern gardeners, though some prodigious crops have been achieved, even in England. If the orangery at Versailles is the most generally famous European example, the one at Beddington in Surrey was, in the 1690s, yielding ten thousand fruits a year (4). Oranges had been grown at that location before 1595 (66), and Daniel Defoe (25) described them thus in the early eighteenth century: 'The Orange trees continue, and are indeed wonderful; they are the only standard trees in England, and have moving houses to cover them in winter; they are loaded with fruit in summer, and the gardeners told us, they have stood in the ground where they now grow above 80 years.' Of course, oranges were most commonly grown in tubs and overwintered in special premises, from September to late May, though the Beddington arrangements for these trees planted outside echoed an earlier method used by the Duke of Parma (22).

Oranges had been known in Italy long before the Duke's experimental success. The Romans had imported bitter oranges from the East, though they seemed not to be able to grow the plants. The uses of the fruit were mainly medicinal, and Pliny (80) said that the seeds were chewed to sweeten the breath.

Later the bitter or Seville orange was given a Mediterranean distribution by the Arabs during their expansion through North Africa to Spain. The first references to the crop date from the eleventh century (93), though it is not clear if Italian gardens (those at Chiaramontesi had several thousand trees in the thirteenth century (20)) were stocked from Spain or North Africa. It seems that some of the original trees survived for a very long time; Commelin describes some growing at Rome that were supposed to be five hundred years old, and as he was writing in 1683 (22), that makes the trees part of the first introduction (cuttings from them were being grown at Versailles in the eighteenth century).

The sweet orange, with its delicious taste, was introduced to Europe some time in the fifteenth century (93). Its introduction is often ascribed to Jean de Castro, a sixteenth-century Portuguese warrior (76), though he is a bit late. The plants came from China, where they had long been cultivated, though derived from the same place of origin as the Seville orange: eastern India.

Naturally its popularity rapidly outstripped that of the Seville, and everybody wanted plants. To speed up dissemination, the Seville type was used as a rootstock, and the sweet orange grafted upon this. The flowers have a less powerful perfume than the Sevilles and so were themselves less in demand. They also failed to supplant the medical uses of the Seville, the juice of which was used in scurvy, for malaria, for menorrhagia and, as orange flower water, for nervous disorders and hysteria (66).

By the sixteenth century, oranges, of whatever sort, played an important part in all aspects of the life of the upper classes. Orange leaves were chewed, like the seeds, to sweeten the breath; orange flowers were used as decoration and in nosegays or, beaten with sugar, were turned into pastilles to protect against pestilence and agues. Their perfume was extracted with almond oil and used to perfume gloves, or they were dried and used to perfume linen in the chest, or extracted with brandy and taken as something to 'shrink the gut' – an early slimming idea (22). The flowers were also distilled, or boiled in several changes of water, to provide both orange-flower water and crystallized flowers (13). The former is still used in moderately grand desserts and in cosmetics. The young fruits, pea-sized, were strung together and used for necklaces and bracelets by seventeenth-century ladies, 'because of their good and sweet smell' (22). The mature fruits were stuck with cloves as a pomander to perfume the clothes press and, of course, orange-flavoured desserts were immediately popular. Further, orange juice, especially of the bitter sorts, was widely used as a sauce for fish, asparagus, artichokes, straw-berries and even kidneys and cutlets (it is quite good with all of these, though best in moderation).

Some of the odder variants of the orange were grown early. Blood oranges were grown by the seventeenth century, and even in the nineteenth were still believed to be ordinary oranges grafted on pomegranates (76). The oddest, the Cloiser apple, was sometimes thought to be an orange but is in fact closer to the lemons (q.v.).

The mandarin and tangerine were introduced to Britain in the very early nineteenth century (76). Both species had a Far Eastern origin and are not closely related to the true orange (93). Both, too, make much better plants for today's greenhouses, being smaller than the orange and growing to fruiting size in a faster time (oranges can take at least twelve years). The small 'oranges' commonly seen in florist's shops are calamondins, another Far Eastern type, and really too bitter to eat, though they can make quite a good conserve or an excellent dessert if stewed in a light syrup until the skin is tender and served with whipped cream.

All the oranges are of easy cultivation. If you have room, the best way is to train them as standards. They were often given a mushroom-shaped top, with the branches being kept fairly open by constant pruning, with only one fruit on each branch (45). Though Commelin found the fruit ready in fifteen months, Jacob wrote in 1717 of English fruit: 'Oranges are four or five Years a Ripening with us, but in other Countries they ripen yearly.' Plants kept in British greenhouses take a shorter time. In my garden, plants kept out of doors scarcely grow. Most are hardy to at least a degree or two of frost. In orangeries, before thermo-meters became common, when water kept in a saucer froze, a small fire was put in the fireplace. Too much heat dried out the plants or set them growing; both dangerous states. It is worth following Jacob's advice to keep the plants open, for they are apt to become far too crowded with leaves. While this does not look too bad, it becomes very difficult to exterminate the crop's main pest: scale insect. A nasty thing this, the exudate from the animals coats the leaves and encourages a black fungal growth which eventually ruins the plant.

# Parsley
## (including Hamburg Parsley)

*Petroselinum crispum*  (MILLER) A. W. HILL

*Origin:* southern Europe and western Asia

It is now the most widely grown of all the herbs, a state of affairs
that has existed in Britain at least since the end of the seventeenth
century. Earlier, however, it seems not to have been especially
popular, although it must have been introduced by the Romans.
They made extensive use of it as a flavouring for soups, stews and
salads and as a medicinal herb (93). Both flat and curly kinds
were grown (the flat sort is still widely used on the Continent and
has a slightly lighter and sharper flavour than the curly sorts
grown here), and there was some debate about which sort was
male or female. Perhaps because the flat sort was more easily
mistaken for one of the poisonous umbellifers, it was used at
funerals (Pliny said that the Sardinian parsley was actually
poisonous). Even in the sixteenth century, in England, parsley
was sometimes accused of causing epilepsy and, more often, of
poisoning small birds (66). The flat-leafed parsley, because the
leaf stalks are longer than those of the curled, can be blanched
like celery and makes a pleasant vegetable. Seedlings of the flat
type can easily be converted to curly ones if they are 'rowled' just
after germination – at least, that is what Liebault wrote in 1570.
For more magic, the leaves of any parsley, rubbed against a glass
or tumbler, will break it (77). It does actually produce a very
high-pitched 'ring', though perhaps modern parsley has lost its
virtue, for it has broken nothing of mine. However, I certainly
would not try it on a thin eighteenth-century wineglass.

Parsley seed was used for all the usual ailments susceptible to
the properties of the rest of the family. 'Reines', bladder stones
and strangury were especially helped by parsley (21), and it was
also used in the sixteenth century to 'cast forth strong venome or
poyson' (34). Not only humans found the herb beneficial; it was
commonly thrown into fish ponds if the fish became ill, and sheep
were fed on it to cure them of liver fluke or 'rot' (77).

Hamburg parsley is a variant grown for the swollen root. It is

Hamburg parsley, a new crop when this plate was drawn

supposed to be only of nineteenth-century origin (93). However, parsley roots of some sort were eaten as winter fare in Scotland in the late seventeenth century (84), so there may have been earlier selections of this type. In any case, Miller grew some imported from Holland in 1727, and by the last edition of his *Gardener's Dictionary* it was fairly common in the London markets. It is, as Miller says, tender and sweet, though personally I do not find it sufficiently superior to parsnip to make it worth growing as anything but an occasional curiosity. The leaves can be used in the same way as curly parsley but are tough in texture and with a slightly rank taste.

# Parsnip

*Pastinaca sativa* LINNAEUS

*Origin:* native; widespread elsewhere

Native to much of Europe, the root of most wild plants is narrow and woody. However, there must have been some good early forms, for the Emperor Tiberius had his annual supplies from Germany as part of the tribute sent to Rome (though see Carrot). However, some less good varieties had been used much earlier, being well known to the Greeks (93). The seed was much used as a medicine, and the roots were used in ceremonies associated with Vulcan's wife, and also as a supposed aphrodisiac (77). As food, the root was eaten raw or boiled, and if cooked, the woody core was removed (necessary with other unimproved umbellifer roots like fennel and dill). The fleshy and sweet part was served with a sauce made from mead (77).

Much improved varieties without such a woody core seem to have been developed during the Middle Ages (93) and were much esteemed. It was then (and until recent times) commonly served with salt fish dishes and formed a staple food during the Lent fast (77). The root, of course, is very sweet (almost too much so for some tastes), a property early exploited in Europe. It was used as a source of sugar until overtaken by the sugarbeet in the nineteenth century – the parsnip's juices were evaporated, and the remaining brown liquid used as 'honey' (77). It was also used as a base for alcoholic drinks, the wine supposedly being nearly as good as Malmsey, and parsnip beer was a common substitute for the real thing in Ireland (66). Parsnip 'marmalade' (the word has only recently become completely attached to orange preserve) was thought good for nineteenth-century invalids. Gerard mentions parsnip bread, and Platt describes 'sweet and delicate' parsnip cakes. The parsnips were sliced, dried and powdered, with the resultant flour mixed with two parts of wheat flour. Made without spice or sugar, they seem to have been admired throughout the seventeenth century.

As is fairly common among crops now thought innocuous, not everyone was entirely happy with them. One old country name is 'madneps' or 'madde neaps', and Ray (82) wrote that country people thought that eating old roots brought on delirium and madness (perhaps the wrong species of root occasionally found its way into the pot). Parkinson suggests a less alarming possibility: that the name simply applies to parsnips foolish enough to bolt the first year. However, both old and new authors (66, 77) assert that the leaves, especially if handled when wet, can cause bad blistering on arms and hands. Also, as with a number of other crops, some of the early cultivation 'hints' make it surprising that the plants managed to survive; for instance, this from '*Systema Agriculturae*' of 1687: 'When they are grown to any bigness, tread down the tops, which will make the Roots grow the larger. . . .' This was still being advised in the eighteenth century (106).

Even if you are not especially fond of parsnips, it is worth planting a row or two of newly bought seed (it has a short viability), if you can spare the space. Baked parsnips, quartered if they are large, can be delicious. They are also good if sliced and boiled for only a few minutes (to remove some of the sweetness) and then drained and finished off by stewing in butter, then flavoured with a little parsley. Parsnip soup is more common in Europe and America than in Britain, a situation with which we should be happy.

# Passionflower

*Passiflora edulis* SIMS and *P. quadrangularis* LINNAEUS

*Origin:* Central and South America

With such an extraordinary flower, it is not surprising that passionflower species are fairly widely grown. A number of them have fruit with pharmacological properties (the last edition of the *Gardener's Dictionary* reports some in use as counter-poisons, sedatives and appetite stimulators). Miller himself cultivated various edible sorts between 1731 and 1768, though some were in cultivation much earlier in the previous century, with several types being grown by a Mr William Coys in 1604 (37).

As the name suggests, those first introduced from Brazil and the West Indies were thought to have flowers that were religious symbols. Parkinson was very scornful of such ideas and included in *Paradisi in Sole Paradisus Terrestris* this plate showing how a religiously inclined illustrator had distorted the flower's shape to demonstrate the symbols (Parkinson's own illustration also depicted here, is excellent). The earliest name for the passionflower, and a common one, was 'maracock', though some species were called 'Virginian climber'. Few plants ever fruited, and this is still a problem. Hand pollination is generally necessary, the complex flowers defeating native insects. It may be, too, that the plants are self-incompatible, though in any case even in a greenhouse the plants flower so late in the season that a good crop cannot be expected without the use of considerable heat. In the late eighteenth century, and for most of the next, the passionflower was grown in the stove house, and the fruit was therefore only available to a small section of the community. Very few people can be growing their own today; disappointing really, though the flowers of all sorts are something of a compensation.

A passion fruit flower in its symbolic aspect

Parkinson's realistic passionflower, with periwinkles and clematis

# Pea
## (including Sugar Pea)

*Pisum sativum* LINNAEUS (*P. arvense* LINNAEUS; *P. elatius* BIEBERSTEIN)

*Origin:* probably the Near East and eastern Mediterranean region

One of the most ancient crops, the pea is certainly as old as wheat and barley. Smooth-coated seeds (the sort now used for drying) have been found in eastern Mediterranean and European excavations that date from 7000 BC. They seem to have been widely grown all round the Mediterranean, and no clear centre for their evolution can be discerned. The species is not related to any known wild progenitor (93).

The name, too, has survived remarkably well. The Greek word for them was 'pison', which survived in English as 'peason' until the sixteenth century. By the reign of Charles I, 'pease' had become more common, finally being shortened to 'pea' in the following century (77).

The Greeks and Romans consumed them in large quantities but seem not to have had any clearly defined sorts (93). This is surprising in view of the crop's diversity and age. If they were not already grown in Britain (and it is very likely that they were), the Romans must certainly have introduced them. Curiously, early in Elizabeth I's reign, at least certain sorts were seen as 'fit dainties for ladies, they come so far, and cost so dear' (102). They seem to have been imported from Holland at that date. Later Gerard described many sorts (34), including the delicious sugar pea. This, now rather returning to popularity for its high yield, marvellous flavour and economical usage, was described by Parkinson only a few years later as falling out of use. Even odder, Loudon (57) says that they were introduced in 1650, but perhaps this was a reintroduction.

By the early eighteenth century huge numbers of cultivars existed, whole groups of which had been lost to cultivation a century later. Dr Martyn (66) bemoans the loss of rose, rouncival, sickle, tufted and Hotspur peas. Even the 'Hastings' type was then on the way out, surprising in view of the fact that it was winter hardy and could be cropped by May (66). The 'Hotspur' group could go from seed to seed in six weeks (68).

Serious breeding work on the wrinkled seed type of pea (which have a high sugar content that suits them for eating fresh from the pod) started in the late eighteenth century, and by the early nineteenth most of the major sorts now grown were in existence. Modern breeding programmes are extensive, with yield, uniformity, disease resistance and freezing qualities being important. For the home gardener, only yield and disease resistance are especially helpful. Uniformity of ripening simply produces gluts in the kitchen, so that there can sometimes be little advantage in growing the newest varieties. In any case, for small gardens, the sugar pea, in either its climbing or bush forms, seems to offer the best dishful, for it 'is extraordinary sweet; the great Inconveniency that attends them is, that their extraordinary sweetness makes them liable to be devoured by Birds' (68). The birds knew a good thing even in 1707.

Early peas were, and are, a great delicacy. Enormous trouble was taken to procure them, overwintered seedlings being transferred to hotbeds in February (66). The final peas were buttered and served with a little mint at least since the seventeenth century, and later in the season the flavour was enhanced by the addition of chopped asparagus. This is well worth trying with the first few spears, when there is not yet enough to make up a proper dishful (1, 13). Later still, green pea soup was served with pigeons, green goose or veal (13), a combination of flavours that is quite as good today.

# Peach

*Prunus persica* (LINNAEUS) BATSCH

*Origin:* China

This luscious fruit, if slightly less luscious than the very closely related nectarine, is exceptionally hardy and will produce fruit if grown against a good wall at least as far north as the Firth of

A large-flowered peach of 1819

Forth. It has an illustrious history, having been first domesticated in China in ancient times, where it was grown for both its fruit and flowers. It seems not to have been known to Theophrastus or Cato, and three centuries after Cato, Pliny refers to it as being a recent introduction. One route for its arrival in Italy is given as being out of Egypt via Rhodes (76), but it seems likely that the Romans imported it directly from Asia.

Once at Rome, it was rapidly disseminated, Columella (at the end of the first century AD) saying that it grew in Gaul. Peaches must have reached Britain during the Roman occupation but seem to have died out thereafter. However, they were growing in Britain again in the early sixteenth century (76) and may have been reintroduced from France (46). Tusser (102) mentions red and white types; Tradescant the Elder bought many trees for the gardens at Hatfield (37), and Sir Thomas Hanmer grew nineteen varieties as wall espaliers. Ten varieties were grown in Scotland by 1754 (49), where they were often grafted on to the wild gean, though there were three times that number available in London (66). By the end of the century, every walled garden had peaches, whether in the open or under glass, and it was an easily obtained fruit throughout the summer. The suggested yield for each tree was about fifty peaches, but this must have produced remarkably large fruit. For a reasonably large tree, far more can be allowed, though if the gardener is much too greedy and does not thin the fruit sufficiently, quality of flavour does suffer. Even so, the resultant crop still makes excellent preserves, pickles, jam, cheese, wine and chutney (the chutney is sumptuous).

Peach flowers, apart from being decorative (the trees were much planted in eighteenth-century 'wildernesses'), were also once used to make a syrup used to rid children of worms. The young leaves removed when 'stopping' the various laterals were used to flavour blancmanges, custards and puddings (76). Such leaves smell strongly of bitter almonds, so perhaps such desserts were not too healthy. Some were even used to imitate peach brandy, largely an American drink. The peach had been imported to that country by 1565 and, where the climate suited it, soon naturalized (ancient peach varieties can still be found there). The crops were so enormous that large quantities of peach wine were distilled to marc brandy. The rest were fed to pigs, with peach-fed hams being an American gourmet's delight (18).

Though some peach varieties were developed in England during the nineteenth and early twentieth centuries (a few famous ones are still grown), the main breeding centre is now America. Cobbett and others note that ripe peaches are best eaten in the morning, when they have just fallen from the tree. This is true, but there needs to be some way to avoid the fruit getting too bruised on its fall. Cobbett (19) suggests netting stretched between sticks placed beneath the tree. In my garden, under glass, we cover the earth with a thick layer of crumpled newspapers. Either method preserves the fruit and also keeps woodlice (who adore peaches) away from fallen fruit that is not immediately consumed. Woodlice will also climb the trees, and the fruit need regular inspection. A dish of perfectly ripened peaches and a cup of coffee on a summer morning is one of the great human pleasures.

# Pear

*Pyrus communis* LINNAEUS

*Origin:* western Asia

One of the most ancient fruit crops, cultivated in prehistoric times and originating in western Asia (93). Though the species is referred to as *P. communis*, it probably contains genetic material from a number of related *Pyrus* species. Nevertheless, even by 1000 BC, Homer called the pear 'one of the fruits of the Gods', so there must have been some delicious cultivars available three thousand years ago (46) – some modern gourmets still think the pear incomparable. Cato actually described six of the cultivars in the second century BC, and Pliny recorded thirty-five three hundred years later. Columella, in the same century, mentioned early and winter sorts, as well as those only suitable for baking (still worth growing for mid-winter desserts, as they cook marvellously in syrup, or especially with red wine). The Romans used some varieties as a counter-poison for mushrooms (76).

The pear may have been introduced to Britain long before the Roman occupation (46), and it seems to have soon naturalized (trees on their own roots are vigorous, hardy and exceptionally long-lived). By AD 1200 there were extensive pear orchards (46), and by the time Gerard was writing there were vast numbers of native British varieties. They slowly began to be superseded by French and Belgian varieties in the seventeenth century, and by the nineteenth most of our own old ones had vanished (though a few can still be found in specialist nurseries). The improved Continental pears were the result of deliberate selection in the seventeenth century, a process which continued unabated until recent times. One French collection of 1628 contained 254 distinct sorts (46). Today, about a thousand are known (32).

Of good varieties, Parkinson described sixty-four; Rea (83)

said that twenty-one were suited to growing against a wall and that there were thirty-five 'meat' pears and thirteen baking sorts. Worlidge said, in 1677, that there were over five hundred commonly grown. Of the old sorts still sometimes found, 'Jargonelle' is a delicious early summer pear (though not very large) and dates from about 1600; 'Bergamotte' is a lightly perfumed pear of the same century, as is 'Catillac', a splendid baking pear ready from December to April. Those pear trees found in old gardens, whose owners complain that the fruit is as hard as a stone, often have this variety. They should store the produce and cook it during the winter. Modern catalogues often list a 'Bon Chrétien', though what relationship it has to the whole group of pears with this name described by Parkinson is not clear. The 'Bartlett' type is a seedling of 1796 (46), and the famous 'Conference' is a mid-nineteenth-century variety.

However, pears were not only for the dessert table. Certain varieties were the source of perry, which is now beginning to make a welcome return to favour. Perry pear trees are even hardier than the dessert pears and were a widely grown hedgerow tree in all the colder parts of the country. The yield is prodigious, and as the pears scarcely soften, bird damage is slight. Sometimes the pears were harvested from the tree, but more often they were allowed to fall off themselves, piled into heaps and then crushed when time suited (11).

The drink was much consumed by the agricultural classes; gentry often refused it, thinking that it caused 'wind'. However, some sorts of pear gave a very sweet drink with a low alcohol content. This was thought suitable for ladies in spring and early summer, before the warmth re-started the fermentation, upon which it became sour and potent. The white 'horse' pear gave the best perry, which was highly flavoured and strong and could be kept for many years (11).

The pear has little in the way of magic or medicinal associations. For the latter, 'the sower, rough, and chokely Pears, and others that are not waterie, to be eaten raw or backte before meals, do stop the common laske or flowing of the belly, and do fortify and strengthen the mouth of the stomacke' (26). In the seventeenth century they were much planted near houses, being so long-lived and providing good shelter from gales. Ancient trees are, of course, magnificent to look at when in flower.

# Pineapple

**Ananas comosus** (LINNAEUS) MERRILL

*Origin:* Central America

This elegant and delicious fruit, once called the king of the dessert, has been a symbol of luxury and delight from the early eighteenth century to the present day. Throughout the eighteenth century the plant had been cultivated in kitchen gardens all over Britain. The first bulk load of fruit imported directly from the tropics only arrived in 1824, from Bermuda, and two-thirds of the cargo arrived in good condition (76).

The date commonly given for the first plants to be grown in Britain is 1690, and the place given as the gardens of the Duke of Portland (though a number of other gardens lay claim to the honour). The well-known paintings showing a fruit being presented to Charles II date from twenty or so years earlier and were either painted abroad or are of an imported fruit. The one shown looks rather ill-grown. The pineapple seems to have been known much earlier on the Continent than here, for Estienne and Liebault write that young ones were eaten to cure coughs after they had been soaked in rosewater.

Wherever it was first grown here, it was still very rare indeed well into the second decade of the eighteenth century. Lady Mary Montague, staying in Hanover, saw her first one there, being served for dessert (76). By 1719 they were being well grown at the Duke of Chandos' stupendous garden at Canons (9), though even by 1733 the beautiful fruit catalogue issued by Robert Furber shows a very poorly grown plant. Ninety years later, the fruit was common enough for London confectioners to sell pineapple ices at almost the same price as raspberry ones. London gardeners were apparently especially skilful at cultivating them (76). When the British ambassador in Paris, throwing a banquet in 1817, had a look at French produce, he had to send the diplomatic coach to London to fetch some pineapples. The French ones simply were not good enough (71).

Of course, the pineapple is a tropic fruit, and one which may have originated in the lowlands of southern Paraguay. By the time South and Central America were opened up by the Euro-

A well-grown pineapple of the early nineteenth century, just before they were first imported from the tropics

peans, the pineapple was widely grown, though as no remains are found in early excavation sites, it may have been a recent addition to the Indian diet (93). In northern Europe, it had to be grown on hotbeds and under glass. By the end of the eighteenth century, special 'pine stoves' had been designed for growing the fruit, often with sections at different temperatures for rooting crowns and suckers, growing on the resultant plants, and for final fruiting (94). In establishments without space or resources for a proper pine stove, the potted plants were commonly grown on staging beneath the vines in the vine house. Not that vine houses were especially expensive; in 1732, a house costing £48 might cost £5 a year to heat and could be expected to produce slightly over one hundred fruit over the year (49). Home-grown ones usually weighed about four pounds – the plants cropped when they were eighteen months old (57) – though, as is usual with gardeners, there were competitions to produce the largest fruit. To do this the potted plants had metal collars put round the pots, into which rich earth could be piled around the stem to induce more roots (94). One of the largest was grown in July 1821, at Lord Cawdor's Stackpole Court, and weighed 10 pounds 8 ounces and was 10½ inches in length (57).

The plants were cut slightly before maximum ripeness, with about four inches of stalk. This was so that a servant, gloved, could hold the fruit while cutting a slice for whichever plate required it. The tuft of young leaves was carefully reserved and returned to the gardener to turn into another plant.

Many cultivars were grown, generally of West Indian origin, though much seed was sown and good new types selected. The varieties differed in colour, shape and markings of the leaves. Few remain. I find it not an easy plant to grow, the roots quickly rotting if it gets overwatered and too cold. Thrips, mealy bugs, scale insects and aphids are always a nuisance. Eighteenth-century insecticidal fluids contained henbane, walnut juice, nicotine and even mercury, though today's are no doubt more effective. Still, to grow pineapples now is more a matter of garden heroics than economic necessity. They do, though, make handsome plants and, together with the lemon, lend a garden a certain style.

# Plum
## (including Sloe, Bullace and Myrobalan)

Plum: **Prunus domestica** subsp. **domestica** LINNAEUS
Bullace: **P. domestica** subsp. **insititia** (LINNAEUS) C. K.
SCHNEIDER (P. insititia LINNAEUS; P. domestica subsp.
italica (BORKHAUSEN) HEGI)
Sloe: **P. spinosa** LINNAEUS
Myrobalan or cherry plum: **P. cerasifera** EHRHART (P.
divaricata LEDEBOUR)

*Origin:* eastern Europe and western Asia

A very diverse group of plants, especially so in Europe and western Asia (93), and possibly not domesticated until 1000 BC (this making it less ancient than the damson). Both the Greeks and the Romans had a number of plum cultivars, and the difference between cooking and eating types seems already to have been established. The sloe and the bullace are native to Britain, but the plum (possibly some sort of hybrid between *P. spinosa* and *P. cerasifera*) may have been introduced by the Romans. The myrobalan is a native of Russian Asia, Iran and the Balkans.

Of the large number of plum varieties (plums come fairly true from seed, thus giving rise to large numbers of reasonably good but similar-looking cultivars), Parkinson listed sixty-four good ones (all of them available 'of my good friend Master John Tradescant'), Rea listed only twenty-eight, and Sir Thomas Hanmer grew only thirteen. Although many plums are vigorous, which makes them difficult to train, many were used as wall-fruit. East- and south-facing walls were the most popular in the seventeenth century (85), though some varieties (and some green-gages) did well on north-facing ones, where the fruit grew bigger, was less sugary and ripened over a longer period (19).

Bullaces, scarcely grown now, were used for preserves – one part fruit to three of sugar (66), though they were sometimes left on the tree until after the first frosts, which improved their sugar content. Myrobalans, or cherry plums, now generally used only for hedging, were used in the same way. Mirabelles and other cooking plums were used in plum cake, plum pudding, plum bread and the rest (a good way of making plum bread is to use ready baked and sliced bread, and push fresh or preserved plums into the surface, scatter with sugar or preserved plums with their syrup, and bake or grill until beginning to brown).

Of the varieties, 'Coe's Golden Drop' was admired in the late eighteenth century and is still available and excellent (66). The commonly grown 'Victoria', not of the first quality for flavour but self-fertile, seems to have originated in 1840 (63).

Much earlier than that, plums seem to have been regarded with some suspicion, and to eat too many was thought to 'engender naughtie blood' (36). However, as compensation, plum tree leaves were used to relieve swellings of the vulva, throat and gums (26). A gargle also made of leaves cured swollen salivary glands. Even Worlidge, writing late in the seventeenth century, continues the prejudice and writes: 'The common ordinary Plums will grow almost anywhere; they are not worth the planting to be eaten, unless you can find a way to make good wine from them. . . .'

# Pomegranate

*Punica granatum* LINNAEUS

*Origin:* Middle East

A handsome and large bush that will flower and fruit outdoors against a warm wall in southern parts of Britain, though the fruit is of poor flavour (those grown under glass taste better). The plant has been grown here certainly from the mid-sixteenth century, though almost entirely for its vast range of medicinal uses: the fruit rind and stem bark are still sometimes used as astringents, vermifuges (76) and bactericides and for various intestinal disorders (66, 97).

Elsewhere, the plant has been grown since ancient times, though it is probably native to Iran (93). The Romans thought it originated in Carthage, though that is perhaps the location from which they introduced their plants (66, 76). The pomegranate

A handsome pomegranate by Redouté

has been a symbol of marital bliss and fruitfulness, and it may have had a wider association with pleasure: the Greeks thought it grew in the Elysian fields. It is certainly a fine plant, with its translucent pink, white or vermilion flowers, flushed and golden fruit and splendid autumn colours.

The Romans grew nine varieties, some to eat, some sour ones to use for tanning leather, and the flowers of all of them to dye cloth a light red colour called '*puniceus*' (76). They might have brought it to these shores, though the first recorded plants were grown for Henry VIII in 1548 (76). Gerard grew several, but the plant's first fruiting is recorded in the gardens of Charles II (76). Various sorts were collected by John Tradescant, and by the end of the eighteenth century many varieties were grown, with single or double flowers, and some even striped in various colours (65). All are extremely rare today; occasionally seed of the single red sort can be found. Much more common is seed of the dwarf pomegranate, which stays less than six feet high and whose fruits are about the size of nutmegs and have no flavour. The plant is also less hardy than its normal-sized relative.

In the sixteenth century, pomegranates were used for 'weakness and wamblings of the stomach', for agues, for curing 'green wounds', for fastening loose teeth and for 'burstings that come of the falling down of the gut' (24), as well as for sores and ulcers of the 'mouth, privities and fundament'. Francis Bacon thought that it could be used, sweetened, for liver complaints.

It was once believed that pomegranates grew better if they were planted next to myrtles 'in so much as the roots will meete and tangle together with great joy' (36). Whatever the truth of this (I have not tried it), the meeting might be of more magical or symbolic significance than material. With or without myrtle, it is well worth having a plant or two. They grow well as potted plants, outdoors or in the greenhouse, and if space is limited, the dwarf form offers an attractive allusion to the full-sized plant. Both sorts are easily increased, should you need more, by layers or cuttings (45).

# Potato

*Solanum tuberosum* LINNAEUS

*Origin:* Central and South America

An extraordinarily successful crop, generally the main vegetable served for at least one meal a day throughout much of the 'advanced' world, and yet it was hardly eaten, even in Britain, until the 1750s. As late as 1833, Cobbett echoed a common prejudice and wrote that it 'shouldn't be used as a substitute for bread ... I never eat of it myself, finding so many things far preferable to it' (19).

Its early history in Europe is not yet clear. Early documentary sources are few; no one seems to have thought it a sufficiently important discovery to record. The association with various famous Elizabethan gentlemen is probably apocryphal, though it is possible that both Drake and Ralegh did play some part in its distribution once the plant had reached Europe. In any case, it seems that the tubers that reached us in the sixteenth century were not of the sort of potato most suited to their new conditions.

In Central and South America, *S. tuberosum* is just one of a very large number of solanums, and its tubers are bitter and toxic. However, in the wild, various plants can be found with less dangerous roots, and these are occasionally still gathered. Serious cultivation of these types began between 5000 and 2000 BC (93). The Spaniards encountered them in 1537, and the tubers seem to have been shipped back to Spain by the 1570s. These first sorts were from the central Andean region, and the plants do not crop well with long summer days and temperate conditions. Nevertheless, a gardening papal legate sent a few tubers to the equally enthusiastic governor of Mons at Hainault, and he later sent some (in 1598), to Clusius in Vienna (66, 77).

In Britain, the potato was cultivated in the early years of the next century to please aristocratic tastes, and in 1619 Anne of Denmark's household was being supplied at one shilling per pound (77). By 1662 the Royal Society was calling for the potato's extensive planting. Though it was already a popular crop in Ireland, it was only by 1800 that the crop was at all widely grown in England and Scotland. In the latter country, the first field of potatoes had been planted at Kilsyth in 1723, though few farmers copied Thomas Prentice for another fifty years (77).

It is difficult to know why the dislike of potatoes existed, let alone why it survived for so long. That the plant is closely allied to many very poisonous natives was early recognized, and it was thought that the plant must itself be dangerous. A similar belief certainly inhibited the spread of the tomato. Further, in the sixteenth century, little distinction was made between the potato (the potato of Virginia, as it was often known) and the sweet potato. This plant (*Ipomoea batatas*) was commonly used 'to provoke lust' (21), or more politely for 'restoring decayed vigour' (57), and will have formed part of the kissing comfits used by Falstaff (a powder of eringo roots will have comprised the rest).

Perhaps the ordinary potato was regarded by respectable people as having similar properties.

Few seventeenth-century gardening books mention it, and even Mortimer, writing in 1707 and comparing it to the Jerusalem artichoke, thought it 'not so good or wholesome. These are planted either of Roots or Seeds, and may probably be propagated in great quantities, and prove good Food for Swine.' The French upper classes continued to prefer the artichoke until the 1750s, at which time the potato had a brief vogue. The *Gardener's Dictionary* editions of 1768 and 1771, though having an entry under 'potato', do not describe any cultivars, though Dr Martyn's edition of 1807 describes forty-five. In Britain, by that time, gardens in most parts of the kingdom grew a few (presumably Cobbett's did not), though in Europe the dislike persisted. A shipload sent from London to Naples to relieve a famine were not eaten (66). The French poor still would not eat them in 1822 (77).

Some of the early methods of cooking were imaginative; they were often baked in pies, with bone marrow, sugar and spices, or they were preserved and candied (74) or mashed with butter, sherry, egg yolks, nutmeg and a little sugar and baked until brown (13), which is delicious. They were used as an alternative source of starch powder for whitening wigs or adulterating corn bread, and for making soufflés. Pressed, they provided a juice for cleaning cloth, furniture and wainscotting (77).

# Pumpkin
## (including Squash)

*Cucurbita maxima* DUCHESNE, but including parts of *C. pepo* LINNAEUS, *C. mixta* PANGALO and *C. moschata* DUCHESNE

*Origin:* Central America

Long thought to originate in the eastern Mediterranean, the group is American and has been domesticated there for at least ten thousand years (93); other authorities suggest a lesser time of five to six thousand years (106). Though wild forms have tough skins and bitter flesh, they are attractively colourful, and the seeds of all forms taste nice. It seems likely that the seeds were the first sought-for product and that forms were later found in which the flesh was not bitter.

The immense variety of pumpkins, squashes and marrows (q.v.) store well and so might have reached Europe soon after the discovery of the Americas. Once here, they must have spread extremely rapidly, for even some nineteenth-century authors thought that they were introduced to Europe from North Africa and the Levant (apparent references to them in Pliny probably relate to sorts of cucumber and melon). Pumpkins also accumulated a fair amount of magic, though this may have followed them from the New World or have been taken over from other already cultivated cucurbits. Estienne and Liebault wrote: 'To make pompions keep long, and not spoiled or rotted, you must sprinkle them with the juice of a houseleek. . . . A woman having her termes [period], and walking by the border of pompions, gourds, and cucumbers, causeth them to dry and die, or to be bitter.' Their use as rattles in American Indian ceremonies does seem to have been taken up by some European settlers turned quack doctors (77).

Since their introduction they were thought to make more wholesome food than the cucumber (26) and in the seventeenth century were used, mashed, to bulk up bread (12) or were eaten boiled and heavily buttered (34, 77) – still nice. The *Gardener's Dictionary* quotes the American settlers' recipe for roasting pumpkins stuffed with sliced and spiced apples. This is especially good with firm-fleshed musk squashes, if seed can be found, using plenty of butter. By the nineteenth century, pumpkins were used to bulk up stews in impoverished kitchens.

Many sorts are capable of growing to a very large size. Pumpkins weighing two hundredweight were a common sight in the London markets of the nineteenth century, where they were sold as curiosities (77). Even an averagely grown pumpkin of the yellow sort commonly available here, places a strain on the present-day kitchen. Pumpkin pie, however delicious when properly made, becomes tedious in quantity. Probably the winter squashes are the most useful types to grow, though even they take up considerable space in the garden. If you do have room, it is well worth trying the various kinds; almost all of them yield most handsome fruits, though it is a pity that so few are actually offered by British seedsmen. The best way to store what you harvest is to sling the fruits in nets suspended from shelf or ceiling. They bruise if stood on a hard surface, soon begin to rot and collapse into a most dreadful mess. Kept sensibly, they offer a pleasant addition to both decor and diet.

Some squashes are eaten when small, rather in the manner of courgettes. Pumpkins were similarly treated in the eighteenth and nineteenth centuries. Some small ones were pickled and said to be very good (68). The seeds of all sorts are consumed in huge quantities in most Mediterranean countries. In Britain the fresh seeds are good if quickly fried, or baked, and then salted. In the sixteenth century, the seeds were pounded in their own juice with oatmeal, and the resultant mush was applied to the face. It was supposed to bleach freckles and other imperfections (26).

# Purslane

*Portulaca oleracea* subsp. *sativa*  (HAWORTH) ČELAK

*Origin:* probably eastern Mediterranean region

A plant with a crisp and pleasing texture, though with no pronounced taste. Perhaps unfairly, Cobbett wrote (19): 'A mischievous weed, eaten by Frenchmen and pigs when they can get nothing else. Both use it in salad, that is to say, raw.' He omits to say that it is an important ingredient of the delicious '*potage bonne femme*'.

It is indeed a weed, now distributed worldwide in temperate and tropical countries. It may have been first cultivated in the eastern Mediterranean region and is probably ancient. First mentioned in British herbals in 1562 (99), it was already used as a salad, as pickle and as a medicine, being available in several varieties.

It was well known in Scotland by 1694 (84), where it was sown in hot-beds early in the year and then transplanted outdoors (I find it hard to grow well, needing more water and shelter than I can give it, though it does excellently under glass if the greenfly can be kept at bay). A few years later, green, red and yellow leafed varieties were widely grown, at least in England (68). The red sort had dropped from use by 1885 (105), and today only the green sort seems to be available.

Once it was used for bladder and kidney pains, though it was thought to make the blood watery. The juice, mixed with vinegar and oil, was poured on the head to quell sunstroke and could also be used for erysipelas and 'ulcers of the fundament' (26).

# Quince

### *Cydonia oblonga* MILLER (*Cydonia vulgaris* PERSOON)

*Origin:* eastern Mediterranean region and Middle East

A really lovely small tree, in no way to be confused with the pink- or red-flowered bush quince (*Chaenomeles* sp.). The true quince has large pinkish or white flowers with fragile-looking petals, wiry branches with oval leaves covered, in youth, with thick down, and golden pear-shaped fruits with a voluptuous perfume.

Jewish tradition says that this is the oldest of the fruits – wild forms can still be found in western Asia (65), that it grew in the Garden of Eden and was actually the tree in which the snake resided with such success. A shadow of this belief seems to have persisted into sixteenth-century Britain, for the Lyte translation of the Dodoens herbal explains that, 'Women with child that eat quinces will bear wise children.' Elsewhere in the ancient world, in cultures with no knowledge of original sin, the quince was an emblem of happiness, love and fruitfulness and was dedicated to Venus. Brides ate one before entering the marriage bed (65, 76). This is possible in the Near East and countries bordering the Mediterranean, where varieties of quince ripen sufficiently to be eaten directly off the tree. Their association with pleasure lasted a long time; Columella mentions it in the first century AD, and even Renaissance grandees with good gardeners kept potted plants to decorate the frescoed halls of their houses. Quinces may also have been the golden apples of the Hesperides (76).

Pliny the Elder (80) says that many sorts were grown in the Roman world, of all colours and sizes, though there seems to be

Early eighteenth-century quinces

no record of its introduction to northern Europe and Britain at that time. However, such was the quince's importance for both its cosmetic and medicinal properties that settlers must have taken plants with them. It was certainly in cultivation by Gerard's time; he said that it was commonly grown to protect vineyards.

New sorts were being introduced in the early seventeenth century, and the currently available variety called 'Portugal' was brought in by the Tradescants (3) – it is juicier, earlier and less acid than the others, though it can be a shy bearer. It makes an attractive tree if allowed its head but can also be used against a wall and does especially well if trained as an espalier (65).

During the same century, the quince played an important part in people's lives, being used in all sorts of ways. The down was scraped from fruit and leaves, mixed with honey and used as a hair-restorer (21). The fruits cured patients spitting blood, having swollen spleens or dropsy (the affected areas were rubbed with juice), various gut disorders (76), asthma, inflamed eyes or skin ulcers (again the juice was used, or the mucilage obtained by boiling the seeds), or simply with unruly hair (the mucilage was used to keep the hair in place) (65).

The fruit was also widely used in the kitchen. The Portuguese word for quince is *marmelo*, and only gradually did this word become used in this country to denote a preserve of oranges. True marmalade was made by cooking the flesh soft, sweetening to taste and boiling the mixture to setting point. Another name for the same preserve was 'Codignac' or 'Contignac', made similarly, but with honey in fifteenth-century methods and sugar later on. Meech (65) said that the preserve was better if not boiled to setting point but only warmed through after the sugar was added. More of the exquisite flavour reached the jar. The seeds should be discarded at the very beginning, as they can impart an unpleasant flavour.

Quince wine was also popular, both for pleasure and invalids. For this, the fruits were finely grated, and the juice from this process was sweetened at the rate of two pounds of sugar to every gallon of liquor (1). Whole quinces, baked, were a popular way of ending a meal in the sixteenth century (26), as was anything made with the fruit. It was thought that the quince 'looseneth the belly, and closeth the mouth of the stomacke so fast, that no vapours can come forth, nor ascend up to the braine: also it cureth the headache springing from such vapours' (26).

# Radish

*Raphanus sativus* LINNAEUS

*Origin:* probably western Asia

A popular and immensely variable crop, grown since such ancient times that any connection with a wild species seems to have been lost. Maximum diversity is found between the shores of the eastern Mediterranean and the Caspian Seas. Black-skinned sorts, probably long-season like the present-day varieties, are shown in Egyptian tomb paintings of *circa* 2000 BC (93) and are described by Herodotus even earlier. A few sorts seem to have reached China and Japan between 500 BC and AD 700, giving rise to further types in the East that were subsequently re-imported to the West.

In ancient Greece, certain sorts were used as votive offerings to Apollo at Delphi – turnips were presented on lead dishes, beet on silver ones, radishes on gold (77). Numerous varieties were grown in Rome, from tiny ones that were almost transparent to huge ones that Pliny said could weigh up to forty Roman pounds. Large ones of this type were grown in Europe into the sixteenth century, when Googe wrote that the radish exceeded all other roots in 'greatnesse'. However, to get the roots to enlarge, the leaves as they grow 'must still be trampled downe and trodden upon, whereby the roote shall grow the greater, otherwise it flourisheth with leaves and given encrease to the leaf, and not the roote . . .'. Googe, following Roman precedent, thought radishes acted as an antidote to poison. Large radishes continued to be grown into the late eighteenth century (36) but do not seem to be available in Britain today.

The small round types now so popular, swiftly brought to maturity, and in shades of red, pink, rose and white, seem to have been developed in eighteenth-century France (93), though perhaps from earlier progenitors. The white sorts came first, followed by the red, purples and the rarely seen yellows. The long narrow sorts may be much older but taste just as good. All have always been eaten as a salad, especially with salt, bread and cheese, though sometimes they have been added to stews, or even cooked as a hopeful substitute for asparagus (77).

For winter eating, 'Black Spanish' and 'China Rose' are generally easily obtained in this country; elsewhere in Europe, several shapes of a black one can be found, though all taste similar. They are extremely good if grown fairly fast; if not, they become too woody and blunt both grater and teeth. Well-grown ones go into the winter salad (Evelyn used them as thin shavings, still the best way) or make an excellent sauce for beef if lightly stewed in butter, with plenty of cream added at the end of cooking.

If you have part of a row of early salad or of winter radishes left uneaten, do not throw the plants away. Leave them to flower (if there is room, since the inflorescences take up a lot of space), for the young seed pods pickle deliciously in lightly spiced vinegar. The pods should be young enough to eat fresh; as soon as the inner membrane becomes papery, it is too late to pickle them. They were a well-known seventeenth-century accompaniment to roasts, or an addition to salads (30), and amply repay the trouble of their harvesting.

Not surprisingly for such an ancient crop, there were numerous medicinal uses, embracing everything from reducing the pains of childbirth, increasing milk production, stopping ringing in the ears and also stopping worms in the gut (28), to reducing the pain of bladder and kidney stones and gravel (74).

# Rampion

***Campanula rapunculus*** LINNAEUS

*Origin:* Europe

Rarely seen today, it was once a common kitchen garden plant and one of several esculent *Campanula* species. The plant, a biennial, is native to most of Europe, though it is thought to have been introduced to Britain. Certainly, it was common enough in sixteenth-century soups and stews, or as a salad. The Lyte-Dodoens herbal suggests that if 'eaten with vinegar and salt, [it] stirreth up appetite or meat lust, and provoketh urine . . .'. A salad could contain the leaves, but more often it was the fleshy white roots, gently boiled or steamed, that were eaten cold with oil and vinegar (that is the way that Parkinson liked them).

By the early nineteenth century the use of rampions was dying out in Britain, though they were still being extensively grown in France and Switzerland (66). Cobbett thought that one square yard of garden ground devoted to them was enough for any family. By the end of that century the rampion seems to have vanished. If you do come across seed, it should be sown in May or June, the roots being harvested from October and November and then throughout the winter.

There seem to have been few medicinal uses, though the chopped leaves were mixed with lupin flowers to 'cleare and beautifie the face, and the other parts of the bodie . . .' (26).

*Campanula rapunculoides* also has edible roots and is a more frequently seen plant. It is also quite nice to look at but once in the garden is impossible to remove. It is best grown in a bucket, like the most invasive of the mints. The more polite plant C. *persicifolia* is also edible, though the roots are so stringy that it is a brave cook who tries it. The double white and double blue forms make splendid additions to the flower garden, if not the kitchen garden.

# Raspberry

**Rubus idaeus** LINNAEUS (some modern cultivars contain genetic material from other species)

*Origin:* Europe

The specific name derives from Pliny's belief that the first raspberries came from Mount Ida in Greece, though in fact the plant is native to most of Europe. Perhaps Mount Ida produced a superior sort. In any case, the berry was not held in much esteem by either the Greeks or the Romans and seems to have been more used (mixed with honey) as a cure for bloodshot eyes or erysipelas (76) than as a dessert.

There are several old English names for the plant, including 'hindberry' and 'Raspis', though the first mention of either seems to be in Turner's *A new herball* of 1551. Even Gerard thought them inferior to blackberries. Though anyone fortunate enough to live near a clump of the wildlings will know that their flavour is rather good, larger and perhaps better flavoured sorts seem to have originated in Belgium (the very old variety 'Antwerp' is still occasionally seen) in the late seventeenth or early eighteenth century. Mortimer described a large kind as opposed to the wild sort (still then grown in gardens), as well as a white-fruited kind, first recorded in 1588 (72), though not the yellow one first recorded in 1601 (72). The pale-coloured ones are supposed to have an excellent flavour, so it is worth trying a plant or two if you come across them.

The European raspberry reached America in the eighteenth century (it was sold in commercial quantities by 1771) and soon began to hybridize with local species (46). Black, purple and autumn fruiting varieties were soon discovered, the autumn types being available in Britain by the early nineteenth century (19). They were further developed in France (93). Flavour and yield of the initial hybrid types was poor, and the more recent and better ones have only been widely planted in recent years.

As well as pies, puddings and jams, raspberries were used for removing tartar from teeth (66) – raspberry is still sometimes used as a flavouring for dental preparations, and in late Georgian London huge quantities were bought to flavour ices and to make raspberry brandy and raspberry vinegar. The wine was helpful for 'ardent fevers' (76) and faintness, and an infusion of the leaves is still reportedly good for speeding and easing childbirth (97).

Present-day breeding continues apace, though almost entirely to help commercial users (largely the jam-makers). Large fruit size, uniformity of ripening, firmness of texture and seed colour are all important characters. For the kitchen garden, season of fruiting and flavour have to be considered, but the most important factor is whether the stock is virus free. Virus seems always to have been troublesome, even if the cause went unrecognized. Mortimer writes that the plants always get 'lice' (greenfly), badly, and that the beds need completely renewing every ten years. Greenfly transmit viral infections from one plant to another. Later, Dr Martyn suggests that the beds need stripping out every three or four years. Perhaps the problem had got worse over the period from 1707 to 1807.

# Redcurrant
## (including Whitecurrant)

*Ribes rubrum* LINNAEUS (used here in its widest sense)

*Origin:* Europe

'It is one of the great fruits of England,' wrote Cobbett (19). Of course, it was grown in other parts of north-western Europe too and has probably been collected from the wild since earliest times. It seems not to have been known to the Greeks or Romans, their herbalists and gardeners in any case having rather few plants coming from countries where the redcurrant is native.

As a cultivated plant, it is first mentioned in German sources of the early fifteenth century and is illustrated by 1484 (72). In Britain, it is not mentioned by Tusser, though it does seem to have been common by the late sixteenth century; Gerard only mentions it in connection with gooseberries (q.v.). There seems at that time to have been some confusion between those two species, for Googe says that the redcurrant is 'now a common bush for enclosing of gardens, and making of borders and arbours' (36). However, as he goes on to say that it is not a good plant to twine about summer-houses because of 'his sharp prickles', he either did not know the plant well or was confusing it with a red-berried gooseberry.

Any confusion must soon have cleared, for it became a very common plant indeed during the seventeenth century. New types continued to be introduced and were soon grown by every cottager. John Tradescant the Elder brought in a large Dutch type called 'Great Red Currant' which became very widely grown. An alternative word for 'currant' was 'corinth', deriving from the redcurrant's likeness to the small raisins imported from that city (68). Parkinson felt it necessary to point out the difference in 1629.

By the early eighteenth century the old English currant had been entirely ousted by the Dutch one, which 'becoming Native of our Soil, has been so much improved in moist rich Grounds, that it hath obtained the higher Name' (68). Whatever the sort of redcurrant, they were used by all classes of society for jam, jellies

Translucent redcurrants, and attendant, by Redouté

and cooling drinks – whitecurrants were considered to make the best wine, being less sharp in taste, and it cost one shilling a bottle in 1813 (69) – as garnishes and for flavouring brandies and punch. The flavour from the fruit was thought better when the plants were grown against north-facing walls, though the plants were grown against walls of all aspects which gave the gardener and cook a long season for the ripe fruit. With the last berries being harvested in late autumn, they were found to store easily and could be kept for a year or two if packed gently into glass jars (76).

# Rhubarb

*Rheum rhabarbarum* LINNAEUS

*Origin:* probably China

All rather a mistake really, for the plants first brought to Europe in the sixteenth century as an important medicinal herb turned out to be the wrong species. The correct one (*Rheum palmatum*) was eventually brought here in the eighteenth century, but it has long dropped out of use (though sometimes seen as a decorative), while the first comer is now found in almost every garden.

A plant called 'rheum' or 'rhabarbarum' was known to the Greeks, probably as dried roots imported from southern Russia or China. Dioscorides used it for chest, stomach and liver complaints as well as ringworm (76). The ancient Chinese used it too, though a herbal of 2700 BC suggests its use only as a laxative (93).

By the sixteenth century, at least in western Europe, it had become known as a cure for the two main venereal diseases (the most serious a recent import), and large quantities of the root were imported via Izmir (76, 93). Two ounces of dried root and half an ounce of parsley were boiled in two quarts of water, and the solution then reduced by two-thirds. The resultant bitter drink was taken several times a day (76).

However, the truly official species are R. *officinalis* and R. *palmatum*, but the plants brought out of China, either via Goa in 1535 or direct from China in the following century, were of another species that we now all know and love. Its inability to offer either a cure for disease or a laxative was early recognized; Gerard called it the 'bastard rhubard'. It became used as a pot-herb, though it seems to have been the leaves that were used — sharp-tasting, like sorrel (66). Presumably they were used in small quantities, for a friend of Gerard's tried to cure an unwary

Seventeenth-century rhubarb, showing the root of so much interest
to the herbalist

butcher's boy who had an ague. Four leaves of the herb 'wrought extremely downwards and upwards within an hower after, and never ceased until night. In the end, the strength of the boie overcame the force of the phisicke.' No doubt he survived, even if still with his ague. Herbalists who stuck to the book and used the dried and imported root used it against 'Wamblings of the gut', convulsions and cramps, sciatica, 'Yeoring' and mange, and to cleanse 'the bodie from pale and wan spots (or the Morphew), . . . and bloody fire' (26).

At the end of the eighteenth century, the root's main property seems to have been as a laxative, and the value of the imports was estimated at £200,000 a year. However, seeds of the officinal species reached London from Russia in 1762, and the Society for the Encouragement of Arts, Manufactures and Commerce began to encourage cultivation. In 1791 Sir William Fordyce was awarded a gold medal by the Society for planting out three hundred rhubarb plants, and later prizewinners planted up to a thousand (57, 76). The roots were kiln-dried, though they were found by various hospitals to be slightly less effective than the imported material. As a bonus, it was also found that the roots could be made to yield a fine red dye, which, before the advent of synthetic dyes, had been a very expensive colour to produce.

However, by the time that landowners were winning gold medals, *Rheum rhabarbarum* was already being forced for the London fruit markets, the petioles being used for early spring desserts. The discovery that the leaf stalks were delicious to eat, and did not have any unfortunate effect on the innards, seems to have taken place in France in the eighteenth century, though French cooks did produce a rhubarb *marmelade* in which the stalks were cooked in honey (66) – used as a very mild laxative – and which might suggest an earlier, and pre-cane-sugar, date.

# Rocket

*Eruca vesicaria* (LINNAEUS) CAVANILLES subsp. *sativa*
(MILLER) THELLUNG

*Origin:* Mediterranean region, western Asia

Half a dozen plants sown every week throughout the summer
make a very pleasant addition to the salad bowl. The flowers,
white with pale grey veins, are also edible, and autumn-sown
plants will often overwinter quite well. The flavour, though, goes
less well with winter chicories than it does with summer lettuce.
There are, or were, hazards for '. . . if Rocket be eaten alone, it
causeth headache, and heateth too much, therefore it must never
be eaten alone, but alwaies with lettuce or purcelaine . . . the use
thereof stirreth up bodily pleasure, especially of the seed' (26).
This last property of rocket was widely believed (21, 28).

Whatever the leaves might do to one, the oil extracted from the
seeds was widely used medicinally since early times and was said
to cure both major and minor ailments. Seed was mashed in
honey and used to clear the face of blemishes. A sixteenth-
century herbalist states that 'Men say, that who so taketh the
seede of Rocket before he be beaten or whipt, shall be hardened,
that he shall easily endure the paine, according as Plinie writeth'
(26). The juice of the boiled roots was also believed to draw out
shards and bone splinters from a wound.

Though once widely used, by the late eighteenth and early
nineteenth century it was 'little known, having been long rejected
on account of its strong ungrateful smell' (66), though its reputation might equally have accounted for its fall from grace in an
increasingly moralistic society. Perhaps it simply was not grown
well; plants in poor soil and those left too long in any soil do have
a rather gross taste.

# Rosemary

*Rosmarinus officinalis* LINNAEUS

*Origin:* southern Europe and Turkey

A widely grown though little used herb, and if it is still used to flavour an occasional roast chicken or piece of beef and to perfume cosmetics, such uses are but pale shadows of the vast range of essential services that rosemary once rendered.

In ancient Rome it was used for garlands and coronets, was associated with fidelity in love (its use at weddings and funerals persisted in Britain until modern times and is still common in other parts of Europe), and, as with several other heavily-perfumed shrubs, was thought good for head and heart (77, 66). Tragus said that the ancient Germans used it as a spice, and the plant has been used as a cure for everything from bubonic plague to bad eyesight and jaundice (28).

It may have been introduced to Britain by the Romans and was certainly widely grown throughout the medieval period. Alice Coats (17) quotes an interesting letter from the Countess of Hainault to her daughter Queen Philippa, for both of whom rosemary was important: 'The leves layde under the heade whanne a man slepes . . . doth away evell spirites and suffereth not to dreeme fowle dreemes ne to be afearde. but he must be out of deedely synne for it is an holy tree . . . and ffolke that have been just and rightfulle gladlye it groweth and thryveth. . . .'

Gerard thought that one type was indigenous to Lancashire, though in fact the plant is native to southern Europe and to Asia Minor. By the time Gerard was writing, rosemary was considered valuable enough to train it against walls of house and garden, where it must have looked splendid. By the early seventeenth century, however, it began to be displaced by fruit, though it remained on Scottish walls until the end of the century (84). The leaves, as now, were used for flavouring roasts, and a rosemary sprig was sometimes used to add more savour to a glass of sherry (30). However, the flowers were in as much demand either pickled in vinegar (30) or candied. They have a very powerful taste, and the pickled ones must have been used very sparingly in the salads for which they were intended. A conserve of the flowers was used to 'comfort the heart' (21) and to cure loss of the voice (26). One can only admire the patience of sixteenth-century housewives who had the task of collecting sufficient flowers for such purposes. Dried leaves were smoked in a pipe for coughs and consumption, and branches were burnt in the streets in the belief that the odour stopped the spread of the plague (it certainly has a nice smell).

Even in the nineteenth century, the disinfectant power of rosemary was still accepted in French hospitals, where it was burnt with juniper berries to improve foul air (77). It may also have been one of the reasons why rosemary was a popular strewing herb for seventeenth-century floors (68). Bunches of it were hung in wardrobes to keep moths from the clothes (giving them a nicer smell than that of wormwood). The ashes of burnt rosemary could fasten loose teeth and formed an early dentrifrice (26).

Other uses, for it was the most powerful of the 'cephalic' herbs, were to cure headaches, giddiness, palsies, hysterias and loss of memory (66). Further down the body, it also cured dyspepsia. Nowadays the oil is used in perfumes, bath oils, cosmetics and insect repellents and as a cure for neuralgia (97).

Though most gardeners will be aware that rosemary is available in several varieties, the range was once much wider. The white-flowered sort is still occasionally seen, double-flowered types were available in the early eighteenth century (68), and Miller described some with yellow or silver striped leaves (the 1807 edition of the *Gardener's Dictionary* says that all the silver ones were killed off in the great frosts of 1740, but perhaps some survived somewhere and their descendants might still be found). The 'gilded' rosemary was more fortunate and can be found in connoisseurs' gardens. There are also some lovely tender forms, and the one called 'Tuscany Blue', which has deep blue flowers, ought to be in a pot somewhere in every garden.

# Rowan

*Sorbus acuparia* LINNAEUS (there are numerous
subspecies)

*Origin:* Europe, Asia Minor and North Africa

Native to the mountainous parts of Britain and of similar areas in
Europe, Asia Minor and North Africa. When kitchen gardens
were hedged, the rowan was an important element and provided
berries for rowan bread, rowan perry and rowan brandy.
However, it was also grown for its magic properties, such as
keeping evil visitors away. Perhaps because the tree grows happily at altitudes well above that of other tree species, it has long
been a venerated tree and associated with all sorts of magic. In
Scotland and Wales a surprising amount of this belief persisted
until at least the end of the eighteenth century, and houses can
still occasionally be found with a protective rowan by the front
door.

Old names current in the seventeenth century were 'witchen',
'wicken' and 'Quicken-tree' (29), and rowans were commonly
found near standing stones, circles and ancient burial places.
Scottish dairymaids used to drive their beasts to summer pastures
with a rowan rod, and drive them down in autumn with the same
carefully preserved piece of wood. In some parts of the country,
sheep were made to jump through rowan hoops on 1 May. In
Wales, churchfolk used to wear a cross of rowan twigs on one day
a year to protect them from evil spirits and hallucinations (66).

The crop was never sufficiently important in Britain for the tree
to be carefully cultivated. The tree was, and is, an important
decorative, though rowan jelly is good in its own right and can be
an excellent flavouring for apple jelly if you do not have room for
a crab.

# Rue

*Ruta graveolens* LINNAEUS

*Origin:* probably Mediterranean region

An extraordinary plant, now grown for sentiment in herb gardens or by gardeners needing the curious blue of its leaves for a colour scheme, but almost never put to use. Yet once it was an essential and beneficent plant to be found in quantity in every piece of cultivated ground, well meriting its old name of 'Herbegrace' or 'Ave-grace'.

In ancient Greece, the garden plots were edged with rue or parsley, and the proverb 'You are not yet arrived at the parsley and rue' was the ancient equivalent of 'Don't count your chickens'. The modern and unfortunate belief of some gardeners that stolen plants grow better than those acquired by other means, was applied to rue by the Greeks (77) – perhaps echoed by the sixteenth-century belief that, 'It should be sowed with cursing, as Cumin, and divers others' (76). Pliny wrote that it was more regarded than any other herb, being used to flavour wine (how odd), as a counter-poison, as a cure for insect and reptile bites and stings – rue juice was stored in brass or copper containers (80) – and as a means to preserve the sight of engravers, painters and sculptors (they had to eat the leaves). All these beliefs survived at least until the sixteenth century and were enshrined in the verse:

> Rue maketh chaste and preserveth sight,
> Infuseth wit, and Fleas doth put to Flight (21).

The chastity it preserved seems to be that of the male, for 'because the nature of Women is waterish and cold, the Rue heateth . . . therefore it stirreth them more to carnal lust; but it diminisheth the nature of men . . .' (21). Even the last edition of the *Gardener's Dictionary* says that it is a stimulant 'peculiarly adapted to phlegmatic habits, or weak and hysterical constitutions, suffering from retarded or obstructed secretions'.

Rue is described in Turner's *A new herball* of 1551 but was certainly known in Britain much earlier. Gerard says that it grew wild in parts of Lancashire and Yorkshire, perhaps a remnant of Roman cultivation. In the kitchen it was used as an occasional

*Tab.170.*

Rue, from *Icones Plantarum*

addition to soups and stews and was often pickled to use as a relish with meat (66). However, to eat too much was thought to be, and is, dangerous. It can be poisonous in quantity (97), though earlier, too much was thought to dry up either 'seede' or milk. In moderation, it cured coughs, sciatica, fevers, 'the gnawing torment of griping paine of the belly called the trenches' (26), earache, face spots, scurvy, scrofula and 'hard swellings of the throat', it drew buboes and, with vinegar, was used as smelling-salts (26). It was also used in nosegays, held to the nose to prevent inhalation of infection.

If you plant it in your garden and do not like either adders or lizards, then it should be useful in keeping them away (28), according to a sixteenth-century belief.

# Runner Bean

*Phaseolus coccineus* LINNAEUS

*Origin:* Central and South America

May the 10th, 1679. I steep'd runner beans first in sack five days, then being taken out, I put them in sallet-Oyle Five days, then in Brandy four days, and about noon set them in an Hot-Bed against a South-wall, casting all the Liquor wherein they had been infused (and reserved in several pots), negligently about the Holes, within three Hours Space (that is, about two-o-clock), Eight of the Nine came up, and were a foot high, with all their Leaves, (as other growing beans use to have), and on the morrow a foot more in height; the Third Day they blossomed, and in a week were podded, and full ripe, and some even black-eyed. . . .

Thus a letter from Mr Gifford, minister of Montacute, quoted by Evelyn in *Acetaria* of 1699. Perhaps Mr Gifford's gardeners were having fun with their master, but that no doubt worthy man seemed convinced enough of the efficacy of his treatment. It was rather a fashion of those years to experiment with the effect of soaking all sorts of seeds in all sorts of fluids, an experimentalism that both looked back to the magical transformation of crops in the previous century, and forwards to the eighteenth century when science was replacing magic.

Mr Gifford probably did not pick his pods for the dinner table. Runner beans may have been introduced some time early in the sixteenth century (93), though the date often suggested is 1633, the date at which Johnson wrote 'that it was procured by Mr John Tradescant, and grew in his time in our gardens . . . that his flowers are large, many, and of an elegant Scarlet colour; whence it is vulgarly termed by our florists, the Scarlet Bean' (48). And a florist's flower it was, used in nosegays and garlands as it was very long-lasting (66). As a garden decoration it was grown around garden houses and arbours. Even Phillips, writing in the early nineteenth century, could remember them being thus used, and there was no thought of gathering the pods and taking them to the kitchen, though Miller himself is credited with being the first gardener adventurous enough to cook them.

Later still, Vilmorin-Andrieux wrote in 1885, 'In small gardens, they are often trained over wire or woodwork, so as to form summer houses or coverings for walks.' Of course, by then the pods were as much valued at table as they are now. Certainly it sounds a nice idea to form a shady, floriferous and productive retreat in the kitchen garden, from which to watch everything coming to ripeness.

The crop is another introduction from South and Central America where it grows in cool, humid upland conditions and is always perennial (it can be treated here as such, if the roots are lifted like dahlias). In Mexico, archaeological datings show cultivation at least two thousand years ago (93). Various sorts were in cultivation in Britain in the seventeenth century, some with white flowers (91) or with immensely long pods. A hunt round present-day seed catalogues will reveal many equally interesting sorts.

# Sage

*Salvia officinalis* LINNAEUS

*Origin:* southern Europe

Recorded from 1573, but certainly in cultivation in Britain very much earlier, though a native to southern Europe. It is now widely used as a flavouring for stuffings for chickens and other meats (indeed, it is often over-used). Before the eclipse of herbal remedies it was much more widely used as a medicine than as a flavouring.

Stylized sage in a sixteenth-century plate in a seventeenth-century book

Another very aromatic plant (see Lavender and Rosemary), it was thought to be good for the head, especially for the faculty of memory, and also because it 'comforteth the hart' (26). However, as one of the chief ways of taking it was to have it stewed in wine, it might well have made the drinker more cheerful, if scarcely helping his memory (26). The Latin name is derived from a word meaning healing; it was used for a vast range of ailments from ancient times. It increased the fertility of women when taken as tea (28, 77), quickened the senses when taken as sage ale (77), was used as a gargle, to tighten loose teeth, to cure ulcers, to dry up suppurating wounds (26) and to cure coughs, the 'bloody fire' and 'night sweats', and was used by the common people as a fomentation. Nowadays it is mainly used as a pharmaceutical flavouring, though it is sometimes recommended to reduce lactation and to relieve anxiety and depression (97).

In the kitchen, young shoots, especially of the purple sage, were added to spring salads (79), and it was a common custom in May to eat them for breakfast with new butter (30). Sage oil was sometimes added to butter for a little extra flavour at other times of year (79). The shoots were also pickled for winter use. Sage tea was widely taken for pleasure, as well as medicine, and Evelyn noted that the Chinese preferred our sage tea to their own and happily exchanged three chests of theirs for every one of ours (30). It was also used in the seventeenth century to give its distinctive smell to cheeses, a practice which, having been nearly extinct in the nineteenth century (77), is now sadly on the increase.

In the garden, purple sage was considered the most useful and was a common border plant in the seventeenth and eighteenth centuries (68). The variegated kind, still fairly common, was available in the sixteenth century, and the now much rarer 'painted' sage (its green leaves prettily splashed with cream and pink) is supposed to have been found by John Tradescant senior in a country garden (66). One very rare sort was called the wormwood sage and had frilled leaves. I hope one day to come across a plant. However, all the sages had a degree of danger in their use. 'At all times,' wrote the author of *Adam in Eden* in 1657, 'be sure you wash your Sage, for fear that Toades, who as I conceive come to it to relieve themselves being overcharged with poyson, should leave some of their venom upon the leaves, the danger whereof is upon record; and therefore it is good to plant Rue amongst your Sage, and then they will not come near it' (21). Whatever toads' predilections, it makes good garden sense, as rue and all the sages look well together. Incidentally, a popular wine in the early eighteenth century was made from sage and raisins, an alarming-sounding combination of flavours.

# Salsify

*Tragopogon porrifolius* LINNAEUS (and rarely the yellow flowered *T. pratensis* LINNAEUS)

*Origin:* southern Europe

'Salsify' is nowadays restricted to *T. porrifolius*, a good garden vegetable that provides delicious roots until January (thereafter they lose flavour) and then even more delicious flowering shoots in April and May. Plants left in the ground go on to produce large dull purple flowers and immense thistle-heads of seed. The plant is a native of Mediterranean countries and may first have been taken into cultivation in Italy in the early sixteenth century (97), reaching Britain in the latter part of the seventeenth century.

Earlier British references (even Evelyn regards 'salsifix' as a synonym for 'Goat's beard') may refer to *T. pratensis*. Certainly, the salsify grown by both Gerard and Parkinson had yellow flowers characteristic of that species. *T. pratensis* is native to Britain and has probably been eaten since earliest times. It was used in the same way as modern salsify.

Most recipes suggest that the roots should be boiled or stewed, de Bonnefons (12) pointing out that the roots are much more easily peeled after parboiling (with a little skill, the skins can be made to slip off like gloves, though even then peeling is time-consuming). Boiling should last for twenty minutes, and then the peeled roots should be sliced and finished off in butter. They can be served like that, or the butter turned into a white sauce. The soup is also good. Of the flowering shoots, the top six or eight inches are tender enough to eat, preferably steamed, served with plenty of butter and a dash of vinegar. The flavour is subtle enough to serve them (hot or cold) as a first course, rather than as a vegetable to accompany meat.

# Samphire

### *Crithmum maritimum* LINNAEUS

*Origin:* native

A native plant growing on sea cliffs all around the British Isles, which has been admired as a delicacy since early times. The Italian name for it was *Herba di San Pietro*, often abbreviated to *Sampetra*, being related to the English 'samphire'. Earlier still,

True samphire, from *Icones Plantarum*

Pliny wrote that Theseus had a meal with samphire before going off to meet the Minotaur (77). The Romans used it in salads but also took it in wine to clear the complexion and give a happy expression.

Gerard said that it was a common ingredient in sauces for meat, and it was often pickled for winter consumption. Some attempt seems to have been made to cultivate it (not easy), and it was sown at the foot of a south- or west-facing wall or in pots (68). However, it seems more often to have been harvested by seaside dwellers, pickled by them and sent to inland markets (77). Demand outstripped supply, and either the glasswort (*Salicornia*) or the golden samphire (*Inula crithmoides*) was substituted (66, 77). Neither is especially edible.

# Savory
## (including winter and summer sorts)

Winter savory: *Satureja montana* LINNAEUS
Summer savory: *S. hortensis* LINNAEUS

*Origin:* southern Europe, Turkey and North Africa

Both sorts of savory have a similar taste and similar uses; the perennial *S. montana* was once widely grown in Britain, and is naturalized in various places, whereas the annual has not managed to establish itself. Unless needed in large quantities (unlikely), the shrub is the one to grow.

The two species are native to southern Europe, Asia Minor and parts of North Africa. In ancient times, huge quantities of savory grew at Thymbra, near Troy (77), though whether for local consumption or export is not clear. As Virgil says that both sorts should be planted extensively near bee-hives, it may have been for the production of honey.

The Romans were devoted to it, both for flavouring meat dishes and sausages and in sharp sauces for lettuce. Because it was thought to reduce the intestinal winds, it was much used in dishes of beans, peas and pulses (34). Of course, a little savory added to any of these, especially fresh beans, makes them taste absolutely delicious. The Romans must have brought it to Britain, though the first description seems to be in Turner's *A new herball* of 1551.

Gerard says that the plant was used as a slimming tonic and that it was also used to flavour cakes and puddings. In the early eighteenth century it was used in stews and ragouts. Medicinally, it seems to have been regarded as a substitute for thyme (26) and may also have been used as an aphrodisiac. It is still sometimes used in gastric complaints (97).

# Scorzonera

*Scorzonera hispanica* LINNAEUS (*S. stricta* HORNEMANN)

*Origin:* southern Europe

A plant superficially resembling salsify, except that the roots are black skinned, the flowers yellow, and the plant will be perennial if allowed. It is a native of southern Europe, though it has been cultivated here at least since the 1560s and probably much earlier. Mainly used as a winter vegetable, it seems never to have been widely popular. Evelyn, ever experimental, said it was good peeled, soaked (to remove some of the bitter latex) and eaten raw. Cooked, even he said it was better done with bone marrow, spices and wine. In Scotland it was boiled, sliced lengthways and fried in butter to a finish. The flower stalks were considered better than asparagus (49) – they are good, rather better than those of salsify. In Europe the young leaves were added fresh to salads, a use that seems not to have caught on here.

Scorzonera's wavering popularity can be judged from Martha Bradley's description in 1770, as 'a new dish just getting into use at some great tables and is, though not expensive, very elegant as well as pleasant . . . nothing can be taken by way of Food restores decayed Nature like it . . .'

Well worth growing, though the roots are a fiddle to prepare. If space is restricted, six or seven, kept as perennials, will throw up enough flowering shoots in the spring to provide a few delicious 'starters' (as well as a couple of seed-heads if a row or two of roots are ever needed in the future).

# Seakale

*Crambe maritima* LINNAEUS

*Origin:* native

One of the culinary delights from the garden in April and May (earlier if forced), and a handsome plant for most of the summer and autumn. It has large silvery-blue leaves and dense branches of white, scented flowers. It 'groweth naturally upon the bayche and brimes of the Sea, where there is no earth to be seen, but sand and rowling pebble stones' (34) but must once have been far more commonly seen there, for it was only brought into formal cultivation in the late eighteenth century, three hundred years after Gerard so picturesquely described its location (66, 69). Before its cultivation, the wild population seems to have been enough to supply the markets, which themselves supplied both grand tables as well as ships' stores. For the latter, the young leaf shoots were stored in oil barrels, a use noted by Pliny, although the plant does not grow on Mediterranean shores (76).

On the beach, the young leaves were blanched by heaping sand or shingle between six and twelve inches deep over the crowns. In the garden, ashes, sand or earth were used (19, 105), though special seakale-pots were once made and can still be found in forgotten corners of old kitchen gardens. For an early crop the pots were put over the dormant plants, and manure was heaped around the pot, warming it and forcing the young buds to expand. A well-grown plant yields three crops each spring, thereafter being left to produce leaves, flowers and seed.

A nice plant, far too rarely seen, quite capable of being used in the decorative flower borders, though excellent to give a little visual drama to the kitchen plot. The blanched leaf shoots can be boiled or baked, taste rather like a combination of the most delicious cabbage and very fresh hazelnuts, and should be served with plenty butter or a cream sauce. By the end of the season the plants get quite large and can swamp anything else planted too close. If you need more, they are easily increased by root cuttings; indeed it is sometimes difficult to eradicate if you have too many.

# Service

*Sorbus domestica* LINNAEUS, and sometimes *S. torminalis* (LINNAEUS) CRANTZ

*Origin:* southern Europe

Though Cobbett wrote, 'It is totally unfit to be eaten and, therefore, I shall say no more about it', it had once been popular garden fruit and was still being widely grown in Italy as a dessert when Cobbett wrote so rudely of it in 1833.

The Romans had been exceptionally fond of the four sorts they grew, and Cato had even suggested that they should be used preserved and that they were far better than medlars (q.v.). The medical properties of the service were the same. The true service tree is a native to southern Europe and the Mediterranean region and, the Romans being so fond of it, it seems likely that they would have brought it with them to Britain. They were certainly responsible for spreading it through France and Germany. In Britain the tree and its fruit seem to have remained popular into the sixteenth century, when they were commonly part of the kitchen garden hedge, though Francis Bacon treated them more politely and grew services in his fruit garden (76). In the latter part of the seventeenth century, with all the improvements then taking place in other fruit crops, the service began to lose favour (83). Even so, several varieties were available and remained so throughout the following century. Furber, in his marvellous series of monthly illustrations (a nursery catalogue, in fact), published in 1732, shows the 'Italian service' as a fruit for October and the 'English service' as one for November. Even in the early nineteenth century, Phillips (76) reports country-folk bringing the fruit to London, with the fruit bunches threaded onto canes or twigs so as to form a cylinder of berries about a yard long. After purchase they were hung up in the garden until dew and frost had sufficiently altered the flavour to make them fit for eating.

The wood was much in demand as well, as the blocks for woodcuts, for archers' bows, for pulleys, spindles, pistol stocks (68) and rulers (66) and by cabinet-makers (76). In the seventeenth and early eighteenth centuries, ebony was often simulated

Service; a plate from the nineteenth century, when the berries
were still marketed

by varnishing service wood with boiled linseed oil.

The fruit seems hardly ever eaten these days, and even the handsome tree is not often met with. A pity really, for it looks good at all seasons. The other species (*S. torminalis*) is a native of Britain but seems not to have had such a good flavour as its relative and to have been less widely used.

# Shallot

*Allium cepa* LINNAEUS (though it was once given specific rank as *A. ascalonium*)

*Origin:* possibly the Middle East

A useful and delicately flavoured bulb maturing in midsummer, and one of the myriad sorts of onion. It was thought to originate in the ancient city of Ascalon.

It may have arrived here by 1548 (77), but Mortimer, writing in 1707, says that, 'it is now from France, become an English plant. . . . They give a fine relish to most Sawces, and the Breath of those that eat them is not offensive to others . . .' which makes it sound as if it was a relatively new introduction. Not that it is a recent garden plant; Pliny also said that it was excellent for sauces.

In the garden, they were sometimes used, like chives, as edgings to the vegetable plot borders. Though we now only use the bulbs, the leaves were also once used as a substitute for chives. One of the simplest and most delicious ways of having a good fried steak is to throw a finely chopped shallot into the pan a moment or two before the steak is done, a popular dish at least since the early nineteenth century (77).

# Skirret

*Sium sisarum* var. *sisarum* LINNAEUS

*Origin:* northern Europe

Once much grown as a winter root, the seed is now only very occasionally offered by specialist seed merchants. I have never managed to get it to germinate, and suspect that it has a short period of viability. This seems always to have been a problem, the

Skirret; a sixteenth-century woodcut

seed either not germinating or giving rise to very variable plants. Propagation was generally by root cutting from good plants (105).

The root consists of several long, fleshy tubers, the thickness of a little finger, that surround an inedible woody core. To cook them, they were stewed in butter or rolled in flour and fried (66). The flavour is said to be sweet and floury (105) or of 'a sweet taste disagreeable to many palates' (66). The mysterious root, variously thought to be carrot or parsnip, that was sent to the Emperor Tiberius, was believed by Evelyn to be the skirret (30). The plant is not native to Britain, though it is found in other northern European countries. It was certainly cultivated in Britain by Gerard's time and already had an older name (skir-wort), so possibly it was an early introduction.

Medicinally, it was used to cure wounds and ulcers and was yet another plant thought to be good against the plague. The leaves were sometimes put into salads (28).

If you do find a plant, or seeds, the leaves fall entirely from the root in October. In the eighteenth century, each plant was marked by a little stick so that it could be found when needed (49).

# Sorrel
## (and Herb Patience)

Sorrel: **Rumex acetosa**, and more rarely **R. scutatus** LINNAEUS
Herb Patience: **R. patientia** LINNAEUS

*Origin:* possibly native; widespread elsewhere

An excellent kitchen garden plant, somewhere between a vegetable and an herb, making excellent sauces for any of the coarser-flavoured fish, for pork, for goose and also various good soups and, in moderation, a splendid filling for an omelette. As a vegetable, it is piled in a pan with a little butter and steamed like spinach. For serving, the sharpish taste is softened by the addition of an egg yolk and plenty of cream, making a really delicious dish (77).

The roots produce leaves very early in the spring, long before the first spinach is ready, and the first crop is the most delicious of all. Throughout much of the year, and all of it if the winter is mild, the leaves can be used in salads, though they need to be finely shredded and used in not too great a quantity. Mature plants try to flower in early summer; so cut them right down to the ground. A new crop soon forms, and in any case you will not miss them at that time of year. A dozen plants are enough for most families. They need moving every couple of years, to stop them getting too firmly anchored and exhausting the surrounding soil.

Various sorrels have been grown since earliest times (Pliny said that they were used with meat, making it easier to digest), though for a long time the 'French' sort (*R. scutatus*) has been considered the best. Widely used until the seventeenth century, sorrels began to fall from favour in the eighteenth, and by the nineteenth were to be found in Britain 'only on fashionable tables' (77). Nevertheless, the immense range of medicinal uses remained, while the plant fell from grace in the kitchen, until those too dropped out of use.

Almost all of the plant was used; the leaves were prescribed as a mild laxative or, powdered with oil of roses and saffron, were used to 'dissolve impostumes of the head' (26). A poultice of leaves was used to cure agues (28) and putrefaction of the gums, as well as to tighten loose teeth (75). The juice of the leaves was taken in consumptions or to cleanse suppurating ulcers (77). Less alarmingly, it was used as a general tonic for the liver (34). The flowers and flower stalks, as well as restoring lost voices to singing birds (77), were used to cure the 'bloody fire' in human beings, 'Wambling panes of the stomach' (26), scorpion stings, jaundice, mange and 'wild festereing and consuming scabbes' (26). The roots were boiled and the liquid used for swellings behind the ears (26), but the same juice, because it has a fine red colour, was also used as a dye for hemp and flax (77) and to colour various drinks, especially barley water (77). Nowadays sorrel is said to have diuretic, laxative and antiseptic properties, and the poultice is sometimes used to cure acne (97).

The English word 'sorrel' is close to the French *l'oseil* though the Scots 'sourock' is virtually the same as the seventeenth-century Dutch word *surick* (36).

# Spinach
## (and Orache)

Spinach: *Spinacia oleracea* LINNAEUS

*Origin:* south-western Asia

Orache: *Atriplex hortensis* LINNAEUS

*Origin:* temperate Europe and Asia

Spinach, a plant of south-western Asia, was introduced to Britain, possibly from Spain, in the sixteenth century (93). Turner's herbal states that it 'is an herb lately found, and not long in use' (101). It was not known to the Greeks or Romans but was used by later Arabian physicians, and no doubt the Arab expansion carried the plant to the Iberian peninsula. No medicinal properties seem to have survived from the Moorish past to Renaissance herbals. Most of the latter seem only concerned with its cooking; steamed, beaten, drained and then made into little balls when mixed with butter (36), or a sort of quiche called 'Italian pie' (28), made with spinach, butter and eggs, baked in an open pastry case.

A much more elaborate pie is described by Gervase Markham. In this, the spinach is boiled in white wine, drained, flavoured with rosewater, sugar and cinnamon, and then cooked again until as thick as marmalade. This filling was used for putting into elaborate and heraldic pastry cases, often designed as the coats of arms of the host or guest. Markham notes, under his section on quinces, that at a prosperous banquet about half of all the dishes were for show alone and not meant to be eaten.

The juice left from the steaming of spinach was early admired for its intense green colour, and much used for colouring cakes and desserts well into the nineteenth century (13, 77). It was regarded as preferable to the poisonous copper-based dyes of the day. The juice was also used to make touchpaper for eighteenth- and nineteenth-century fireworks, for paper that had been soaked in it, and dried, smouldered well.

Prickly and round-seeded sorts seem to have been introduced at the same time, though the smooth-seeded one was preferred. The prickly one is probably the most primitive sort (93). Many leaf types were available, and a few of the 'savoyed' types can still be found, all looking nice in the garden, though they are difficult to clean. Vilmorin-Andrieux (105) said that the plants established more vigorously if the seed was soaked for a day before planting.

Orache seems to have been cultivated before the introduction of spinach and is still an important crop in some parts of Europe (66, 105). It was much used in seventeenth-century soups and stuffings.

# Strawberry

Modern garden strawberries: *Fragaria x ananassas* DUCHESNE

    *Origin:* initial hybridization in Europe, of American species

Wild and alpine strawberries: *F. vesca* LINNAEUS

                                     *Origin:* Europe

Musk strawberry: *F. moschata* DUCHESNE

                                     *Origin:* Europe

Other species of *Fragaria* are sometimes found in the kitchen garden, including *F. viridis* DUCHESNE and *F. virginiana* DUCHESNE

The sorts of strawberry now most often grown are almost entirely hybrids of various American species, most of them introduced to Europe in the seventeenth and eighteenth centur-

The 'Bath' strawberry; an early nineteenth-century strawberry

ies. However, the wildling has an ancient history, being cultivated in Roman gardens, if not earlier. Its fruit has always been
thought delicious, and a number of superior sorts seem to have
been selected early on. Long-season ones are mentioned by the
fourteenth century (93), and sorts with fruit the size of a mulberry
by the sixteenth century (41). Runnerless sorts were also available by that date. Gerard grew various colour variants, of which
the white-fruited sort was said to have the most delicate flavour
(68). The green one (*F. viridis*) was much grown in the seventeenth century, being one of the latest to mature, and also the
sweetest (107, 68).

The small-fruited sorts now generally referred to as 'alpine'
have sometimes been thought of as a separate species (66, 105)
but are now regarded as part of *F. vesca*. They, too, were known
in the sixteenth century but are supposed not to have been
cultivated until the middle of the eighteenth century (72, 103).
Other variants are the rare and charming 'Plymouth' or 'prickly'
strawberry found by John Tradescant the elder at Plymouth, the

*fraise de Versailles* or *F. vesca* var. *monophylla*, that has a single leaflet instead of the usual arrangement of three (a very invasive garden plant) and a useful variegated form.

A central European species, *F. moschata*, was also once widely cultivated. The dark-coloured fruit have a remarkable musky perfume, and even though both male and female are needed to obtain fruit, they are remarkably vigorous, and it is hard to see why they have become such a rarity. It was introduced to this country in the sixteenth century, and Parkinson, growing it in the seventeenth century, called it the 'Bohemian' strawberry.

However delicious the European strawberries, they must always have been regarded as a nuisance to pick. The introduction of large-fruited American species was widely hailed as an advance, and they were quickly taken up by the cultivators. *F. virginiana* – abundant in Virginia, especially in new woodland clearings (72) – reached Europe by 1556 and was grown in Britain in the early seventeenth century. It was grown by Parkinson and was much admired. Mortimer's comment is that, 'Some esteem that the best of all which hath not long since been brought from *New England*: It is the earliest ripe of all *English* Fruit, being ripe many Years in the first week of May.' Later on, it was also the type most used for forcing (76). *F. chiloensis*, long cultivated by American Indians (93) who also grew various colour types, was first grown in Spain (93) but spread to the rest of Europe by the early eighteenth century. Hybrids between the two species (and referable to *F. x ananassas*, so called after their early name of 'pine strawberry') soon began to appear, and Miller was growing them by mid-century. Many of them were produced in France, and some of those created by Amedée Frezier at Versailles were extensively cultivated. However, the first major breeder was British (46). T. A. Knight produced hundreds of varieties in the early nineteenth century, amidst widespread interest. Perpetual-fruiting sorts, still not enough grown in modern gardens, were available by 1866.

Wild, alpine and Virginian strawberries were eaten fresh but dressed with sugar and red wine – claret and burgundy were thought to be best (77) – a way of eating which was popular well into the nineteenth century (if not especially effective). Eighteenth-century Frenchmen liked them dressed with orange juice, a practice still sometimes followed and certainly useful for some of the thinly flavoured modern varieties. Even some of the early hybrids were not perhaps too strong-tasting, for Cobbett, having recently discovered the alpine strawberry on the advice of Sir

Charles Wolseley, wrote, 'but a bed of these strawberries surpasses all others in fragrance, and, I think, in flavour' (19). A mixture of alpine sorts and *F. ananassas* ones tastes good too, but ignore statements that the birds do not eat alpines. They do, and you will lose a good proportion of your crop unless you grow them under the same netting as their lusher relatives.

Medicinally, strawberries have the wide range of uses that one might expect for such an old crop. A decoction of the plant, including the roots, was thought to stop menstrual flows, cure mouth ulcers and stop bad breath (26), was good for 'Heart Qualms and Faintnesse' (21) and is reported to have been used as yet another cure for gonorrhoea (97). The fruit, regarded as a general tonic, especially for invalids, was beneficial also because 'taken even in large quantities they seldom disagree with the stomach. They promote perspiration, impart a violet scent to the urine, and dissolve the tartarous incrustations upon the teeth' (66). They also helped people with gout or kidney stones if eaten in quantity, and must have offered a very pleasant cure, if of dubious efficacy.

# Swede

**Brassica napus** LINNAEUS

*Origin:* probably central Europe

A dull vegetable, hardier than the turnip because of its lower water content, and therefore useful for a few midwinter meals. First recorded by Caspar Bauhin in 1620, it may have originated in medieval gardens, possibly in Bohemia (63), where kale and turnip were growing side by side (93). It was introduced to Britain from Sweden (hence its name) in the 1770s and was soon widely grown for both beasts and man. In the field, hares and pheasants are said to prefer the swede to the turnip (66), not a taste I share, though there are variations in flavour between some of the numerous varieties. If you have only a small garden, it is probably not a culinary field worth investigating. Space is better left for the more interesting root crops.

# Sweet Cicely

*Myrrhis odorata* (LINNAEUS) SCOPOLI

*Origin:* Europe

Perhaps a native to Britain, and certainly so in the rest of Europe. It was once in very widespread domestic use, and so its geographical range may have been drastically enlarged. Its use was once medicinal, though this had largely vanished by the sixteenth century, when Gerard and like-minded gardeners all grew it. It was used very like chervil (q.v.), the young leaves for salads and the roots boiled and eaten cold with oil and vinegar. Sometimes, because of their extreme sweetness, they were put in tarts (66). Parkinson wrote (77): 'Some commend the green seeds sliced and put in a sallet of herbs . . . comfort the cold stomach of the aged . . . the preserv'd or candid rootes are of singular good use to warm and comfort a cold flegmaticke stomak, and is thought to be a good preservative in the time of plague.'

In the north of England the ripe shiny and black seeds were used in the eighteenth and early nineteenth centuries as a polish, especially on oak floors, to which they imparted their pleasing smell (66).

# Swiss Chard
## (including Ruby Chard and Leaf Beet)

*Beta vulgaris* var. *cicla* LINNAEUS

*Origin:* Europe

The chards and the beetroot (q.v.) show two extremes of selection from the same species (leaf beet is a primitive form occupying the mid-ground between the two). Whereas the beetroot is grown for its rootstock (though the leaves are perfectly edible and are sometimes used in parts of Europe and Russia), the chards have been selected for leafiness and for the fleshy leaf stalk and midrib. The crop seems to have been introduced to Britain in the mid-sixteenth century. Of it, Gerard wrote that the 'leaves [are] very great and red . . . the midribs of the leaves are very broad and thick, like that of the cabbage leaf, and they are equal in goodness with the leaves of the cabbage, being boiled. It was brought unto me by that courteous merchant Master Lete; and grew with me in 1596 to the height of eight cubits, and did bring forth his rough seeds very plentifully.' Gerard clearly had ruby chard, which has, to my taste, a less good flavour than the white-stemmed variety. Had he grown this, he might have been more enthusiastic. In the next century, Parkinson admired 'the ribbes eaten in sallets with oyle, vinigar, and pepper, and is accounted a rare kind of sallet, and very delicate'. Some years later, John Evelyn stewed the leaves of his chard in their own juices (like spinach) and served them on buttered toast (30), still a good way of doing things, though the toast does need lashings of butter. Also in the seventeenth century the French *potage maigre* contained spinach, sorrel, chard and cabbage (30). Since that time chard has been consistently grown but never achieved a great deal of popularity.

Modern seed catalogues and cook-books usually suggest chard as a dual-use vegetable, eating the leaf stalks and midribs separately from the green leaf blade. As they have different cooking times, this is useful. The greenery makes quite a nice early spring substitute for spinach, though it is vastly improved by the addition of a little of the first sorrel. The sharpness of the latter lightens texture and taste. The leaves together also make an excellent soup.

The white (or red, if you insist), parts are quite pleasant if gently stewed in butter until soft, and served as Evelyn suggested, on toast. The stalks are naturally quite salty, so take care with any addition. European cuisine handles chard more imaginatively, and there are some excellent pork pies that contain plenty of chard to add flavour and reduce the pie's fattiness.

Both ruby and white chard are handsome plants when well grown. They are fairly immune to pests, though the large leaves are easily damaged by storms. Both make a useful visual addition to the kitchen garden. In the nineteenth century, varieties of chard existed that had frilled and curly leaves; I have not managed to discover seed of these types, though perhaps they still exist somewhere.

# Tarragon

*Artemisia dracunculus* LINNAEUS

*Origin:* possibly western Europe

'French' tarragon seems to be a sterile and aromatic clone that has originated from the fertile and rank-flavoured 'Russian' tarragon, which species is actually native to southern and eastern Russia. The Dodoens herbal of 1578 says that tarragon has only lately been brought out of France but seems to suggest that there were two tarragons, 'the little Dragon of the garden' being used in salads with lettuce. 'French' tarragon shoots are good in salads, so perhaps the 'little Dragon' did originate in France, and in the sixteenth century or earlier. *Dragon* remains the German name.

Wherever and whenever the little tarragon arose, it is unlikely to have been made 'of linseed prikt in many places of the head of a red onion, the strongest and sharpest that may be found, and put into well-manured earth'. So wrote Estienne and Liebault in 1570, echoing an earlier method quoted by Ruellius, in which a radish or sea squill substituted for onions (28). Presumably, strong-flavoured onions were chosen to give a more powerful taste to the resultant tarragon.

By 1596 Gerard was growing the right sort, and thereafter it was much used in salads to counteract the 'coldness' of the other vegetation and soon became used to flavour vinegar and pickles, as well as roasts. By the end of the seventeenth century it was used in perfumery as well (97). It seems, though, to have had few medicinal uses, perhaps supporting its comparatively recent introduction to the garden. It was thought to stimulate the appetite, loosen the belly and prevent choler (26).

A floppy and untidy herb, suitable for some out-of-the-way patch where its habit will not offend, it is essential for the kitchen. It needs to be bought, or begged from friends. Tarragon seed sold by seed merchants is the wild and unimproved species, taller and more rampant than French tarragon, invasive and, if you let it flower and seed, sowing itself everywhere.

# Thyme

Various **Thymus** species, including **T. vulgaris** LINNAEUS
(*T. aestivus* REUTER and WILKOMM), **T.**
**herba-barona** LOISELEUR-DESLONGCHAMPS, etc.

*Origin:* southern Europe

A herb comprising several species and many hybrids, all part of a huge and complex genus and with an illustrious past. Though less in demand today than was once the case, it is still worth having as many different types as possible in the kitchen or flower garden.

Most of the highly aromatic species are native to Mediterranean countries, and there deliberate cultivation can hardly have been necessary. In ancient Greece, thyme was thought to give courage and revive the spirits (77). Thyme honey was then, and still is, much admired. The Romans made extensive use of thyme as a medicine, many of the uses surviving into the nineteenth century. In the kitchen, they also used it as a flavouring for roasts and stews, and even to flavour sheep on the hoof; thyme-fed lamb was an expensive delicacy (77).

Though mentioned by Gerard, it must certainly have been introduced by the Romans and, because of its medical importance, must have been widely grown. Sixteenth-century authors followed Greek and Roman belief that thyme 'is profitable for those that are fearful, melancholicke and troubled in spirit or mind' (26), and it was also used for headaches, falling sickness (28), hangovers (66) and 'bleared and waterie and painful eyes' (26), as well as toothache. It was supposed to be good for sleep, and sixteenth- and seventeenth-century beds were often hung with bags of it, one to each of the four posts. Thyme was also supposed to drive away fleas, which might have been an additional help. Though thyme was largely a 'cephalic' herb, it was also helpful for the lower parts of the body, being good for wind, belly-ache, coughs and 'clammy fleume' (26), 'sharp humours' and 'corruption of the blood' (26) and to ease the pain of the gout. Thymol, first extracted from the plant in 1725 (97), is still much used in pharmacy.

The decorative possibilities of thyme were also early recognized, and in seventeenth-century gardens '. . . a Border of it is a considerable and necessary Ornament in a kitchen Garden' (68), a use that persisted well into the nineteenth century. Various thymes were used as flower-garden borders in late Georgian cottage gardens. Gold- and silver-leaved sorts were the most used, though the practice was falling out of use by 1830 (77). Some are still very suited to such a use and can look very pretty. At least in my garden they do, though they seem not to like draughts and do best with a certain amount of shelter. Some of the grey-leaved culinary sorts need very sharp drainage, or they can rot at the roots during the winter. The favourite sort here, collected at San Remy, has a plant or two overwintered in a pot in the cold greenhouse, just to make sure.

# Tomato

*Lycopersicon esculentum* MILLER

*Origin:* South America

'*Pomme d'amour*', 'love apple', 'golden apple' are all early names for the now so familiar fruit and suggest some of the awe in which it was once held. Indeed, on its introduction, probably from Mexico in the sixteenth century, it was thought to be poisonous.

The wild form, the 'cherry tomato', rather similar to some varieties grown by gardeners (such as 'Gardeners Delight'), is an aggressive weed of South America (93). There were many different sorts already in widespread cultivation by the time of the Spanish invasion. Why what was so obviously a crop plant for the American Indians should be regarded as poisonous in Europe is not clear, though of course the flower and fruit do quite closely resemble a number of very poisonous European members of the family. This culinary barrier seems to have broken first in Italy, and then the habit of actually eating tomatoes spread around the Mediterranean and gradually northwards (93). Dodoens reported, in 1578, that they were eaten with salt, pepper and oil, though he added, 'This is a strange plant, and not found in this Country, except in the gardens of some herborists . . . and is

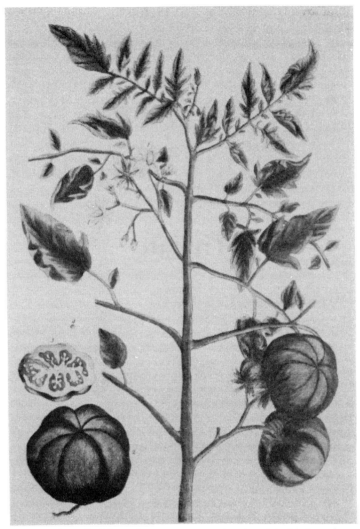

An early eighteenth-century tomato, showing a lobed fruit

dangerous to be used.' Estienne and Liebault wrote that tomatoes were also boiled or fried, though they gave rise to wind, choler and 'infinite obstructions'. Parkinson grew them, but only as decoratives. He was, though, aware by this date that they were eaten with delight in other countries. He also thought that they might be used to cure the 'itch', but of what sort he does not say.

Early introductions included red, yellow and white forms, with the red in two varieties: small and round, and large, flat and lobed. This last sort was thought to have the best flavour (it still has) and is nowadays referred to as part of the 'Marmande' group (66).

Even in early nineteenth-century Britain, caution persisted. Though the tomato had long been used in Jewish cuisine and had even become fairly common on upper-class tables, Phillips could write: 'I do not find that they are used by the middle and lower classes of English families, who have yet to learn the art of improving their dishes with vegetables. . . .' Cobbett, in 1833, mentions all three colour forms, saying that they were sold at high prices. In other parts of Europe, caution about the tomato persisted into the twentieth century (93).

Almost every new vegetable (at least those new in the sixteenth, seventeenth and eighteenth centuries), seems to have been thought of as an aphrodisiac. The 'love apple' was no exception, and this may account for the awe in which it was held; it certainly lends a certain romance to those awful ketchup bottles in forlorn cafés. However, the tomato also became used for glaucoma, cataplasms and St Anthony's fire (77), though none of these uses appears in seventeenth-century herbals.

During the late nineteenth and early twentieth centuries, tomato-growing became big business, and soon no salad was complete without a few pinkish slices, and no fish dish was eaten without a dollop of tomato sauce. What had once been rare, mysterious and exciting became hackneyed and hardly regarded. Developments in tomato breeding have not helped. Breeders have much increased the plant's yield and disease resistance but also greatly reduced the flavour. If you have space and conditions to grow any of the Marmande group, or even 'Gardeners Delight' (sweet and strong-flavoured, but without the fragrance and delicacy of the other), you will feel nothing but pity for less fortunate people who have to buy those uniform, plastic-wrapped and plastic-tasting tomatoes on supermarket shelves. A good tomato can be very good indeed.

# Turnip

*Brassica rapa* subsp. *rapa* LINNAEUS

*Origin:* eastern Europe and western Asia

An ancient crop, and a very variable one, the western sorts (probably originating in the Mediterranean region) mostly selected for their swollen roots, the eastern sorts (probably originating in Afghanistan and Pakistan) being selected for their succulent leaves. A third type, possibly originating in India, has been widely grown for the oil in its seeds – colza oil, important for lighting European rooms at least from the thirteenth century (93).

The Romans seem to have had several varieties, though it may have been a crop associated with poverty: Roman armorials sometimes bore pictures of turnips to denote a benefactor of the poor (77). Medicinal uses seem mostly to have been concerned with the feet, the turnips being baked and mixed with suet to cure frostbite, chilblains and various diseases (77).

Turnips may already have been grown throughout Europe (there are old Saxon names for them), by the time of the Roman Empire. Since then, they seem to have remained a widespread though minor crop until the seventeenth century. Cutlers used a mixture of turnip juice and earthworms to quench newly forged knives (28), and the medical uses eventually expanded until turnips became used to cure smallpox, measles (28), coughs and sore throats – as syrup (77) – and were even fermented and distilled for spirit (66).

Their use in the kitchens of the past seems to have been more imaginative than it is in those of today. Roots were baked and served with butter and sugar (30), the soup was common, turnip sauce was necessary for seventeenth-century ducks (it is still used in France) and for all dishes using salted meats. In spring the overwintered roots were allowed to produce young and edible flower shoots (still a popular vegetable in much of Europe, and worth trying here, though the shoots of some varieties seem to me rather rank tasting).

Essential as turnip was for salted meat, it eventually became the means of avoiding salt meat altogether. Beasts used to be

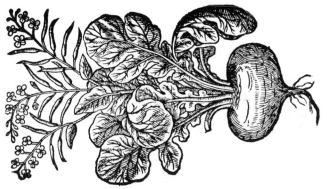

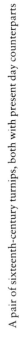

A pair of sixteenth-century turnips, both with present day counterparts

salted down for winter because there was not then enough greenstuff to keep them all alive and healthy. However, turnips, once only a kitchen garden crop, became used on a field scale, usually as a late summer crop on stubbles. The plants' ability to keep growing well into the hard weather, and their cold-tolerance thereafter, meant that fresh fodder was available throughout the winter, and so fewer animals needed to be killed.

The practice reached Britain in the mid-seventeenth century (66) but took a while to oust the old procedures. It did not become common until well into the next century. It was also realized that turnips grew well on very light and poor soils but that after a few seasons under turnip the soil became so enriched with animal manure from the wintering beasts that it became able to support much more valuable crops. Agriculturally speaking, the eighteenth century became the 'age of the Turnip', and immense tracts of previously unproductive land came under profitable cultivation.

The small, fast-growing and white-skinned sorts make the best eating to my mind. They do well if your garden is reasonably free from root fly and finger-and-toe disease. The seed should be sown in small amounts throughout the spring and summer, with the first few lots being grown in the greenhouse or under cloches. Of the larger sorts for winter use, I often wonder how many of the plants grown ever actually get eaten; can any family need more than a dozen?

# Vine

*Vitis vinifera* subsp. *vinifera* LINNAEUS (*V. vinifera* subsp. *sativa* HEGI)

*Origin:* probably eastern Mediterranean region

A crop with a most ancient and illustrious history. The wild plant, of the eastern Mediterranean area (46), has reasonably good fruit which can be used to produce a tolerable wine. No doubt good variants were cropped by nomadic peoples of earliest times. Legend says that the vine was first domesticated in Armenia (93), and there are records showing cultivation in the Middle East by 4000 BC (46), Egyptian manuals on viticulture from 3000 BC (93) and Greek records from around 1000 BC (Homer seems not to have known the pleasures of wine).

Early Romans either treated wine with great respect or simply did not have many vineyards, for all women and young men under thirty were forbidden to drink it. Later on, it became so plentiful that the expansion of vineyards began to inhibit other forms of agriculture. In the first century AD Domitian tried to halve the area devoted to vines (76). However, by that date big vineyards were being set up in Germany (93); Burgundy was beneath vines by Antonine times, and they were certainly grown in Britain by AD 280.

The plant itself rapidly extended its range of cultivation, and there was also a very extensive early trade in raisins. Varieties of grape with high sugar contents will dry, in a warm climate, without rotting. The resultant raisin contains eighty per cent of sugar, and so it is sweet and delicious and will store almost indefinitely. It is also easily transported. They were produced all around the Mediterranean, those from Damascus being thought the best (66). Even fresh Damascus grapes were shipped to Rome, packed in chaff in earthenware jars. Each fruit was supposed to be the size of a pigeon's egg and was of exquisite taste, and bunches of them commonly weighed twenty-five pounds (76).

Wine, too, was an important article of commerce. Pliny described eighty kinds of wine, Greek ones being the best and most expensive. Even at the grandest banquets, they were served only once. Old wines, then as now, were in demand and expensive; Pliny mentioned some that were over two hundred years old, and there were many wine auctions.

Once the vine reached Britain, it seems to have been widely cultivated, at least south of Derby, an early northern limit (66). After the collapse of the Roman occupation, the vineyards may have collapsed as well, the extensive cultivation of the vine returning perhaps with the Norman invasion. Vineyards are mentioned in the Domesday book and remained common well into the medieval period, until French wines were imported in quantity in the fourteenth century (66). Interest seems to have revived in the late sixteenth and early seventeenth century, when many Tudor and Stuart mansions had extensive vineyards – the gardens at Hatfield were given thirty thousand vines by the wife of the French ambassador (37). The Tradescant garden catalogue of 1634, and also Sir Thomas Hanmer's list, shows that about seven varieties were grown. Parkinson lists twenty-three in 1640, and Lawrence fifty-two in 1718. However, interest in home-produced wines waned throughout the eighteenth century, and by the end of it only a few magnates bothered to make their own wine. The vineyard is nowadays making a modest recovery, though wine production in Britain is never likely to be more than a very pleasant novelty, more suitable climates producing a cheaper and generally better product.

Of course, grapes were not grown only for wine. Dessert grapes were widely grown, very often against the walls of the kitchen garden, the terrace or the house. Even the southern parts of Scotland could produce, in a good summer, excellent crops of fully ripened fruit (buttressed walls were especially helpful, the vines being planted at the buttress, and the fruiting arms being trained into the sheltered areas between them). In any case, unripe fruit was still of use, for it was pressed and the resultant 'verjuice' used in sauces for meat, game and fish. The leaves of the vine were used for roasting small birds (76) – especially for cooking wheatears, though, failing these, even a chicken roast in a covering of leaves is delicious – as a sauce for pigeons (the finely chopped leaves were quickly fried in butter, then sharpened with vinegar (60)) and for fritters. This lovely eithteenth-century recipe has the leaves soaked in lemon juice and brandy (white wine will just do), and then they are fried after coating with a batter made with flour, white wine and eggs (13). Some seventeenth-century gourmets followed Roman precedent and tried eating the young tendrils, fresh or pickled. They taste quite sweet, but the ones in my garden seem always to be rather fibrous.

When glasshouses became widespread in the early eighteenth century, growing grapes for dessert became an important occupation for the gardener. The earlier buildings called orangeries, with their solid roofs, had never been suitable for permanently bedded-out inhabitants. The new structures, generally a 'lean-to' on the south-facing wall of the kitchen garden, were ideal. With plenty of height, easily ventilated, vines thrived, could be forced and yielded heavily. To produce large bunches of grapes for presentation to one's friends became something of a pastime. In 1781 the Duke of Portland sent to his friend the Marquis of Rockingham a bunch of grapes that had been grown in his garden at Welbeck. The bunch weighed 19½ pounds, was 4 feet in circumference and 22 inches long. There is no record as to the quality of the flavour (57).

Curiously, in spite of the crop's ancient history, its association with various Classical deities and its use in the rituals of several religions, there seems to be little magic associated with it. There are similarly few medicinal uses: the leaves were used to cure diarrhoea and haemorrhaging and as a styptic. The sap was once used to cure calluses and specks on the cornea (76).

The main skill needed when growing a vine is in knowing how much to thin the young fruit bunches. Training the vine itself is easy, though one needs an iron determination not to let the plants have their way. Anyone with wall space, or room in a cold greenhouse, would find it worthwhile trying. Yields can be prodigious, and the flavour of a well-grown bunch of a good variety of grape, straight from the vine, is something quite special. Anyone who can put a little heat into the glasshouse should grow some of the Muscat types. The flavour is even more special, and if you can find the variety 'Muscat Frontignac' you will be growing a variety that once flourished in ancient Athens (46).

Not only are the cultivars themselves long-lived; individual plants will also survive for a long time. Pliny mentions a plant that was reputed to be six hundred years old, and Columella writes that Seneca had a vine that produced two thousand bunches of fruit a year (the 'Black Hamburg' vine at Hampton Court has done better). Vine wood was sometimes used as a timber in its own right, and the great doors of Ravenna Cathedral were made of vine planks (76).

# Walnut

*Juglans regia* LINNAEUS

*Origin:* central Asia

Not really a plant of the kitchen garden proper, as it is an imposing tree, and one which does not take kindly to pruning. However, because of the value of both its fruit and its timber, it was widely planted in the seventeenth and eighteenth centuries, and because its deep roots do not take much nourishment from the upper layers of the soil, it was commonly to be found in

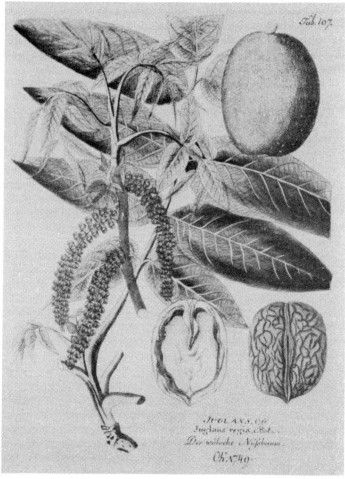

Walnut in flower and fruit (nineteenth century)

the shelter belts that surrounded the better planned kitchen garden.

The species normally grown (there are many edible species of *Juglans*, a few known in Britain since 1629) is native to the area between the Carpathians and northern India. The Greeks found it in Persia, and from their gardens Vitellius took it to Italy during the reign of Tiberius (46, 76). It was certainly in England by

1562, but it is difficult to imagine that a plant so important to Roman medicine was not introduced during their occupation. It was already quite common by Gerard's time, so if it was not brought in by the Romans, it may have been introduced during the fifteenth century. Certainly its beautiful timber became popular for furniture and wainscot only in the seventeenth century (the wood is wormproof), by which time ancient trees must have been sufficiently plentiful to supply the market.

As usual, sixteenth- and seventeenth-century usage followed Roman ideas. The nuts were used at the beginning of meals as a vermifuge (walnuts were originally pickled so that worms could be expelled throughout the year) and as a counter-poison (Gerard believed them effective). They were also used to suppress onion-scented belches, and by 1714 walnuts were being used as a sauce for fish, as well as cold meats (1). Because the kernel of the nut looks so much like a brain, it is not surprising that nuts or bits of the root were hung around the neck to cure epilepsy (21), frenzy, 'Passions of the Brain' (21) and other mental disorders. Powdered walnut root also 'provoketh Urine, and purgeth the liver and the kidneys. Being boiled in wine and drunk, it purgeth the Blood, and is good for women in child-bed, to purge their Seconds and Termes . . . it helpeth the grippings of the Belly, helpeth the Cholick, cleaneth the Guts . . . defendeth against the Strangury, the biting of Serpents, and the spleen; and having Castoreum boiled with it, it helpeth the palsie and the stone . . .' (21).

The leaves, too, were useful. Macerated, they were often part of various insecticides and were commonly used to kill off worms in bowling-greens and lawns (68) – the worms were then suitable for use by anglers (76) – as well as ringworm on human scalps (though, mixed with boar fat, they were also a useful hair-restorer). Decoctions of the leaf were used to dry up running ulcers and sores (74), while dried leaves were placed among clothes in the press to stop the depredations of moths (78). Extracts from the green nut shells were used to stop toothache, and from the ripe shells to give a deep yellow dye. For reasons which I cannot discover, the green nuts were preserved, keeping the purity of their colour by storing in the pressings of crab apples after their verjuice had been pressed out (78).

The oil from ripe nuts was of enormous importance, as a frying and cooking oil (marvellous, too, if you can find it), as a base for paints and varnishes, and in oil lamps (66). The wood, however worm-proof (66), was too fragile for structural timbers and so was used for the finest items of furniture and panelling and for the bodies and wheels of coaches (68).

To have a kitchen garden ringed by walnuts was not, however, without its dangers; it was not thought safe to sit beneath them without a hat, as the trees' effluvia were hurtful (76). Perhaps, though, the hat was necessary as an ancient mark of respect for a tree sacred to Jupiter. Even so, as late as the nineteenth century, walnuts were not planted near houses or near strawberry beds (76).

# Welsh Onion

*Allium fistulosum* LINNAEUS

*Origin:* China and Japan

Rather a useful member of the onion tribe, and too little seen. The plant scarcely produces a bulb, though the lower fleshy parts of the leaves do swell slightly. Their advantage is that they form early in the year and are also generally happy to remain in the ground all winter. The clumps increase in girth rapidly and need splitting up every year or so. The plant has all the uses of the onion, though skinning a large quantity of them can be a tiresome business. I find them excellent for soups, pizzas and stuffings. The greenery can be used instead of chives, and so they are particularly useful in winter when the chives are beneath the soil.

The Welsh onion, of course, does not come from, or have any connection with, Wales. The name probably originated from a German word meaning 'foreign'. This it certainly is, for it comes from China and Japan where it has been cultivated since earliest times. From those countries it may have travelled to Russia, for it was supposed by early British gardeners to come from Siberia. It seems to have been grown here at least since the early seventeenth century (77), though a plant of similar name is mentioned by Chaucer (93). It may once have been thought of as an aphrodisiac (see Onion).

The plants can be grown from seed, though the resultant seedlings can be very variable. Probably the best way to get Welsh onions is to ask gardening friends for a plant. Almost everyone who grows it will have an excess and, with luck, they will have a good and productive variety.

# Wormwood

*Artemisia absinthium* LINNAEUS

*Origin:* native; widespread elsewhere

A bitter-tasting and acrid-smelling herb of vigorous and quite handsome growth, though now never used in the kitchen, unless by the experimental gardener trying to make his or her own vermouth or absinthe. However neglected now, it was once in considerable demand.

'Artemisia' may have been named either after a Carian princess or after one of the aspects of the goddess Diana (77), who presided over the illnesses of women. The Egyptians seem to have used it in the worship of Isis, and at Rome it was widely used as a tonic, the prizewinners of chariot races being obliged to drink a cup of it. This may have been so that its bitterness counteracted the sweetness of winning, or simply to ensure their good health. There were dozens of less glamorous uses. As the modern name suggests, it was used to expel worms from the gut; its smell was thought to bring sleep to invalids, and its ashes were mixed with oil of roses to blacken fading hair (77).

Many of the ancient uses persisted, certainly to the sixteenth century. At that time it was in use as an antidote to mushroom poisoning and was pounded with honey to relieve bloodshot eyes, and its insecticidal and bactericidal properties were in use. It was thought to stop all sorts of putrefaction, to stop beer turning to vinegar (it was similarly used long before hops were used in ale) and to keep moths from clothes (26). Even in the seventeenth century, Platt suggests that 'tapistry' brushed with the flowering tops was proofed against the moth (I wish I could try that). It was also a rodent-deterrent, for 'inke made with the infusion or decoction of Wormewood keepeth writings from being eaten with mice or rats' (26). The Romans used it in the same way when writing on parchments. The oil of wormwood was rubbed into wood to keep woodworm away (77), though a floor or beams so treated must have smelt bad.

Even if you do not have bloodshot eyes or moth-eaten tapestries, it is quite a nice plant to grow, if rather rampant. It is quite a useful filler for the herbaceous border, and the tall and elegant plumes of greenish-grey flowers are effective. They cut well, which is useful, for if left on they produce huge quantities of seed. Lastly, even if you do not want your clothes to smell of it, it is also supposed to keep the Devil away (77).

# BIBLIOGRAPHY

1  Anon., 1714. *A Collection of Receipes in Cookery, Physick and Surgery*
2  Aiton, William T., 1810–13. *Hortus Kewensis*, 2nd edition
3  Allan, Mea, 1964. *The Tradescants: their plants, gardens, and museum*
4  Amherst, Alicia, 1895. *A History of Gardening in England*
5  Arber, Agnes, 1912, 1938. *Herbals, their Origin and Evolution*
6  Austen, Ralph, 1665. *A Treatise on Fruit Trees*, 3rd impression
7  Austen, Ralph, 1657. *The spiritual use of an orchard, or garden of fruit trees*
8  Bacon, Francis, 1625. *Of Gardens: an Essay*
9  Baker, C. H., Collins, and Muriel, I., 1949. *The Life and Circumstances of James Brydges, 1st. Duke of Chandos, Patron of the Liberal Arts*
10  Baker, Thomas, 1640. *The Countryman's Recreation, or the Art of Planting, Grassing and Gardening in 3 books*
11  Beale, John, 1657. *Herefordshire orchards; a pattern for all England*
12  Bonnefons, Nicolas de (trans. Evelyn), 1658. *The French gardiner; instructing how to cultivate all sorts of fruit trees and herbs for the garden*
13  Bradley, Martha, 1770? *The British Housewife*
14  Candolle, Alphonse L. P. P. de, 1883. *Origine des plantes cultivées*
15  Castlehill, Lady, 1712. *Receipt Book* (ed. Hamish Whyte)
16  Clapham, A. R., Tutin, T. G., Warburg, E. F., 1958. *Flora of the British Isles*
17  Coats, Alice M., 1963. *Garden shrubs and their histories*
18  Cobbett, W., 1821. *The American Gardener*
19  Cobbett, W., 1833. *The English Gardener*
20  Coffin, David R., 1972. *The Italian Garden*
21  Coles, William, 1657. *Adam in Eden; or, nature's Paradise*
22  Commelin, Jan, 1683. *The Belgick or Netherlandish Hesperides*

23 Cotton, Charles, 1681. *The Planter's Manual*, 2nd edition
24 Culpepper, Nicholas, 1652. *The English physitian*
25 Defoe, Daniel, 1724–6. *A Tour through the Whole Island of Great Britain*
26 Dodoens (Dodonaei, Rembert), 1578. *A niewe Herball or Historie of Plants* (trans. H. Lyte)
27 Duhamel du Moncea, Henri Louis, 1768. *Des Arbre Frutier*
28 Estienne, C. and Liebault, J., 1570. *Maison Rustique, or the Countrie Farme* (trans. Richard Surflet)
29 Evelyn, John, 1664. *Sylva*
30 Evelyn, John, 1699. *Acetaria. A discourse on Sallers*
31 Evelyn, John (published 1932). *Directions for the gardiner at Sayes-Court*
32 *Flora Europaea*, ed. Tutin, T. G. *et al*, 1964–8
33 Gardener, Master John, 1440. *The Feate of Gardening*
34 Gerard, John, 1597. *The Herball*
35 Cockayne, Rev. Oswald (trans.), 1864. *Glastonbury Herbal*
36 Googe, Barnaby, 1578. *Foure Books of husbandrie, collected by Conradus Heresbachius . . . newly englished and increased by B.G.*
37 Gunther, R. W. T., 1922. *Early English Botanists and their Gardens*
38 Hartlib, Samuel, 1645. *Discourse of Husbandrie used in Brabant and Flanders*
39 Herklots, G. A. C., 1972. *Vegetables in South East Asia*
40 Hill, Sir J., 1757. *Eden; or a complete Body of Gardening*
41 Hill, Thomas, 1558. *A most briefe and pleasaunte treatise, teaching how to dress, sowe, and set a garden*
42 Hitt, Thomas, 1757. *A Treatise on Fruit-trees*
43 Hogg, Robert, 1875. *The fruit manual*
44 Hughes, William, 1665. *The complete vineyard*
45 Jacob, G., 1717. *The Country Gentleman's Vade-Mecum*
46 Janick, Jules and Moore, James (eds.), 1975. *Advances in Fruit Breeding*
47 Jashemski, W. F., 1979. *The Gardens of Pompeii*
48 Johnson, T., 1633. *The Herball, or general historie of plants* (by John Gerard), enlarged and amended by T. Johnson
49 Justice, James, 1732. *Scots Gardener's Director*
50 Justice, James, 1759. *The British Gardener's Calendar*
51 Kidner, Alfred W., 1959. *Asparagus* 2nd edition
52 Langford, T., 1681. *Plain and full instructions to raise all sorts of fruit-trees that prosper in England*
53 Laurence, John, 1718. *Gardening improv'd*
54 Lawson, William, 1618. *A New orchard and Garden*
55 Lemmon, Kenneth, 1962. *The Covered Garden*
56 Lindley, John, 1841. *Pomologia Britanica*
57 Loudon, J. C., 1822. *Encyclopaedia of Gardening*

58 Lovelock, Yann, 1972. *The Vegetable Book: an unnatural history*

59 McIntosh, Charles, 1829. *Flora and Pomona*

60 Markham, Gervase, 1637. *The English Housewife*

61 Markham, Gervase, 1695. *The Country Farm*

62 Mascall, Leonard, 1569. *The booke of Arte and maner, howe to plante and grafte all sortes of trees*

63 Masefield, G. B., Wallis, M., Harrison, S. G., Nicholson, B. E., 1969. *Oxford Book of Food Plants*

64 Mawe, T., 1767. *Everyman his own gardener*

65 Meech, W. W., 1896. *Quince culture, an illustrated handbook*

66 Miller, Phillip, *Gardener's Dictionary* (many editions from 1724, used here. Unless stated otherwise, in Dr Thomas Martyn's edition of 1807, published as *The Gardener's and Botanist's Dictionary*)

67 Morris, C. (ed.), 1949. *The Journeys of Celia Fiennes*

68 Mortimer, John, 1707. *The Whole Art of Husbandry*

69 Neill, Patrick, 1813. *On Scottish Gardens and Orchards*

70 Neill, Patrick, 1817. *Journal of a Horticultural Tour through some parts of Flanders, Holland and the north of France*

71 Niewhof, M., 1969. *Cole Crops: botany, cultivation and utilisation*

72 Oldham, Clarke, H., 1946. *The cultivation of berried fruits in England*

73 Palissy, Bernard de, 1563. *A Delectable Garden* (trans. Helen M. Fox)

74 Parkinson, John, 1629. *Paradisi in Sole Paradisus Terrestris*

75 Parkinson, John, 1640. *Theatrum Botanicum*

76 Phillips, Henry, 1820. *Pomarum Britannicum*

77 Phillips, Henry, 1822. *History of cultivated vegetables*

78 Platt, Sir Hugh, 1653. *The Jewel House of Art and Nature*

79 Platt, Sir Hugh, 1660. *The Garden of Eden* 2nd edition

80 Pliny (Plinius Secundus), (trans. Philemon Holland), 1634. *The History of the World*, commonly called the *Natural History* . . .

81 Raffald, Elizabeth, 1769. *The Experienced English Housekeeper*

82 Ray, J., 1686–8. *Historia Plantarum*

83 Rea, John, 1665. *Flora, or a Complete Florilege*

84 Reid, John, 1683. *The Scots Gardiner*

85 Rohde, Eleanour Sinclair, 1933. *The Garden Book of Sir Thomas Hanmer* (from an MS of 1659)

86 Rose, John, 1666. *English Vineyard Vindicated* (edited by John Evelyn)

87 Sands, Mollie, 1950. *The Gardens of Hampton Court*

88 Scot, Reginald, 1574. *A perfite platforme of a hoppe garden*

89 Sharrock, Robert, 1660. *A history of the propagation and improvement of vegetables by the concurrence of art and nature*

90 Shaw, J., 1794. *Plans of Forcing Houses in Gardening*

91  Sibbald, Sir Robert, 1684. *Scotia Illustrata*
92  Simmonds, A., 1948. 'A Horticultural Who was Who', in the *Royal Horticultural Society Journal*
93  Simmonds, N. W. (ed.), 1976. *Evolution of Crop Plants*
94  Speechley, William, 1779. *A Treatise on the Culture of the Pine-apple*
95  Stillman, Jan, 1920. *Theophrastus Bombastus von Hohenheim, called Paracelsus*
96  Strabo, Walahfrid, *c.* 842. *Hortulus* (trans. 1966, Raef Payne)
97  Stuart, Malcolm (ed.), 1979. *The Encyclopedia of Herbs and Herbalism*
98  Sturtevant, E. Lewis, 1919. *Notes on Edible Plants* (edited by U. P. Headrick)
99  Sweet, Robert, 1827. *Hortus Britannicus: or, a catalogue of the plants cultivated in the gardens of Great Britain*
100  Switzer, Stephen, 1729. *Method for Raising Italian Broccoli, etc.*
101  Turner, William, 1551. *A new herball*
102  Tusser, Thomas, 1572. *Five Hundred points of good husbandry*
103  Varro, Marcus Terentius, 37 BC. *De Re Rustica* (trans. 1955 Ash, Furster and Heffner)
104  Vavilov, Nicolai I., 1949. *The origin, variation, immunity and breeding of cultivated plants*
105  Vilmorin-Andrieux, Mme, 1885. *The Vegetable Garden* (English edition edited by William Robinson)
106  Whitaker, Thomas W., and David, N., 1962. *Cucurbits: botany, cultivation and utilisation*
107  Worlidge, John, 1677. *Systema horti-culturae*
108  Worlidge, John, 1687. *Systema Agriculturae*

# INDEX

# INDEX

*Page numbers in bold type denote the
beginning of each crop's main entry*

*A complete list of Alan Sutton books,*
*including country titles*
*is available from:*
*Alan Sutton Publishing, Dept CB,*
*30 Brunswick Road, Gloucester, GL1 1JJ*